Wonderful
WORLD 3

TEACHER'S BOOK

Katrina Gormley

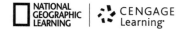

Wonderful World 3 Teacher's Book
Katrina Gormley

Publisher: Jason Mann
Director of Content Development: Sarah Bideleux
Commissioning Editor: Carol Goodwright
Development Editor: Lynn Thomson
Assistant Editor: Manuela Barros
Project Editor: Amy Smith
Production Controller: Denise Power
Art Director/Cover designer: Natasa Arsenidou
Compositor: Rouli Manias

Acknowledgements
Recorded at Motivation Sound Studios and GFS-PRO Studio.
Production at GFS-PRO Studio by George Flamouridis.

The publisher would like to thank the following sources for permission to reproduce their copyright protected photos:
Cover: left to right, top to bottom: (Jim Richardson/ National Geographic), (George Steinmetz/ National Geographic), (Medford Taylor/National Geographic), (David Edwards/National Geographic), (Eduardo Rivero/Shutterstock Images), (Richard Nowitz/National Geographic), (Dick Durrance II/National Geographic), (Guy Needham/National Geographic), (Scott S. Warren/National Geographic), (Michael Poliza/National Geographic), (Fritz Hoffmann/National Geographic), main image (Jim brandenburg/Minden Pictures/ National Geographic).
Inside: Photos.com – pp. 169, 178 (a-c), 179, 180, 189 (a), 199 (a), 204. All other photos courtesy of Shutterstock.

ISBN: 978-1-111-40222-8

National Geographic Learning
Cheriton House
North Way
Andover
Hampshire
SP10 5BE
United Kingdom

Cengage Learning is a leading provider of customized learning solutions with office locations around the globe, including Singapore, the United Kingdom, Australia, Mexico, Brazil and Japan. Locate your local office at:
international.cengage.com/region

Cengage Learning products are represented in Canada by Nelson Education, Ltd.

Visit National Geographic Learning online at **ngl.cengage.com**
Visit our corporate website at **www.cengage.com**

Printed and bound in Lebanon at Arab Printing Press
2 3 4 5 6 7 8 9 10 11 – 16 15 14 13 12

Contents

Contents of Pupil's Book	4
Introduction to Wonderful World	6
Introduction Unit	8
Unit 1	12
Unit 2	19
Review 1	26
Unit 3	28
Unit 4	34
Review 2	40
Unit 5	42
Unit 6	48
Review 3	54
Unit 7	56
Unit 8	62
Review 4	68
Unit 9	70
Unit 10	77
Review 5	83
Unit 11	85
Unit 12	91
Review 6	97
National Geographic DVD Worksheets	99
Notes on the Play / Surprise!	103
Listening script	105
Photocopiable Cartoon DVD Worksheets	112
Photocopiable Extra Tasks (for early finishers)	124
Extra Tasks Key	136
Workbook Key	138
Project Book Key	148
Grammar Book Key	153
Unit Tests Key	162
Unit Tests	166
End of Year Test	202

Contents of Pupil's Book

Unit	Reading	Vocabulary	Grammar
Introduction Hello! p 4-9		The Alphabet, Numbers, Days, Months, Dates, Seasons, Colours, The Body, Time, Classroom language	*a/an* Plurals *This/These – That/Those*
1 Family and Friends p 10-17	The Cortuga Mystery Emperor Penguins My Best Friend!	family members adjectives for people	*Be* Possessive Adjectives Possessive – *'s*
2 My Favourite Things p 18-25	The Cortuga Mystery The NG Kids' Shop What's your favourite thing?	toys possessions home entertainment	*Have got* *There is, There are* Prepositions of place
Review 1 p 26-27	Vocabulary and Grammar tasks / Song		
3 School Life p 28-35	The Cortuga Mystery Schools in Japan Anna's school	school subjects school equipment	Present Simple (aff, spelling) Present Simple (neg, question) Adverbs of Frequency
4 Hobbies p 36-43	The Cortuga Mystery Luna Park What do you do on Saturdays?	equipment for hobbies kinds of entertainment	Question words *Can* (ability, permission)
Review 2 p 44-45	Vocabulary and Grammar tasks / Song		
5 Celebrate! p 46-53	The Cortuga Mystery Carnival Crazy! Special Days around the World	parties fancy-dress costumes	Imperatives, Object pronouns, *Let's* Countable and uncountable nouns *Some/any*
6 Food! p 54-61	The Cortuga Mystery Food fun Food around the World	food, drink and restaurant-related words	*Much/Many, How much …/many …* *A lot of/Lots of/A little/A few*
Review 3 p 62-63	Vocabulary and Grammar tasks / Song		
7 Sport p 64-71	The Cortuga Mystery Thai Boxing Ice Dancers	sports verbs of motion	Present Continuous (aff, spelling) Present Continuous (neg, question) Present Continuous (for the future)
8 People and Places p 72-79	The Cortuga Mystery Modern Cowboys Welcome to Scotland!	homes buildings jobs	Present Simple and Continuous *must*
Review 4 p 80-81	Vocabulary and Grammar tasks / Song		
9 Holidays and Travel p 82-89	The Cortuga Mystery Up, up and away! Cool Holidays!	means of transport holiday equipment	Past Simple of *be* Past Simple regular (aff, spelling) Past Simple irregular (aff)
10 Fame! p 90-97	The Cortuga Mystery Who was Walt Disney? Lessons in Fame	jobs in entertainment music films	Past Simple irregular (neg, question) *Wh …* questions in the Past Simple
Review 5 p 98-99	Vocabulary and Grammar tasks / Song		
11 Animals p 100-107	The Cortuga Mystery Presidents' Pets My clever pet!	wild and domestic animals adjectives to describe animals	Comparative Superlative Comparative and Superlative
12 Weather and Nature p 108-115	The Cortuga Mystery Nature in danger Looking for Tornados!	weather landscapes	*Be going to* Future Simple
Review 6 p 116-117	Vocabulary and Grammar tasks / Song		

National Geographic DVD Worksheets   p 118-123
Play   p 124-125
Irregular verbs   p 126

Listening	Speaking	Pronunciation	Functional language	Writing
Introduction of Cortuga Mystery characters Song	Dialogue introducing yourself		Introducing yourself	Personal fact file
Label pictures True or False Song	Talk about yourself	silent letters	Making friends	Punctuation Email
Multiple choice True or False Number correct order	Talk about favourite things Find differences between pictures	*the*	Playing games	Connectors *and* and *but* Advert
Blank filling Tick the correct school subjects Complete the table Song	Talk about everyday life	*oo* sounds	Talking about everyday life	Word order Description
Match Two-option lozenge Complete cinema information	Talk about your hobby Describe pictures	*w* sounds	Talking about hobbies	Verb forms Letter
Tick the correct box Match	Talk about special days	*s* and *sh* sounds	Making suggestions	Reference words Description
Tick the correct picture Tick or Cross things on a list Song Number pictures (recipe)	Talk about your favourite restaurant or café Dialogue	*ch* and *sh* sounds	Talking about food	Time words: order of events Recipe
Number the sports Write Yes or No Song	Describe the picture Talk about sports	*ea*, *ee* and *i* sounds	Talking about sport	Time expressions: word order Email
Complete the table Number jobs Multiple Choice	Talk about your home Find the differences between two pictures	Complete a poem (rhyming words)	Talking about places	Connectors: *because* and *so* Description
Tick the correct picture Number the places Song	Talk about your last holiday	*-ed* in Past Simple	Talking about travel	Adjectives Postcard
Multiple Choice Tick the correct film Complete the table	Play 'Guess the star' Practise a dialogue	*c, g, s, y* sounds	Talking about favourite stars	Paragraphs Review
Complete the table True or False Song	Compare these animals	*a* and *u* sounds	Talking about animals	Spelling Advert
Number the pictures Complete the table Number the pictures	Talk about your plans for the weekend Make predictions	*a* sounds	Talking about the weather	Checking for mistakes Letter

Introduction to Wonderful World 3

Course Components

Wonderful World 3 Pupil's Book

The pupil's book is divided into an Introduction, twelve topic-based units, each containing a unit opener and three two-page lessons, and six reviews. Each lesson begins with a reading text that approaches the topic from a slightly different angle. In Lesson 1 pupils listen to and read an episode of *The Cortuga Mystery*. They follow Jake, Kate, Robbie and Mandy on their adventure around the world to find the pieces of the puzzle. Lesson 2 teaches pupils about the world we live in through a non-fiction reading passage inspired by National Geographic, and Lesson 3 links the theme of the unit to the pupils' reality through a variety of text types such as emails, dialogues, articles and so on.

Each unit also contains:
- topic-related vocabulary tasks that practise and build on vocabulary in the reading texts.
- clear and concise grammar presentations followed by one or two tasks that practise form and usage.
- topic-related listening tasks and speaking tasks that allow pupils to practise vocabulary and grammar presented in the lesson.
- a *Sounds of English* section that provides pronunciation practice.
- a *Say it like this!* section that focuses on functional English to aid communication.
- a strong writing sub-skill syllabus that enables pupils to write well from the start.

The Introduction revises basic vocabulary and grammar from primary level and introduces the main characters in *The Cortuga Mystery*. *Wonderful World 3 Pupil's Book* also contains six reviews, one after every two units, that consolidate vocabulary and grammar taught within those units and a song.

At the back of the pupil's book, there are three DVD worksheets that accompany the National Geographic video clips on *Wonderful World 3 DVD*, a play that can be performed by pupils and an irregular verbs list.

Wonderful World 3 Workbook

The workbook accompanies *Wonderful World 3 Pupil's Book*. Like the pupil's book, it is also divided into an Introduction, twelve units and six reviews. Lessons 1 and 2 of each unit consolidate vocabulary and grammar from the relevant lesson of the pupil's book. Lesson 3 also includes consolidation of the *Say it like this!* functional language and the writing sub skill found in the pupil's book lesson. In the reviews there is a non-fiction reading text inspired by National Geographic and vocabulary and grammar multiple choice tasks. At the back of the workbook, there are six wordsearches for further practice of key vocabulary.

Pupils will be motivated by the full-colour pages, lively illustrations and captivating National Geographic photographs, and the workbook's clear and simple format means that it can be used at home as well as in class.

Wonderful World 3 Grammar

The grammar progression in *Wonderful World 3 Grammar* follows that in the pupil's book. Each lesson begins with a cartoon presentation designed to introduce the grammar in an amusing way. This is followed by grammar theory accompanied by plenty of example sentences. *Remember!* boxes appear often and serve to remind pupils of things they should be aware of. The lesson then continues with a selection of graded tasks before finishing with a speaking task, which allows pupils to practise the grammar they have learnt in realistic situations.

There is a review after every two units of *Wonderful World 3 Grammar*. Each review contains a variety of tasks designed to consolidate the grammar covered in the preceding two units. The review ends with a non-fiction Writing Project featuring National Geographic photography. Pupils then have the opportunity to do their own Writing Project. At the back there is an irregular verbs list and a word list of key vocabulary used in the grammar book.

There is also a Grammar Test section with six tests: one test for every two units of the Grammar Book. The answer key is provided. The class may do the tests at home and check their own answers as a pupil-based resource.

Project Book

The Project Book is designed for pupils to use either in class or out of the classroom, as homework.

Projects

There is one project for each unit of the course and they are linked thematically to each unit. Each project is designed to be carried out once the children have completed the unit. Each project consists of a series of short activities, which revise vocabulary and language, which may be done in class, before the children embark on a short project, which can be completed at home. The project often involves drawing a picture, making a poster or booklet, or making a model and then sharing the finished work with other members of the class. The projects all involve items (such as paper, colouring pencils, paint etc.) which can be found easily at home.

The aim is to encourage the children to be creative and to have fun with the topic they have been studying. It is hoped that all the children will participate and that those weaker pupils particularly, and/or those who are artistic and creative, rather than academic, will have a chance to shine in class. Time should be set aside for the `show and tell' element of each project, so that the pupils can complete the pair work tasks in each project and enjoy sharing their work with the rest of the class.

The teacher should not formally mark or assess each project, but instead, display the projects on the classroom walls or in the corridor (if either are possible) and encourage the children to bring in their work and to look at and admire each other's efforts. The children could vote for the project(s) they find most interesting, colourful. Be sure to praise all the children's work, particularly those who have made a real effort or have been enthusiastic.

The Project Book Answer Keys and teacher's notes are on pages 148-152 of the Teacher's Book.

Wonderful World 3 Teacher's Book

Wonderful World 3 Teacher's Book provides objective boxes, clear lesson plans with detailed instructions and the key to all tasks from the pupil's book. There is a section of photocopiable support material at the back which contains Extra Tasks for early finishers and worksheets to accompany the animated episodes of *The Cortuga Mystery* found on the DVD component. Listening scripts with justification for the answers to listening tasks underlined, and the key to *Wonderful World 3 Workbook* are also included.

Wonderful World 3 Interactive Whiteboard Software

Wonderful World 3 Interactive Whiteboard contains the pupil's book, including the audio material and the DVD. Most of the tasks found in the pupil's book are interactive and have been developed to be easy to use by both pupils and teachers alike. Justification for reading comprehension and listening tasks is available at the touch of a button, as is the key to all tasks. The DVD can be played with or without subtitles and the song lyrics change colour as they are sung to make it easier for pupils to sing along. *Wonderful World 3 Interactive Whiteboard* is compatible with any interactive whiteboard hardware.

Wonderful World 3 CD-ROM

Wonderful World 3 CD-ROM is designed to recycle vocabulary and grammar from each unit in the pupil's book in a fun way. The CD-ROM also contains a variety of games that increase pupils' motivation for what they are learning. It is compatible with both PCs and Macs.

Wonderful World 3 DVD

Wonderful World 3 DVD contains animations of the twelve episodes of *The Cortuga Mystery* found in Lesson 1 of the pupil's book, and three National Geographic videos that provide pupils with real-life knowledge of the world around them. The narration for these National Geographic videos has been carefully graded so it is appropriate for beginner level. There are photocopiable worksheets in *Wonderful World 3 Teacher's Book* for classroom use with the animated episodes of *The Cortuga Mystery*, and there are DVD worksheets for use with the National Geographic videos at the back of *Wonderful World 3 Pupil's Book*.

Wonderful World 3 Audio CD

Wonderful World 3 Class Audio CD contain the recordings of *The Cortuga Mystery*, the listening tasks, the *Sounds of English* pronunciation sections, the songs and the play found in *Wonderful World 3 Pupil's Book*.

Professional actors are used in all recordings to ensure clarity and accurate intonation and pronunciation.

Introduction

Objectives

- Revising key expressions to talk about ourselves
- Revising the alphabet and practising writing
- Revising number and word forms of numbers 1-100
- Revising the days of the week, months, dates and seasons
- Listening to a description and colouring a picture
- Matching body parts to their names
- Revising telling the time
- Practising classroom language
- Revising a / an; plurals; this / that – these / those
- Completing a personal fact file
- Reading first part of the cartoon story, *The Cortuga Mystery*, and meeting the characters

Materials needed

- coloured pens, pencils or crayons: blue, brown, green, grey, orange, pink, purple, red, yellow
- photo of each pupil

Way in

- Introduce yourself and go round the class asking each pupil to say his or her name.
- Explain to pupils that the course book you will be using is *Wonderful World 3*.
- Explain to pupils that the Introduction will revise basic English that they should already know from junior classes, and that they will meet the main characters in the cartoon story in the book.

Hello!

Background Information

The picture shows parrots called scarlet macaws. There are 17 different species of macaw, and they live in the rainforests of Central and South America. The size of the scarlet macaw ranges from 30 to 100cm and they mainly eat nuts, seeds, fruit, insects and snails. For further information go to www.nationalgeographic.com and follow the link for 'birds'.

- Ask the class to look at the picture on page 4. Ask *What kind of birds are they? How many birds are there? What colour are their feathers? Where are the birds?*
- Read the two sentences on the picture about scarlet macaws to the class. Use the background information in the box above to give the pupils further information about these birds if they are interested.
- Ask the pupils what parrots do that other birds don't (*talk*). Explain that one of the macaws is called Polly and the other is called Max. Then ask them to complete the dialogue between the two birds.
- Pupils can do the task individually, but check the answers as a class. You could get the pupils to practise the dialogue in pairs.

Answers

1 Hi!	**3** I'm fine, thanks.
2 My name's Polly.	**4** I'm thirteen.

Extra Class Activity

Put the pupils into pairs and tell them that they are going to practise the dialogue in the *Hello*! section, but this time asking and answering the questions about themselves. Role play the dialogue with one of the pupils. Encourage them to ask you the questions. Answer about yourself so the pupils know that they should speak about themselves. End the activity by quickly asking the questions round the class so that each pupil gets to pupil a question.

Teaching Tip

Always try to give pupils extra speaking practice by getting them to use new words and phrases to speak about themselves where possible.

The Alphabet

A

- Ask pupils if they remember the English alphabet and encourage them to say it out loud as a class.
- Ask pupils if they know what we call the animal in Task A (*a snake*). Tell them that they are going to complete the alphabet by filling in the missing letters. Explain that they should write the capital letter and the small letter for each one. Demonstrate what you mean by writing *B* and then *b* on the board.
- Once they have filled in the missing letters, check the answers as a class. Then ask them to use the missing letters to write the name of the animal in the box provided under the illustration.

Answers

Aa	Ee	Kk	Nn	Ss

SNAKE / snake

B

- Tell pupils they are going to hear words being spelt out on the recording. Explain that they should write the word they hear on the lines provided.
- Do the first one together as a class. Play the CD and ask pupils which word they hear. Ask them to write the word and then check the spelling. Then play the rest of the recording.
- Play the recording again. Tell pupils to check their answers the second time and fill in any missing information.
- Check the answers as a class. Write each word on the board to make sure pupils have the correct spelling. Then go round the class and ask pupils to say the words out loud and correct their pronunciation where necessary.

Answers

1 boy	**2** car	**3** desk
4 horse	**5** pencil	**6** school

Numbers

A

- Ask pupils to say the numbers 1 to 20 out loud as a class. Then write the numbers *30, 40, 50, 60, 70, 80, 90* and *100* on the board. Ask pupils to say these numbers in English. If time allows, write random numbers between 20 and 100 on the board and ask pupils to say them out loud.
- Before pupils do the sums, make sure they are familiar with the symbols and how they are referred to in English (three *plus* one; seventeen *minus* two; ten *times* two, twenty *plus* twenty *equals*).
- Ask pupils to complete the task individually, or in pairs, and then check the answers as a class.

B

- Ask pupils if they remember how old Polly the scarlet macaw is (*thirteen*). Then ask several pupils how old they are.
- Ask pupils to answer the questions about themselves by writing the *number* and the *word*. Approach this task with sensitivity if you sense pupils may have a problem discussing their weight.

Answers

Pupils' own answers

Extra Class Activity

If there is time at the end of the lesson, play a numbers game by getting the pupils to say the numbers one to a hundred out loud. Put the pupils in a row; the first pupil says one, the second pupil says two, the third pupil says three and so on. Carry on until they get to a hundred. If a pupil makes a mistake, they sit down and start from the beginning again. If you feel you have a strong class, you could tell them that instead of saying five and any multiples of five (*ten, fifteen, twenty*, etc) they can say *macaw*.

Days of the week

- Ask pupils what day of the week it is. Then ask them what day it was yesterday and what day it will be tomorrow.
- Ask pupils what the first day of the week is and get them to write the word on the line for 1. This may vary from culture to culture, so accept the answer that is correct in your context.
- Tell pupils to use the wordbank and to fill in the rest of the answers. Check the answers as a class. Correct pupils' pronunciation where necessary.

Answers

1	Sunday	**5**	Thursday
2	Monday	**6**	Friday
3	Tuesday	**7**	Saturday
4	Wednesday		

Tuesday is the missing day.

Months

- Ask pupils how many months there are in a year. Then ask several pupils which month they were born in.
- Ask pupils to complete exercises A and B individually, but check the answers as a class.

Answers

A

January	July
February	August
March	September
April	October
May	November
June	December

B

Pupils' own answers

Dates

- Tell pupils what today's date is and write it on the board both in numbers and words. Quickly revise the ordinal numbers by writing 1st - *first*; 2nd - *second*; 3rd - *third*; 4th - *fourth*; 5th - *fifth* on the board. Then introduce some two digit ordinals, 11th - *eleventh*; 21st - *twenty-first*; 32nd - *thirty-second*, 43rd - *forty-third*. You could ask some pupils what date their birthday is and write these numbers on the board.
- Ask pupils to complete the exercises individually, but check the answers as a class.

Answers

A		**B**	
1	st	**1**	twelfth
2	nd	**2**	seventeenth
3	rd	**3**	twenty-first
4	th	**4**	thirtieth
5	th	**5**	ninth
6	th	**6**	twenty-second
7	th		

C

Pupils' own answers

Seasons

- Ask pupils if they know the names of the four seasons of the year. Correct their pronunciation if necessary. If pupils don't know the seasons, then teach each one separately, asking the pupils to repeat them after you.
- Ask pupils to look at the pictures and say which season it is in each one. Tell them that each set of jumbled letters can be used to spell out one of the four seasons. Ask pupils to use the letters to write the correct season under each picture. Check the answers as a class.

Answers

1	winter	**2**	autumn	**3**	summer	**4**	spring

Colours

- To get started, point to objects in the classroom and ask pupils what colour they are. Make sure you include the following colours: blue, brown, green, grey, orange, pink, purple, red, yellow and white.

- Tell pupils that they are going to listen to a description of the Planet Od and colour the picture in their books so that it matches what they hear on the recording. Ask them to look at the picture and tell you what they can see. Make sure pupils are familiar with the words; *tree, flower, car, dog, duck, sun, sky* and *bird* before they listen.
- When you play the recording, stop the CD after each sentence so the pupils have a chance to colour in the picture.

Answers
Make sure pupils have coloured the picture as follows:
- trees – purple
- flowers – yellow
- duck – pink
- the sun – red
- the sky – grey
- dog – green and white
- birds – orange
- car – brown
- Ziggy – blue
- Bleck – red

The Body

- Ask pupils how many fingers they have. If they say 20, tell them that you only have 10 fingers and wiggle your fingers at them. Then point to your toes and remind them that we call them toes in English, if necessary.
- Ask pupils to look at the picture of the girl jumping. Tell them that they are going to match the parts of the body labelled a to l with the words numbered 1 to 12. Do the first two together as a class and then ask pupils to complete the exercise on their own. Check the answers as a class.

Answers
1 b	**2** g	**3** i	**4** a	**5** c	**6** l
7 j	**8** k	**9** e	**10** f	**11** h	**12** d

Extra Class Activity
If you have time, you could play 'Simon says …' with the class. Tell them to stand up and that they should point to the part of the body that Simon tells them to ('Simon says point to your nose', etc). Explain that if you don't say 'Simon says' then they shouldn't point to anything ('Point to your head'). Any pupil who points to the wrong part of their body or who points when you haven't said 'Simon says', sits down and is out of the game. The pupil left standing at the end is the winner.

Telling the time

- Ask pupils if they can tell you what time it is now. If no one is wearing a watch or there isn't a clock on the wall then draw a clock face on the board showing the time. Revise the time in English by changing the position of the hands on the clock you've drawn and ask the pupils to tell you what time it is.

Make sure they are familiar with the phrases: *o'clock, quarter to, quarter past, half past.*
- Ask pupils to complete the exercise and explain that they should look at the clock faces to help them fill in the gaps using the words in the word bank.

Answers
1 past		**2** o' clock		**3** quarter	
4 to		**5** twenty-five		**6** quarter	

Teaching Tip
Give pupils plenty of practice in telling the time by asking them at least once every lesson to tell you what time it is. Giving them a reason to tell the time in English will allow them to develop this skill.

Classroom Language

- Ask pupils to look at the pictures and ask them where the people are (*in classrooms*). Explain that they are going to learn some useful words and phrases that they can use in the classroom during the year.
- Ask pupils to do the task individually, but check the answers as a class. Once pupils have matched the words and phrases correctly, you could get them to practise by acting out the dialogues together.

Answers
1e	**2**a	**3**f	**4**b	**5**d	**6**c	**7**g

a or an

- Write *a hand* and *an arm* on the board. Ask pupils to tell you why we have *a* before *hand*, but *an* before *arm*. If they don't know, explain that we use *an* before the vowel sounds a, e, i, o, u. (*At this stage they don't need to know about semi-vowel sounds.*) Ask them to tell you words that have *a* before them and make a list under *a hand*. Try to include the words *watch, country, life* and *man*. Do the same for *an*.

Teaching Tip
It would be a good idea to draw a table on the board with four columns. Put the words with *a* in the first column and the words with *an* in the third column. Leave columns two and four blank so that you can write in the plurals of the words when introducing them in the next section.

- Ask pupils to do the task individually, but check the answers as a class.

Answers
1	a		**6**	a
2	a		**7**	an
3	an		**8**	an
4	a		**9**	a
5	an		**10**	an

Plurals

- If you have drawn the table on the board as suggested in the previous *Teaching Tip*, elicit from pupils that the plural of *hand* is *hands* and write *hands* in the second column to the right of *a hand*. Ask them to tell you which other words in the table form the plural by adding *-s*. Ask them to tell you the plural form of the other words you have listed and complete the table.
- Make sure pupils understand that words ending in *-x*, *-s*, *-ss*, *-ch* and *-sh* form the plural with *-es*; words ending in *-y* form the plural with *-ies*; some words ending in *-f* or *-fe* change to *-ves* and that some words ending *-o* form the plural with *-oes*, but others with *-s*. Explain that irregular plurals need to be learnt by heart. Encourage pupils to make a note of how plurals are formed when recording vocabulary in their vocabulary notebooks.
- Ask pupils to do the task individually, but check the answers as a class.

> ## Answers
> Accept answers 2 to 5, and 8 to 10 in any order.
>
> 1 toy, toys
> 2 box, boxes
> 3 bus, buses
> 4 glass, glasses
> 5 tomato, tomatoes
> 6 family, families
> 7 knife, knives
> 8 child, children
> 9 foot, feet
> 10 mouse, mice

This/These-That/Those

- Start by holding up an object that belongs to you, (*your bag*, *a book*, *a pen*) and ask pupils *What is this?* When they tell you the correct answer say, *Yes, this is a ...*, etc. Then point to something far away from you and ask *What is that?* When they tell you the correct answer say *Yes, that is a ...* . Repeat the procedure to practise *these* and *those*.
- Ask pupils to look at the pictures in their books and make sure they understand how to use these words. Then ask pupils to work in pairs and create their own sentences using the words in the word bank.
- You could extend this exercise by asking pupils to write their sentences down.

> ## Suggested answers:
> - This is a red bag.
> - These are books.
> - That is a board.
> - That is a clock.
> - Those are desks.
> - That is a brown door.
> - These are blue pens.
> - Those are pencils.

Fact File

- Tell pupils they are going to make a fact file containing information about themselves. Ask them to stick a photo of themselves onto the fact file.
- Make sure they understand the words *favourite* and *hobbies*. Then ask them to fill in the information about themselves.

- You could ask pupils to make a fact file on a separate sheet of paper for homework so that you can display them on the wall. In the next lesson, you could allow pupils a few minutes to read each others' files. This way they will get to know each other better.

The Cortuga Mystery

- Explain to pupils that the first lesson in every unit of *Wonderful World 3* starts with an episode of the ongoing cartoon story called *The Cortuga Mystery*.
- Tell pupils to look at the cartoon on page 9 and ask them where they think the story takes place.
- Write the names of the main characters on the board. They are: *Jake*, *Mandy*, *Robbie*, *Kate* and *Uncle Oliver*.
- Ask pupils to read the cartoon on their own. Then assign roles to pupils and ask them to read their parts out loud. If you have a large class, you can repeat this task using different pupils each time.
- Explain any vocabulary pupils don't know and correct their pronunciation where necessary. Make sure they realise that the *s* in *island* is silent.
- Tell pupils they are going to listen to the dialogue and the Cortuga Island song. Ask them to listen carefully to find out why Robbie, Kate, Mandy and Jake are on Cortuga Island and why Uncle Oliver is there.
- Play the song once and ask why the children are on the island (*They are on holiday.*) and why Uncle Oliver is there (*He lives there*). Explain any words pupils have a problem with.
- Play the song again and ask pupils to sing along.

> ### Extra Class Activity
> Divide the class into two teams. Tell them you are going to ask them questions based on the cartoon. Ask each team one question at a time. The team who answers the most questions is the winner.

Questions

1 Who is 8 years old? (*Mandy*)
2 Who is Robbie's cousin? (*Kate*)
3 Which children have got an uncle? (*Jake and Mandy*)
4 Who is Jake's sister? (*Mandy*)
5 How many animals are in the picture? (*3*)
6 Who has got a map and hat? (*Uncle Oliver*)
7 Who has got red trousers? (*Kate*)
8 Who has got glasses? (*Jake*)
9 What is Uncle Oliver? (*a scientist*)
10 Which children have got brown hair? (*Mandy and Jake*)

Family and Friends

Teaching Tip

Begin each lesson by quickly revising key language from the previous lesson.

Way in

- Ask pupils what colour the macaw birds were in the Introduction. Then ask different pupils to come and write each of the colours they learnt on the board or to spell them for you to write on the board.
- Write *nodMay*, *hrsTduya*, *Sudatrya* on the board and ask pupils to unscramble the letters and tell you the days of the week. Then ask pupils to say all the days of the week in the correct order.
- Ask pupils to say the months of the year and the seasons out loud.
- Ask pupils to count how many people there are in the classroom. Then ask them to say the numbers 1 to 20 as a class.
- Spell the words: *animal*, *mouse*, *watch*, *tomato*, *foot*, *child*, *knife*, *box* and *family* and ask pupils to write them down individually or ask different pupils to write them on the board. Then ask pupils what the plural of each word is.

Quiz

- Ask pupils to open their books at page 10 and to say what animals they can see (*chimpanzees* or '*chimps*').
- Explain that chimpanzees are very sociable animals that live in family groups like humans. Tell them that the theme of Unit 1 is *Family and Friends*.
- Ask pupils to read the information about the chimpanzees on page 11 to find out where they live (*in a special park in the Congo*), and if the chimps are brother and sister or friends (*friends*).
- If pupils are interested, give them further information on chimpanzees using the Background Information box below.

Background Information

Chimpanzees are an endangered species of mammal that live in Africa. They live for around 45 years in the wild. They grow to be between 1.2 to 1.7 metres tall and usually weigh between 32 to 60 kilograms. They eat fruit and plants, but sometimes eat insects, eggs and meat. The chimpanzees in the picture come from the Congo, which is in central Africa. For further information go to www.nationalgeographic.com and follow the link for *animals*.

- Ask pupils to do the quiz individually, but check the answer as a class. Explain that Tarzan is a man who lives in the jungle with his friend Jane and Cheeta the chimpanzee. The original story of Tarzan was written by Edgar Rice Burroughs in 1912.

Answer

c

Extra Class Activity

You could extend the quiz by writing the names and animals below on the board in two columns and asking pupils to match each name to the correct animal. Try to introduce the word *shark* here to pre-teach it for the reading text in Lesson 1.

Rex	kangaroo
Garfield	dog
Skippy	shark
Black Beauty	horse
Jaws	cat

Answers

Rex – dog
Garfield – cat
Skippy – kangaroo
Black Beauty – horse
Jaws – shark

Lesson 1

Objectives

Reading	The Cortuga Mystery
Vocabulary	text-related words, adjectives describing people
Grammar	be – affirmative, negative, question and short answers
Listening	labelling a picture
Speaking	asking and answering personal questions
Writing	writing sentences about a friend

Teaching Tip

Before introducing each episode of *The Cortuga Mystery*, quickly discuss what happened in the previous episode and revise any new words they learnt there.

The Cortuga Mystery

Explain to pupils that they are about to see or hear Episode 1 of *The Cortuga Mystery*. Ask pupils if they can remember the characters they met in the *Introduction* and any information about them. Elicit who are brother and sister (*Mandy and Jake*) and who are cousins (*Kate and Robbie*). Ask what Uncle Oliver is (*a scientist*).

For teachers using the DVD

- Make sure each pupil has a copy of the DVD Worksheet found on page 112.
- Ask pupils to work in pairs to do the *Before You Watch* task to encourage discussion.

Answers

1 Mandy (*girl with the blue top and shorts*)
 Kate (*girl with the pink top and shorts*)
 Jake (*boy with the purple top and green shorts*)
 Robbie (*boy with the red and orange swimming shorts*) ➡

2 Uncle Oliver (*man in pictures* 4 *and* 5)
3 on the beach

• Play the whole episode without interruption before pupils do any more tasks on the worksheet. Ask pupils to watch the DVD carefully.

While you watch

• Ask pupils to look at the *While You Watch* task so they can work out what information they need to find when they watch the episode for the second time. Play the whole episode without interruption and ask pupils to watch the DVD.
• Give the pupils a few minutes to complete the task and ask them to check their answers with a partner. If necessary, play the DVD again and ask pupils to fill in any missing information.

Answers			
1	Mandy	**4**	Kate
2	Jake	**5**	Robbie
3	Mandy	**6**	Uncle Oliver

After you watch

• Ask pupils to read the story out loud. Assign the roles of Jake, Mandy, Robbie, Kate and Uncle Oliver to different pupils. If you have a large class, you may have to repeat until all pupils have had a turn.
• Explain any vocabulary pupils don't know and correct their pronunciation where necessary.
• Ask pupils to answer the questions, in the *After You Watch* section of the worksheet individually, but check the answers as a class.

Answers	
1	Mandy, Kate and Robbie
2	Kate and Robbie
3	Robbie
4	Mandy
5	on the beach
6	science
7	Jake

For teachers using the audio CD

• Ask pupils to look at page 12 in their Pupil's Books and to work in pairs. Tell them to point to each of the children and Uncle Oliver and to say their names (*Mandy is the girl with the blue top and shorts. Kate is the girl with the pink top and shorts. Jake is the boy with the purple top and green shorts. Robbie is the boy with the red and orange swimming shorts. Uncle Oliver is the man in pictures* 4 *and* 5.). Alternatively, hold your book up so everyone can see it. Point to each character and ask pupils what their names are. Ask pupils where the children are (*at the beach*).
• Tell pupils that they are going to listen to and read the first part of the story. Ask them to look at the pictures and to follow the story as they listen.
• Play the recording once and ask the pupils what trick Robbie plays (*He pretends to be a shark.*). Ask the pupils what happens in the story (*The children meet each other and introduce themselves.*).
• Ask pupils to read the story out loud. Assign the roles of Jake, Mandy, Robbie, Kate and Uncle Oliver to different pupils. If you have a large class, you may have to repeat until all pupils have had a turn.
• Explain any vocabulary pupils don't know and correct their pronunciation where necessary.

• As a class, ask pupils the questions below to check they have understood the episode.
  1 Who is in the water? (*Mandy, Kate and Robbie*)
  2 Who are cousins? (*Kate and Robbie*)
  3 Who is sorry? (*Robbie*)
  4 Who has got a towel? (*Mandy*)
  5 Where is Uncle Oliver's house? (*on the beach*)
  6 What's Kate crazy about? (*science*)
  7 Who has got a good idea? (*Jake*)

Vocabulary

A
• Explain that the words in the wordbank appear in the cartoon episode. Ask pupils to find the words in the cartoon and to underline them. Explain any words again if necessary.
• Ask pupils to do the task individually, but check the answers as a class. Correct their pronunciation where necessary.

Answers			
1	friend	**4**	scientist
2	shark	**5**	beach
3	idea		

B
• Ask pupils to look back at page 11 and ask them if the chimpanzees are young or old (*young*). Then ask them if the chimps are beautiful or ugly. Accept either answer here as this is subjective, but make sure pupils understand the meaning of the words. Write *young ≠ old* and *beautiful ≠ ugly* on the board and explain to pupils that these are adjectives used to describe people and that they are opposites.
• Teach the other pairs of opposites in the task and build up the list on the board using the cartoon episode as a visual aid. Point to Mandy's hair and say *dark*, then point to Kate's hair and say *fair*. Point to Jake in picture 4 and say *tall*, then point to Robbie and say *short*. Tell pupils that Uncle Oliver is a scientist and that he is clever. Elicit that the opposite of *clever* is *stupid* by asking them if Robbie's trick was *clever*. Remind pupils what the colours *black* and *grey* are but do not add them to list on the board as they are not opposites.
• Ask pupils to look at pictures 1 to 6 to help them circle the correct words. Ask them to do the task individually, but check the answers as a class.

Answers			
1	fair	**4**	tall
2	clever	**5**	beautiful
3	old	**6**	black

Grammar

Be
• Remind pupils that the words in *Vocabulary B* are adjectives that we use to describe people. Tell them that *be* is a verb that we use to describe people and things.
• Read the four uses of *be* in the grammar box and ask pupils to read the example sentences out loud with you.
• Read the forms of the verb in the grammar box to the class and ask them to repeat them after you. Go through the short forms first, and then the long forms.
• Ask pupils to look back at *The Cortuga Mystery* and underline all the examples of *be* in the affirmative. Make sure they understand why '*m*, '*re* and '*s / is* are used.

A

- Explain to pupils that they should read the sentences and then fill the gaps with the correct form of *be*.
- Ask pupils to do the task individually, but check the answers as a class.

B

- Explain to pupils that they have to match the questions on the left to the correct answers on the right. Tell them to pay attention to the subject pronouns in the answers.
- Ask pupils to do the task individually, but check the answers as a class.

Answers

1e	2f	3a	4d	5b	6c

Listening

- Before listening to the recording, ask pupils to work in pairs. Assign each pair one of the people or the dog in the picture to describe using the words they have learnt in the lesson so far. Give each pair a few minutes on their own to talk about their person or the dog and then ask them to describe them to the class. Don't correct any mistakes they make, but make a note of them to pick up on after they listen to the recording.
- Explain to pupils that they are going to listen to Anna describing her friends in the picture. Ask pupils to look at the list of names above the picture and to tell you which are boys' names and which are girls' names. Ask them to listen to the recording and write the names in the correct boxes. Play the recording all the way through twice. Ask pupils to check their answers and to complete any missing information, the second time they listen.

Turn to page 105 for the listening script.

Answers

Top row: Sam, Rocky, Jack
Bottom row: Jane, Becky

Extra Class Activity

Put pupils into two teams. Explain that they are going to play a game describing a person from the other team and that the other team members have to guess who they are describing. The team that gets the most correct answers is the winner.

Speaking

- Explain that pupils are going to work in pairs to ask and answer questions about themselves and their families.
- Remind pupils of the short answers that they learnt with *be*, and tell them that they will use this form to answer most of the questions.
- Go round the class monitoring pupils to make sure they are carrying out the task properly. Don't correct any mistakes at this stage, but make a note of any mistakes in structure and pronunciation.

- Ask each pair to ask and answer one of the questions and repeat until each pair has had a turn.
- Write any structural mistakes that pupils made on the board, without saying who made them, and ask pupils to correct them. Deal with any problems in pronunciation.

Answers

Pupils' own answers

Writing

- Explain to pupils that they are going to write five sentences about one of their friends. Ask them to look back at the sentences in *Vocabulary B* to make sure they understand what a sentence describing someone is. Elicit from them that they can write about the person's hair, if they are tall or short, what kind of character they have, what age they are and what they are crazy about.
- If time allows, ask each pupil to say one sentence about one of their friends. Then ask them to write down their sentences.
- Ask pupils to write the other four sentences. You could set this task for homework if you are short of time.

Answers

Pupils' own answers

Extra Task (for early finishers)

See photocopiable material on page 124.

Lesson 2

Objectives

Reading	factual article – true or false questions
Vocabulary	text-related words, family words
Grammar	possessive adjectives
Listening	true or false statements
Sounds of English	silent letters
Song	song about emperor penguins

Way in

- Ask pupils to tell you the opposite of the following words: *dark (fair), beautiful (ugly), clever (stupid), young (old), tall (short)*
- Ask pupils these questions with *be* to practise short answers.
  - Are you thirteen?
  - Is your dad English / Egyptian / Lebanese?
  - Am I tall?
  - Are your friends scientists?
  - Are we Spanish?
  - Is your brother funny?
- Write the words *beach, friend, idea, scientist* and *shark* on the board and ask pupils to tell you sentences which use them.
- Ask pupils what kind of birds Polly and Max were in the

Reading

Introduction. Explain that they are going to read about another kind of bird, but one that can't fly. If they don't know any, give them more clues to elicit penguins from them (*ask which birds live on ice caps, have large bodies but very small heads and are black and white*).

- Explain to pupils that they are going to read about emperor penguins. Ask pupils to read the pre-reading question and to find the answer while they read the text. Ask them to underline the information in the text that helps them find the answer.
- Check the answer as a class.

Answer

the father penguin (...*the father penguin keeps the egg warm on his feet ... after two months the chick* (baby penguin) *comes out ...*)

- If pupils are interested give them further information on emperor penguins using the Background Information box.

Background Information

Emperor penguins are the largest of all penguins. They grow to around 1.15 metres in height and weigh around 40 kilograms. They live for 15 to 20 years in the wild and can survive in temperatures as low as -60°C. They can dive to 565 metres deep and can stay underwater for more than 20 minutes. They eat fish and squid amongst other things. For further information go to www.nationalgeographic.com and follow the link for 'animals'.

Comprehension

- Ask pupils to read sentences 1 to 5 so that they know what information to look for when reading the text again.
- Ask pupils to read the text again to find out if the sentences are true or false and to write *T* or *F* in the boxes provided. Ask them to underline the information in the text that helps them to find the answers.

Answers

1 T (*Emperor penguins are amazing birds.*)
2 F (*... but they are great swimmers.*)
3 T (*It's very cold in the Antarctic ...*)
4 F (*... the father penguin keeps the egg warm on his feet ...*)
5 F (*The father penguin leaves. He goes back to the sea ...*)

Guess what!

- Ask pupils to read the information in the *Guess what!* feature. Ask them if they know any other birds that can't fly and if they know what kind of bird the picture shows (*ostrich*). Some other birds that can't fly are kiwis, emus, the flightless cormorant and some kinds of duck.

Vocabulary

- Explain that the words in the wordbank appear in the text on emperor penguins. Ask pupils to find the words in the text and to underline them. Explain any words they don't understand.
- Ask pupils to do the task individually, but check the answers as a class. Correct their pronunciation where necessary.

Answers

1	cold	4	egg
2	hungry	5	warm
3	sea		

Extra Class Activity

Divide the class into two teams and explain that they are going to have a class quiz based on the reading passage. Make sure all books are closed during the quiz. Then ask each team one of the questions below at a time. If one team cannot answer a question, or gives a wrong answer, give the other team the chance to answer. The team that answers the most questions is the winner.

Suggested questions

1 Where do emperor penguins live? (*in the Antarctic*)
2 How many eggs does the mother penguin have every winter? (*one*)
3 Where does the mother penguin look for food? (*in the sea*)
4 How far does the mother sometimes walk for food? (*80 kilometres*)
5 Where does the father penguin keep the egg? (*on his feet*)
6 Who doesn't eat for two months? (*the father penguin*)
7 What is a chick? (*a baby penguin*)
8 Why does the father leave when the mother penguin comes back? (*because he is hungry*)

Teaching Tip

If you don't want to set up the extra class activity as a quiz, then you can use the suggested questions to check pupils' understanding of the text once they have completed the true or false task.

Grammar

Possessive Adjectives

- Write the following on the board ... *the father keeps the egg warm on his feet...* . Underline the word *his* and ask pupils what it means (*the father's*). Explain that *his* is a possessive adjective and that we use possessive adjectives to show that something belongs to someone.
- Ask pupils to look at the grammar box and read the first sentence and the example. Ask pupils what *his* means in this example (*Dad's*). Explain that we only use possessive adjectives when we have already mentioned the person that the object belongs to.
- Read through the list of Subject Pronouns and Possessive Adjectives and ask the pupils to repeat them after you. If necessary remind pupils that subject pronouns appear before verbs and tell us who does something.
- Ask pupils to read through the statements in the comprehension task on page 14 again to find a possessive adjective and underline it (*her* in statement 4).
- Explain to pupils that possessive adjectives are always followed by a noun and ask them what nouns follow *his* on the board and *her* in statement 4 (*feet and egg*).
- Read the note in the grammar box to the class. Make sure pupils understand the difference between these words by writing the sentences below on the board.
  - *The dog wants a bone. It's hungry.*
  - *Give the dog its bone.*
  - *You're a great swimmer.*
  - *This is your food.*
  - *He's my dad.*
  - *That's his chick.*
- Ask pupils to read the sentences out loud and correct their pronunciation if necessary.
- Ask pupils to do the task individually, but check the answers as a class.

Answers

1 Her	2 Its	3 Their	4 his
5 Our	6 your	7 my	8 your

Vocabulary

- Read the words in the wordbank and ask pupils to repeat them after you. Correct their pronunciation if necessary.
- Ask them to look at pictures 1 to 6 and ask them to complete the family pairs using the words in the wordbank.
- Ask pupils to do the task in pairs to encourage discussion, but check the answers as a class.

Answers

1 dad	2 sister	3 grandad
4 wife	5 uncle	6 daughter

Extra Class Activity

Ask pupils to work in pairs and to tell each other about their families. They can tell each other what the members of their families are called, how old they are, what they look like and where they live, etc.

Listening

- Explain to pupils that they are going to listen to a boy called Ben talking about his aunt and uncle. Ask pupils to read sentences 1 to 5 quickly to find family words (*uncle*, *aunt* and *daughter*). Then ask them to underline the verbs in the sentences (*is, are, is, isn't, is*). Explain that they need to pay attention to whether the verb forms are affirmative or negative as they listen.
- Ask pupils to read through all of the sentences quickly and make sure that they understand that they have to write *T* if the sentence is correct or *F* if it is incorrect.
- Play the recording once and then ask pupils to compare their answers with a partner. Ask them to justify any answers that are different. Play the recording a second time and ask them to check their answers or fill in any missing information.
- Check the answers as a class and make sure pupils can justify their answers.

Turn to page 105 for the listening script.

Answers

1 T (*He's tall ...*)
2 F (*... and his eyes are blue ...*)
3 F (*She's young – She's twenty-eight years old.*)
4 F (*She's a scientist.*)
5 F (*... she's my cousin ...*)

Sounds of English

A

- Explain to pupils that they are going to hear three words and that they have to listen to see what is special about them. Ask them to read the three words and to pay attention to the red letters as they say them.
- Play the recording and elicit from pupils that the letters in red are silent.

Answer

They are silent letters.

B

- Explain to pupils that silent letters are common in English.
- Ask pupils to work in pairs to say the words to each other so that they can work out which letter is silent in each word together.
- Play the recording and ask pupils to check their answers as they listen.
- Check the answers as a class.

Answers

1 friend	2 listen	3 where	4 two

Extra Class Activity

Explain to pupils that you are going to say some words that have silent letters and ask them to write them down. Suggested words: *white, blue, yellow, autumn, knife*. Check the spelling as a class and ask which letters are silent (h, e, w, n, and k). You might like to explain that although we can't hear the *e* in *white* and *knife*, it changes the way we say *i* in these words.

Song

- Ask pupils what kind of penguins they read about at the beginning of the lesson (*emperor penguins*). Elicit that penguins are a kind of bird that can't fly but that can swim. Ask pupils if they remember what a chick is (*a baby penguin*).
- Tell pupils that they are going to listen to the penguin song and that they should read the song as they listen.
- Play the song and ask pupils who is singing the song (*a penguin chick*). Play it again and ask the pupils to sing along. Play the song a number of times if the pupils enjoy singing along.

Extra Task (for early finishers)

See photocopiable material on page 124.

Lesson 3

Objectives

Reading	personal email – answering open-ended questions
Say it like this!	making friends
Grammar	possessive 's
Writing	punctuation, writing an email

Way in

- Check pupils' spelling of the words they learnt in Lesson 2 by asking them to write down the following words: *cold, egg, hungry, sea* and *warm*.
- Say the following and ask pupils to complete the family word pairs orally: *son and ..., aunt and ..., mum and ..., grandma and ..., husband and ..., brother and ...*.
- Say subject pronouns and ask pupils to call out the corresponding possessive adjectives.

Reading

- Ask pupils if they send emails. If they do, ask who they send them to. Then ask them if they have a best friend. If they do, ask them to tell each other about their best friends.
- Ask pupils to look at the title on page 16 and the two photos accompanying the emails. Ask pupils who the people in the photos might be.
- Explain to pupils that they are going to read the emails and that they should try to find out which best friend is from the same family as the person writing the email.

Answer

Sophie, who is Lara's best friend, is also her mother.

Comprehension

- Ask pupils who the photos on page 16 probably show (*Mike and Greg*, *Lara and Sophie*).
- Ask pupils to read through the comprehension questions so that they know what answers to look for when they read the emails again.
- Ask pupils to read the emails again and then to answer the questions.
- Ask pupils to do the task individually, but check the answers as a class.
- Explain any words that the pupils don't know and correct their pronunciation where necessary. Make sure pupils know how to read the email addresses properly in English, (*errol at epalengland dot com; lara at fra dot com*). Also, explain that although dates are written 8th February, etc, we say the 8th *of* February.

Answers

1	Class 3A	4	France
2	Mike and Greg	5	29 years old
3	8th February		

Teaching Tip

If your pupils get on well with each other, ask them to swap email addresses with each other. Encourage them to email each other in English from time to time. It could be a good way of making sure they find out what homework they have when they miss a lesson.

Say it like this!

- Explain to pupils that they are going to practise using some expressions for making friends. Ask them to work with a partner to ask and answer the questions.
- Ask pupils to role play making friends with each other to answer the questions in the book. You could assign one question and answer to each pair and repeat until all pupils have had a chance to speak.

Answers

Pupils' own answers

Extra Class Activity

You could extend this task by assigning each pupil one of the questions on page 16 to ask the others. Ask pupils to move around the room asking their questions and answering the other pupils' questions until they have all spoken to each other. Then once they sit back down, point to one pupil at a time and ask the others one of the questions about him or her.

Grammar

Possessive 's

- Go round the room picking up things that belong to the pupils. Say who they belong to using *possessive 's* (*This is Maria's pen.*, *This is Harry's ruler*, etc.).
- Read the first part of the grammar box to the class, then write on the board *Ron is the boy's dad.* and *Ron is the boys' dad.* Ask them to tell you what the difference between the sentences is (*the order of the s and the apostrophe*). Explain that in the first sentence Ron is one boy's dad, but that in the second sentence Ron is more than one boy's dad.
- Read the Note in the grammar box and ask pupils what other irregular nouns they know that follows this rule (*men's, mice's*, etc).
- Do the first sentence in the task as a class and make sure that pupils understand which noun needs an apostrophe and why.
- Ask pupils to do the other sentences individually, but check the answers as a class. Write the answers on the board for pupils to see to avoid confusion.

Answers

1	Jane's	4	children's
2	babies'	5	mum's
3	Henry's	6	woman's

Extra Class Activity

Ask pupils to write sentences about the people they read about in the *Reading* section. Write the following prompts on the board:

- Mike and Greg / are / Errol / best friend
- 8th February / is / the boy / birthday
- Greg / is / Mike / twin brother
- Sophie / is / Lara / best friend
- Lara / is / Sophie / daughter

Answers

- Mike and Greg are Errol's best friends.
- 8th February is the boy's birthday.
- Greg is Mike's twin brother.
- Sophie is Lara's best friend.
- Lara is Sophie's daughter.

Writing

Punctuation

A

- Tell pupils to look at the sentences in the previous grammar exercise. Ask them to identify what is included in each sentence as well as the *possessive 's*. Elicit that the sentences include *full stops* (*at the end of each sentence*) and start with *capital letters*.
- Ask pupils to do the task individually, but check the answers as a class.

B

- Explain to pupils that they have to rewrite the sentences using the correct punctuation.
- Do the first sentence together as a class and write the correct answer on the board for pupils to see.
- Ask pupils to do the rest of the task individually but check the answers as a class.

Answers

1 I'm Dan's sister.
2 Are you Rachel's friend?
3 Penguins are amazing animals.
4 My dog's very clever.
5 It's a great house.

Teaching Tip

You might like to extend this task by asking pupils about the different uses of 's in the sentences. Ask which ones are possessive (*Dan's*, *Rachel's*), and which ones are the short form of *is* (*dog's*, *It's*). Make sure they realise that there is no apostrophe in *Penguins* in sentence 3 because it is just the plural form of the noun.

C

- Explain to pupils that they are going to read an email from a French girl called Florence. Tell them that Florence is learning English and that she has made some mistakes in her email. Ask them to read the first sentence and to tell you what mistakes Florence has made (*she hasn't used capital letters correctly*).
- Ask pupils to do the rest of the task individually, but check the answers as a class.

Answers

Hi!

I'm **F**lorence and **I**'m from **F**rance. I'm eleven years old. **I**'m tall with dark hair and green eyes.

My sister Corinne is six years old and my brother **J**ean is a baby.

I'm crazy about sport and my cat, **Felix.**

What are you crazy about?

Email me at:
FlorenceRouen@fra.com

Task

D

- Explain to pupils that they are going to write an email about themselves that is similar to the ones that they have read in the lesson so far. You may have to pre-teach *I haven't got any brothers or sisters*.
- Ask pupils to answer the questions individually, but check the answers as a class. Obviously answers will vary from pupil to pupil, but make sure that structures are consistent.

Suggested answers

Hi!

I'm Roberto and I'm from Italy. I'm nine years old.

My brother's name is Francesco and my sister's name is Laura. Francesco is five years old and Laura is a baby.

I'm crazy about football.

What are you crazy about?

Email me at: RobertoMondi@italia.com

E

- Ask pupils to proofread their email and to check their punctuation.

Teaching Tip

Tell pupils that when they do a piece of writing for you, they should follow a plan like the one in D and proofread their work once they've finished.

Extra Task (for early finishers)

See photocopiable material on page 124.

Project Book

The pupils may do Project 1 now they have completed the unit. The answer key and teacher's notes are on pages 148-152 of this book.

My Favourite Things

Way in

- Give pupils a few minutes to read each others' paragraphs about themselves from Unit 1, Lesson 3. They can do this in pairs, or you could hang the paragraphs on the wall for them to read when they have time.
- Write the sentences below on the board and ask pupils to correct them in their notebooks.
    1 Isnt this Johns' book.
    2 that is Maxs car.
    3 Emperor penguin's are funny?
    4 My best friends brothers' are twins.
    5 The dog hasn't got it's bone.

Answers
1 Isn't this John's book?
2 That is Max's car.
3 Emperor penguins are funny.
4 My best friend's brothers are twins.
5 The dog hasn't got its bone.

Quiz

- Ask pupils what Kate in *The Cortuga Mystery* is crazy about (*science*). Explain to pupils that science is one of her favourite things and that the theme of this unit is *favourite things*. Ask them to work in small groups to tell each other what their *favourite things* are.
- Ask pupils to report back to the class about their *favourite things*.
- Ask pupils to turn to pages 18 and 19 in their Pupil's Books. Ask them to look at the picture and ask what might be the favourite things of the children in the picture. They can continue working in groups if time permits.

Teaching Tip
Spending a few minutes revising the material from the previous lesson will allow you to monitor pupils' progress, and will also mean that any pupils who are late for class won't miss any new material.

- Explain to pupils that they are going to do a quiz based on some of the things in the picture. Ask them to work in pairs to answer the quiz questions, but check the answers as a class.

Answers
a 7
b 30
c 5 pairs (*and 1 individual boot*)

Teaching Tip
If a pupil asks what the name of something is in English that you don't know, ask them to look up the word in a bilingual dictionary (*if there is one in the classroom*). ➡

Alternatively, ask them to find out for homework what it is and make a note to check it before the next lesson. This way, pupils are less likely to lose trust in you and they will take a more active part in the learning process.

Lesson 1

Objectives

Reading	The Cortuga Mystery
Vocabulary	text-related words, toys
Grammar	have got – affirmative, negative, question, short answers
Listening	circling the correct answers
Speaking	asking and answering personal questions
Writing	writing sentences about belongings and favourite things

The Cortuga Mystery
For teachers using the DVD

- Make sure each pupil has a copy of the DVD Worksheet found on page 113.
- Please follow the procedure outlined in Unit 1, Lesson 1 on pages 12 and 13 for teachers using the DVD.

Before You Watch

Answers
1 Uncle Oliver's house
2 to drink lemonade (*Remind pupils of Jake's invitation at the end of the last episode.*)

While You Watch

Answers
1 strange   **4** laptop
2 lizard   **5** mystery
3 message

After You Watch

Answers
1 Uncle Oliver   **5** a puzzle
2 Jake   **6** no
3 at the museum   **7** Mandy
4 no

For teachers using the audio CD

- Begin by asking pupils where Uncle Oliver's house is (*on the beach*) and what he is (*a scientist*). Explain to pupils that Uncle Oliver works in a museum.
- Tell pupils that they are going to listen to and read the next part of the story. Ask them to look at the pictures and to follow the story as they listen.

- Play the recording once and ask the pupils where the children are (*in Uncle Oliver's house*) and why they are there (*for lemonade*). Ask the pupils what the children find (*a puzzle*) and what happens to them at the end (*they disappear*).
- Ask pupils to read the story out loud. Assign the roles of Jake, Mandy, Robbie and Kate to different pupils. If you have a large class, you may have to repeat until all pupils have had a turn.
- Explain any vocabulary pupils don't know and correct their pronunciation where necessary.
- As a class, ask pupils the questions below to check they have understood the episode.

  1 Who has got a pet? (*Uncle Oliver*)
  2 Who has got a message on his mobile phone? (*Jake*)
  3 Where is Uncle Oliver? (*at the museum*)
  4 Has Uncle Oliver's laptop got any computer games? (*no*)
  5 What has Mandy got? (*a puzzle*)
  6 Has she got all the pieces of the puzzle? (*no*)
  7 Who is scared? (*Mandy*)

Vocabulary

A
- Explain that the words in the wordbank appear in the cartoon episode. Ask pupils to find the words in the text and underline them. Explain any words they still don't understand.
- Ask pupils to do the task individually, but check the answers as a class. Correct their pronunciation where necessary.

Answers

1	games	**4**	message
2	things	**5**	strange
3	toy		

B
- Ask pupils to look at pictures a to f and to tell you which things they saw in the picture on pages 18 and 19 (*laptop, teddy bear*).
- Explain to pupils that they have to match words 1 to 6 with pictures a to f.
- Ask pupils to do the task individually, but check the answers as a class.

Answers

1e **2**c **3**b **4**f **5**d **6**a

Extra Class Activity

Ask pupils to think of sentences using the words in *B*. They can write them in their notebooks.

Teaching Tip

Explain to pupils that all the words in *B* are nouns. Encourage them to make a note of what part of speech new words are when they write them in their vocabulary notebooks.

Grammar

Have got
- Ask pupils to look back at the picture on pages 18 and 19. Explain that you are going to describe people and things to them and ask them to identify who or what they are. Say:
  - This person has got blue shorts (*the boy in the paddling pool*).
  - These people haven't got shoes on (*the lady on the sofa and the girl lying across the ball – also accept the boy in the paddling pool as an answer as strictly speaking he isn't wearing shoes*).
  - This person has got a black top (*the lady on the sofa*).
  - These people have got white t-shirts (*the boy sitting on top of the car, the boy in the paddling pool, the man on the sofa*).
  - It has got a pink door (*the children's play house*).
- Explain to pupils that we use *have got* to describe people and things, and to say what belongs to them.
- Ask pupils to turn back to page 21 and read the grammar box to the class. When reading the affirmative forms, read the short forms first and then explain that *have got* and *has got* are the long forms.
- Write the sentences below on the board and ask pupils if *has got* describes someone or something or tells us that something belongs to someone or something.
  - The family have got a big white house (*belongs to*).
  - The girl has got long fair hair (*describes*).
  - The man has got brown hair (*describes*).
  - The boy has got flippers (*belongs to*).

A
- Ask pupils to read through the paragraph to find out who Sasha is (*Liz's cat*). Tell them not to worry about filling in the gaps yet.
- Ask pupils to complete the sentences. Point out that where there is a tick after the gap they should use the affirmative, and that where there is a cross after the gap they should use the negative.
- Ask pupils to do the task individually, but check the answers as a class.

Answers

1	've / have got	**5**	've / have got
2	hasn't got	**6**	hasn't got
3	has got	**7**	has got
4	hasn't got	**8**	hasn't got

Extra Class Activity

Ask pupils if they have got any pets. Ask the pupils who have got pets to describe them to the rest of the class.

B
- Explain to pupils that they are going to write some questions and answers using *have / has got* and the prompts given.
- Do the first one together and remind pupils that in short answers we leave out the word *got*.
- Ask pupils to do the rest of the task individually, but check the answers as a class.
- Alternatively, if you are short of time you could assign this task as homework.

Answers

1 Has Jake got a mobile phone?, he has
2 Have Jake and Mandy got an aunt?, they haven't
3 Have you got a pet lizard, Jamie?, I have
4 Has your sister got a skateboard?, she hasn't

Listening

- Ask the pupils to read through the sentences and options. Ask them how many people they are going to hear about (*three – Bruno, Robin* and *Vicky*).
- Explain to pupils that they are going to listen to five short pieces from a conversation and that there is one question for each of the pieces.
- Play the recording and ask pupils to circle the correct answers.
- Give pupils a few minutes to compare their answers with a partner. Ask them to justify their answers if they are different.
- Play the recording again and ask pupils to check their answers and to fill in any missing information.
- Check the answers as a class and ask pupils to justify the answers.

Turn to page 105 for the listening script.

Answers
1b   2b   3a   4b   5a

Speaking

- Explain that pupils are going to work in pairs to ask and answer questions about themselves and their families.
- Remind pupils of the short answers that they learnt with *have got*, and tell them they will use this form to answer some of the questions.
- Go round the class monitoring pupils to make sure they are carrying out the task properly. Don't correct any mistakes at this stage, but make a note of any mistakes in structure and pronunciation.
- Ask each pair to ask and answer one of the questions and repeat until each pair has had a turn.
- Write any structural mistakes that pupils made on the board, without saying who made them, and ask them to correct them. Deal with any problems in pronunciation.

Answers
Pupils' own answers

Writing

- Ask pupils to work in pairs to tell each other four things that they've got that they haven't spoken about already. Help them with any words that they want to use but don't know.
- Ask pupils to write sentences about the four things they told their partner about and one sentence about their favourite thing. Encourage pupils to give details about the things they describe.
- Go round the class reading their sentences and correcting any mistakes they make.
- Ask each pupil to read out one of their sentences to the class.
- Alternatively, you could ask pupils to do this task for homework.

Lesson 2

Objectives

Reading	website – multiple matching
Vocabulary	text-related words, possessions
Grammar	there is / there are; prepositions of place
Listening	true or false questions

Way in

- Ask pupils to keep their books closed. Show them page 20 in your book. Point to the lizard and ask *What has Uncle Oliver got?* (*a lizard*). Point to Jake's mobile phone and ask *What has Jake got?* (*a mobile phone*). Point to the laptop and ask, *What is this?* (*a laptop*). Then ask *What hasn't the laptop got?* (*computer games*). Point to the puzzle and ask *What has Mandy got?* (*a puzzle*). Then ask *What has the puzzle got?* (*a message*).
- Ask the questions below round the class to pupils at random. Ask pupils to reply using short answers and make sure that all pupils answer at least one question.

  - Have you got a pet?
  - Has your grandad got a skateboard?
  - Have you got any brothers and sisters?
  - Have I got blue eyes?
  - Has the year got twelve seasons?
  - Has your aunt got a toy robot?
  - Have we got English today?
  - Has the week got seven days?
  - Have Kate and Robbie got an Uncle Oliver?
  - Have you got a laptop?

Reading

- Ask pupils if they use the Internet. If they do, ask which websites they visit.
- Ask pupils if they visit the *National Geographic* website. Explain that they are going to read adverts from the *National Geographic kids' website*.
- Ask pupils to read the website on their own and to decide which present they like and which they don't like. Ask pupils to tell you why.

- Explain any words they don't know and correct pronunciation where necessary.

Comprehension

- Explain to pupils that they have to match one of the presents on the website with each of the sentences 1 to 4. Make sure they understand which letters correspond to each product.
- Ask pupils to do the task individually, but check the answers as a class.

Answers
1 D (*There are lots of strange animals from the real world on this DVD!*)
2 SH (*You can walk and feel like an astronaut.*)
3 G (*This is a talking map of the world! … Touch a country with the pen and the globe tells you about it!*)
4 SP (*Do you like tricks? Then this is the toy for you.*)

Extra Class Activity

Scavenger Hunt Game

Write the questions below on the board. Tell pupils they have three minutes to find the answers in the website. Explain that they should scan the adverts for the answers and not read them all carefully. You could put the pupils into pairs for this task and make it into a competition to see which pair gets the most correct answers first.

1 How many legs has a spider got? (*eight*)
2 What is a Komodo dragon? (*a very big lizard*)
3 What presents are good for an eleven year old? (*Interactive Talking Globe, Creepy Creatures DVD and Moon Shoes*)
4 What do you feel like with the Moon Shoes? (*an astronaut*)
5 What present can help you with school work? (*Interactive Talking Globe*)
6 What present is scary? (*Remote Controlled Tarantula*)

Guess what!

Ask pupils to read the information in the *Guess what!* feature. Ask them if they know any other creatures that have a strange number of eyes (*the octopus has only got one eye*) or if they know any creatures that are blind or don't see well (*bats, moles*).

Vocabulary

- Explain that the words in the wordbank appear in the website. Ask pupils to find the words in the text and underline them. Explain any words they still don't understand.
- Ask pupils to do the task individually, but check the answers as a class. Correct their pronunciation where necessary.

Answers
1 country   4 present
2 moving   5 scary
3 exciting

Teaching Tip
Give pupils a few minutes to record the words from the vocabulary task in their notebooks and remind them to write in brackets which part of speech the words are (*1 and 4 are nouns; 2, 3 and 5 are adjectives*).

Grammar

There is, There are

- Point to objects in the classroom or outside the window and describe them using *There is* or *There are*. For example, say, *Look, there's an apple on the tree.*; *There are four boys in the classroom.*; *There's a bus on the road.*; *There's a spider on my desk.*
- Read the uses of *There is, There are* in the grammar box and ask pupils to read the example sentences out loud with you.
- Read the forms of *There is, There are* in the grammar box to the class and ask them to repeat them after you.
- Ask pupils to look back at the website and the comprehension task and underline all the examples of *There is, There are* (in advert 2, *There's a magic pen …*; in advert 3, *There are lots of strange animals …*; comprehension question 1, *There are strange animals …*).

A
- Explain to pupils that they are going to write sentences using the words given. Remind them that we start sentences with a capital letter and end with a full stop or a question mark. Do the first one together as a class and then ask the pupils to do the rest individually, but check the answers as a class.

Answers
1 There aren't any maps at school.
2 Is there a robot in your classroom?
3 There are lots of girls in our class.
4 Are there any spiders here?
5 There isn't a skateboard here.

B
- Ask questions about what *there is / there are* in the classroom and ask pupils to reply using short answers. For example, *Is there a laptop in the classroom?*; *Are there puzzles on your desks?*; *Are there mobile phones in your bags?*
- Ask pupils to do the task individually, but check the answers as a class.

Teaching Tip
If you feel that your pupils need further practice, ask them to turn to pages 18 and 19 and to ask each other about things that *are* or *aren't* in the picture.

Prepositions of place

- Begin by putting an object in various places and telling pupils where it is. You could use a pen. Put it on your desk and say *There is a pen on my desk*. Put it in your bag and say *There is a pen in my bag*. Put it under your desk and say *There is a pen under my desk*. Demonstrate all the prepositions of place in this way.
- Ask pupils to look at the pictures of the frog and the rocks and ask them to say where the frog is in each picture.
- Explain to pupils that they are going to complete sentences about the picture of the children in the bedroom using prepositions of place.

- Ask pupils to do the task in pairs to encourage discussion, but check the answers as a class.

Extra Class Activity

If you have time, you could ask pupils the questions below about the picture.

1 Where is the window? (*behind the girl*)
2 Where are the pens and pencils? (*on the desk*)
3 Where is the rug? (*under the box*)
4 Where is the chair? (*in front of the desk*)

Vocabulary

- Ask pupils to look at pictures 1 to 6 and ask them if they have got any of these things.
- Explain to pupils that they are going to label the pictures with the words in the wordbank.
- Ask pupils to do the task individually, but check the answers as a class.

Answers
1	watch	4	comic
2	globe	5	piano
3	camera	6	ice skates

Listening

- Ask pupils if it's any of their friends' or family's birthday soon. If yes, ask what present they will buy the person. Ask if they would give any of the presents from the website in the *Reading* on Page 22.
- Ask pupils to read the sentences. Explain that they won't hear exactly what is written when they listen to the recording and that they may have to draw conclusions from what they hear.
- Play the recording once and then ask pupils to compare their answers with a partner. Ask them to justify their answers if they have a different one. Play the recording a second time and ask them to check their answers or fill in any missing information.
- Check the answers as a class and ask pupils to justify their answers.

Turn to page 105 for the listening script.

Answers
1 T (*It's my brother's birthday on Friday.*)
2 T (*This is Tom's birthday present.*)
3 T (*A book? Not a very exciting present.*)
4 T (*It's got books and computer games too.*)
5 F (*… but Tom's got lots of DVDs.*)

Extra Task (for early finishers)

See photocopiable material on page 125.

Lesson 3

Objectives

Reading	article – multiple matching
Say it like this!	playing games
Listening	putting objects in the correct order
Speaking	finding differences between two pictures
Sounds of English	pronunciation of *the*
Writing	connectors, writing an advert

Way in

- Go round the class asking questions about objects in the room using *Is / Are there …?*. Explain to pupils they should answer using short answers.
  ### Suggested questions
  - Is there a camera in my hand?
  - Are there globes on the desks?
  - Are there mobile phones in the classroom?
  - Is there a present on your chair?
  - Is there a piano in front of the door?
  - Are there ice skates on your feet?
  - Are there lizards in your bag?
  - Is there a comic in the classroom?
- Give an object to pupils, for example, a pen or a book, and ask them to put it in a specific place. Give the object to one pupil at a time.
  ### Suggested places
  - under a book
  - next to a bag
  - on a desk
  - behind another pupil
  - between your desk and the board
  - in a bag
  - near the door
  - in front of the class
- Ask pupils to write sentences using the following words:
  country   exciting   moving   present   scary

Reading

- Ask pupils to look at the pictures and to guess what each person's favourite thing is. Accept any answer at this stage, but correct their pronunciation where necessary.
- Ask pupils to read the article on their own and then to write the children's names under their photos.
- Ask pupils to work with a partner to compare their answers. Ask pupils what helped them to find the answers apart from the favourite things mentioned (*whether it's a girl's or boy's name and the age given*).

Answers from top to bottom in picture
Tom, Miranda, Dan, Amy

Comprehension

- Ask pupils to read through the questions and explain that they should write the initial of the correct child in each of the boxes.
- Ask pupils to do the task individually, but check the answers as a class.

Answers
1M   2D   3M   4T   5A

Say it like this!

- Explain to pupils that they are going to learn set phrases we use in English when playing games.
- Give pupils a few minutes to role play each of the dialogues in pairs once they have completed them. Then ask each pair to practise one of the dialogues in front of the class. Repeat until all pupils have had a turn. If there is an odd number of pupils, you could role play with one of the pupils.
- Correct pupils' pronunciation and intonation patterns where needed.

Extra Class Activity

Ask pupils what games you might be playing or things you might be playing with if you use the phrases in *Say it like this!*

Suggested answers

- Can I have a go? – computer game, puzzle
- Catch! – ball game
- It's my/your turn! – board game, computer game
- Slow down! – bike, skateboard, ice skating
- Well done! – board game, computer game, puzzle, ball game

Listening

- Explain to pupils that they are going to hear four conversations about toys and games that children have got and that they are going to note down the order that they hear about each toy or game in. Make sure pupils realise that they won't hear the words *skateboard*, *ball*, *computer game* or *board game* on the recording. They have to work out from the language used to talk about each thing, what the children are talking about.
- Encourage pupils to number each object as they hear about them rather than trying to find the answers from a to d respectively. Do the first one together as a class so that they understand how to number the children's things.
- Ask pupils what helped them to find the answer to the first conversation (*It's my turn. Wow – 206. That's great!* and also the noise of the game in the background).
- Play the rest of the recording and ask pupils to number the remaining things, then check the answers as a class. Ask pupils to justify their answers.

Turn to page 105 for the listening script.

Answers

a2 **b**4 **c**1 **d**3

Speaking

- Quickly revise the forms of *have / has got* and *there is / are* with the class.
- Ask pupils to look at the two pictures and explain that there are four differences between them. Tell pupils to work in pairs to find the differences.
- Walk around the room making sure they are carrying out the task properly. Make a note of any mistakes in structure and pronunciation that you notice.

- Check as a class by asking each pair to tell you one of the differences they have found.
- Write the mistakes that you heard on the board, without saying who made them, and ask pupils to correct them. Also correct any mistakes in pronunciation that you heard.

Suggested answers

- In **picture one**, a boy has got / there is a small red kite. In **picture two**, he has got / there is a big red kite.
- In **picture one**, a girl has got / there is one dog. In **picture two**, she has got / there are two dogs.
- In picture one, a girl has got / there is a toy robot. In **picture two**, she has got / there is a teddy bear.
- In **picture one**, a boy has got / there is a comic. In **picture two**, he has got / there is a laptop.

Teaching Tip

During speaking tasks, try not to correct pupils' mistakes constantly as this will make them less fluent and undermine their confidence. Make time to correct mistakes together as a class so that pupils understand why something is wrong rather than just copying the correct form that you tell them as they speak. This way, they will be less likely to make the same mistake in the future.

Sounds of English

- Explain to pupils that in English the word *the* is pronounced in two different ways.
- Ask them to listen to the recording and in pairs to pronounce the different versions.
- Check their pronunciation as a class and play the recording again if necessary.
- Elicit from pupils that the difference in pronunciation is because *computer* and *toy* begin with a *consonant*, but *animal* and *uncle* begin with a *vowel* sound.

Answers

1 and 2 (*the*)   3 and 4 (*thee*)

Writing

Connectors

A

- Write the words *exciting*, *fun*, *new* and *boring* on the board. Ask pupils which words describe something good (*exciting*, *fun* and *new*) and which word describes something bad (*boring*).
- Read the theory and the example sentences with the class. Point out that we use *and* to add something that is similar to a sentence, whereas we use *but* to add something that is different. Remind pupils that *exciting* and *fun* describe something good, so we use *and* to connect them, but that *new* describes something good and *boring* describes something bad, so we use *but* to connect them.

Extra Class Activity

Ask pupils to look back at the article in the *Reading* section in this lesson and to underline examples of *and* and *but*. If you are short of time, then ask pupils to work in pairs and assign one of the children's extracts to each pair. Then check the answers as a class.   ➡

Project Book

The pupils may do Project 2 now they have completed the unit. The answer key and teacher's notes are on pages 148-152 of this book.

B

- Ask pupils to read the sentences and then decide whether *and* or *but* should fill the gaps.
- Ask pupils to do the task individually, but check the answers as a class.

Answers

1	and	**4**	and
2	but	**5**	but
3	and		

C

- Ask pupils to quickly read the advert and then ask them the questions below. Tell them not to circle any answers yet.
  - What colour is the bike? (*blue*)
  - Is it old or new? (*old*)
  - Is it fast or slow? (*fast*)
  - How much is it? (*£60*)
  - Who has got the bike? (*Harry*)
- Ask pupils to do the task individually, but check the answers as a class.

Answers

1 and   **2** but   **3** but   **4** and

Task

- Explain to pupils that they are going to write an advert like the one in *C* for one of their favourite things. Ask them to work in pairs to discuss the thing they will sell and to describe it to each other.
- Ask pupils to write the answers to the questions in their books.

Suggested answer

Skateboard for sale!

It's yellow and it's cool
It's a great skateboard. It isn't new but it's very fast.
It's great for boys but not girls!

Price £30
Ring 210 223 2445 and ask for Bill

E

- Ask pupils to read back through their sentences in *D* to make sure that they have used *and* and *but* where necessary.
- Ask pupils to read some of their sentences to the class. Make sure all pupils have a chance to speak.
- Ask pupils to use their answers from *D* to write a proper advert like the one in *C* for homework. Remind them to proofread their advert. They could also stick on a photograph or draw a picture of the item the advert is about. This way you could display them around the classroom.

Objectives

- To revise vocabulary and grammar from Units 1 and 2
- Song – Skateboard Sharks

Revision

- Explain to pupils that there will be a review after every two units in *Wonderful World 3*. Tell them that *Review 1* revises the material they saw in Units 1 and 2.
- Explain to pupils that they can ask you for help with the exercises or look back at the units if they're not sure about an answer, as the review is not a test.
- Decide how you will carry out the review. You could ask pupils to do one task at a time and then correct it immediately, or ask pupils to do all the tasks and then correct them together at the end. If you do all the tasks together, let pupils know every now and again how much time they have got left to finish the tasks.
- Ask pupils not to leave any answers blank and to try to find any answers they aren't sure about in the units.
- Revise the vocabulary and grammar as a class before pupils do the review.

Vocabulary Revision

- Ask pupils to tell you as many adjectives as possible. Try to elicit *dark*, *fair*, *stupid*, *clever*, *old*, *young*, *tall*, *short*, *funny*, *scary*, *beautiful*, *ugly*, *cold*, *warm* and *hungry*. Ask pupils to tell you about a person or a thing with these adjectives.
- Check that pupils remember family words. Make two columns on the board with the titles *girl / woman* and *boy / man* and ask pupils to put the words related to family into each column.
- Ask pupils what the difference between a teddy bear and a penguin is (*a teddy bear is a toy*, but *a penguin is real*). Then ask one group of pupils to make a list of as many toys and games as possible, and another group to make a list of as many animals as possible.

Grammar Revision

- Write *I*, *you*, *he / she / it*, and *we / you / they* one below the other on the board and ask a pupil to come and write the affirmative forms of *be* beside the subject pronouns. Ask the other pupils to help the pupil who's writing. Then ask individual pupils at random round the class to tell you the negative forms. Do the same for the question forms.
- Write the subject pronoun *I* on the board and the possessive adjective *my* next to it. Then write the other subject pronouns below *I* and elicit their possessive adjectives. Write them all on the board and point to each one and ask pupils to say them.
- Write *Grandads shoes are new.* and *The families houses are big.* on the board and elicit from pupils that the correct possessive form is missing. Ask pupils to correct the sentences to read *Grandad's* and *families'*. Then ask pupils to tell you the difference between *The girl's teacher is nice.* (one girl) and *The girls' teacher is nice.* (more than one girl).
- Ask each pupil to tell you one thing that he or she has got and one thing he or she hasn't got. Then ask one pupil to ask another pupil if they have got something and tell the other pupil to reply using a short answer. Repeat until all pupils have either asked or answered a question. Make sure pupils remember all forms of the verb.

Vocabulary

A

- Ask pupils to say each of the words as a class and then individually. Correct their pronunciation if necessary.
- Ask pupils to go to the first page of stickers at the back of the book and find the stickers for *Review 1*. Tell them to decide which adjective each sticker shows and to stick it in the correct box.
- Check that pupils have put the correct stickers above each word.

B

- Ask pupils to read the words in the wordbank and make sure they understand family, toys and animals. Tell them to look back at Unit 1 Lessons 1 and 2 and Unit 2 Lesson 1 for a reminder if they need to.
- Accept the correct words in each column in any order when checking pupils' answers.

Answers

Family: aunt, daughter, grandma
Toys: board game, puzzle, teddy bear
Animals: lizard, penguin, shark

C

- Ask pupils to choose the correct response to each statement and tell them to look back at the Reading texts in Unit 1 Lessons 1 and 3 and Unit 2 Lesson 1 for a reminder if they need to.
- Then ask them to check their answers with a partner. One pupil should say the statement and the other the response.
- Ask pupils what is happening in each dialogue.

Answers

1 b	2 a	3 b	4 b	5 a	6 b

Grammar

A

- Tell pupils to look at the subject of each sentence before they circle the answer and to be careful with the word order.
- Tell them to look back at Unit 1 Lesson 1 grammar box for a reminder if they need to.

Answers

1	Is	2	are not	3	aren't
4	Am I	5	is	6	Are

B

- Tell pupils to underline the word in the first sentence that relates to the word in bold. Point out that sometimes the word the correct word will begin with a capital letter.
- Tell pupils to look back at Unit 1 Lesson 2 for a reminder grammar box if they need to.

Answers

1	His	2	our	3	His
4	Their	5	Its	6	my

26

C
- Tell pupils to decide whether each word is singular, a regular plural or an irregular plural.
- Tell pupils to look back at Unit 1 Lesson 3 grammar box for a reminder if they need to.

Answers

1	dad's	**4**	children's
2	babies'	**5**	Polly's
3	monsters'	**6**	family's

D
- Point out to pupils that they should read the sentences before trying to fill the gaps to decide if they need the affirmative or the negative. Tell them to find the subject of each sentence to help them get the correct form of *have*.
- Tell pupils to look back at Unit 2 Lesson 1 grammar box for a reminder if they need to.

Answers

1	hasn't got	**5**	hasn't got
2	has got	**6**	have got
3	haven't got	**7**	have got
4	hasn't got	**8**	has got

E
- Explain to pupils that their answers are personal and that they should reply using short answers.
- Tell pupils to look back at Unit 2 Lesson 1 grammar box for a reminder if they need to.

Answers

Pupils' own answers

Song

- Tell pupils they are going to listen to a song about the *Skateboard Sharks*. Ask them to read and listen to the song and to find out where the *Sharks* play on their skateboards (*on the street or in the park*) and why skateboards are sometimes scary (*because they are fast*).
- Play the song again and ask pupils to sing along. You could do this verse by verse and then play it once all the way through.
- To finish, ask pupils to look at the picture of the *Skateboard Sharks* and to find as many things as possible from the song.

When checking pupils' answers to the review tasks, make a note of any problem areas in vocabulary and grammar that they still have. Try to do extra work on these areas so that your pupils progress well.

School Life

Way in

- Give pupils a few minutes to read each other's adverts about their favourite things from Unit 2, Lesson 3. They can do this in pairs or you could hang the paragraphs on the wall for them to read when they have time.
- Write *the ball*, *the skateboard*, *the aunt*, *the emperor penguin* on the board and ask pupils to say them out loud. Correct any mistakes in pronunciation, especially if they make a mistake with *the*.
- Ask pupils to write two sentences, one using *and*, the other using *but*. Ask them to read out their sentences to the class.
- Write the words *amazing*, *beautiful*, *big*, *boring*, *cool*, *exciting*, *scary* and *ugly* on the board. Then ask pupils to look at the picture on pages 28 and 29 and to use the words on the board to tell a partner about their reaction to the picture (*It's cool and exciting. It's scary but amazing.*).

- Ask pupils to read the title of the unit and to say what they can see in the picture. (*The picture shows a girl writing on the board in class.*)
- Ask pupils what subject the girl might be studying (*maths or science*) and then elicit other school subjects by asking what their favourite subjects are.
- Ask them to work in pairs to answer the quiz question to encourage discussion, but check the answers as a class.

> **Answer**
> b

Lesson 1

Objectives

Reading	The Cortuga Mystery
Vocabulary	text-related words, school subjects
Grammar	present simple – affirmative, spelling rules, time expressions
Listening	note-taking
Speaking	asking and answering questions about school
Writing	writing sentences about your school

The Cortuga Mystery
For teachers using the DVD

- Make sure each pupil has a copy of the DVD Worksheet found on page 114.
- Please follow the instructions in Unit 1, Lesson 1 on pages 12 and 13 for teachers using the DVD.

Before You Watch

> **Answers**
> 1 in a classroom
> 2 the other children's clothes

While You Watch

> **Answers**
> a6   b1   c5   d2   e4   f3

After You Watch

> **Answers**
> **A**
> 1 1885
> 2 Tom
> 3 his calculator
>
> **B**
> 1 past
> 2 answer
> 3 The teacher
> 4 magic
> 5 Tom

For teachers using the audio CD

- Begin by asking pupils what Mandy finds in the previous episode of *The Cortuga Mystery* (*a puzzle*) and what happens at the end (*the children disappear*). Ask pupils if they have any idea where they are and tell them they are going to find out.
- Tell pupils they are going to listen to and read the next part of the story. Ask them to look at the pictures and to follow the story as they listen.
- Play the recording once and ask the pupils where the children are (*In a school in the year 1885.*). Ask the pupils who the children meet (*a boy called Tom.*).
- Ask pupils to read the story out loud. Assign the roles of Jake, Mandy, Robbie, Kate, Tom and the teacher to different pupils. If you have a large class, you may have to repeat until all pupils have had a turn.
- Explain any vocabulary pupils don't know and correct their pronunciation where necessary.
- As a class, ask pupils the questions below to check they have understood the episode.
  1. What year is it? (*1885*)
  2. Who isn't very good at maths? (*Tom*)
  3. Who isn't very nice? (*the teacher*)
  4. What has Tom got? (*a piece of the puzzle*)
  5. What does Jake give Tom? (*his calculator*)

> **Teaching Tip**
> Encourage pupils to predict what will happen in the story to generate interest. Ask them where they think the children go at the end of the episode. Accept any answers here and tell them they will find out when they listen or watch the next episode.

Vocabulary

- Explain that the words in the exercise appear in the cartoon episode. Ask pupils to find the words in the text and underline them. Explain any words they don't understand.
- Ask pupils to do the task individually, but check the answers as a class.

Extra Class Activity

Ask pupils to write sentences on a piece of paper using these words. Go round the class to check their sentences while they are writing. Once they have finished, they should hand the sentences in to be corrected. Finish off by asking each pupil to read one of his or her sentences to the class.

Grammar

Present Simple

- Read the uses of the Present Simple in the grammar box and ask pupils to read the example sentences with you.
- Write the sentences below on the board and ask pupils what the verbs are and why we have the *Present Simple*.
  - Teachers work in schools. (work – *general truth*)
  - She brushes her teeth every day. (brushes – *things we do regularly*)
  - Tom lives in a house. (lives - *permanent state*)
  - Jake wears glasses. (wears - *permanent state*)
  - Ask pupils what they notice about the endings of the verbs (*The third person singular ends in –es or -s*).
- Read the rest of the grammar box with the class and explain any words they don't know. Ask them to read the forms with you and correct their pronunciation if necessary.

A

- Explain to pupils that they are going to complete the table with the correct form of the third person singular. Point out that they should pay attention to the ending of each verb and to find a verb with a similar ending in the spelling rules in the grammar box to help them.
- Ask pupils to do the task individually, but check the answers as a class.

Answers

1	stays	3	fixes
2	washes	4	carries
3	fixes	6	gives

B

- Remind pupils to check which person of the verb they need and to refer back to the Spelling rules before they write their answers.
- Ask pupils to do the task individually, but check the answers as a class.

Answers

1	go	5	studies
2	likes	6	has
3	use	7	do
4	play	8	sits

Vocabulary

- Explain to pupils that the eight words are the names of school subjects. Ask them to look at pictures a to h and to match them with words 1 to 8.
- Ask pupils to do the task in pairs to encourage discussion, but check the answers as a class.

Answers

1h **2**c **3**f **4**b **5**e **6**a **7**d **8**g

Extra Class Activity

Tell pupils to work in pairs. Encourage them to tell each other what school subjects they don't like. Once they have finished, ask each pupil to tell the class about their partner's worst subjects.

Teaching Tip

When you see that pupils are getting restless in the lesson, encourage them to get out of their seats and move around the room. You can ask them to speak to each other using language used in the lesson or to practise language from previous lessons. They could also spend some time reading any written work that you have put on the walls.

Listening

- Explain to pupils that they are going to hear four different conversations in a school. Tell them to write down the school subject that each child is doing using the list of subjects in the previous vocabulary exercise to help them. Make sure that pupils understand that they won't hear the actual words they have to write down, but that they have to work out what each subject is from what they hear.
- Play the recording and do the first one together as a class to make sure that pupils understand exactly what they have to do.
- Play the rest of the recording and ask pupils to work individually. Then play the recording a second time and ask them to check their answers and to fill in any missing information.
- Check the answers as a class and ask pupils to justify their answers.

Turn to page 106 for the listening script.

Answers

1 geography **2** maths **3** art **4** sport

Speaking

- Explain that pupils are going to work in pairs to ask and answer questions about school.
- Go round the class monitoring pupils to make sure they are carrying out the task properly. Don't correct any mistakes at this stage, but make a note of any mistakes in structure and pronunciation.
- As a class, ask each pair to ask and answer one of the questions and repeat until each pair has had a go.
- Write any structural mistakes that pupils made on the board, without saying who made them, and ask them to correct them. Deal with any problems in pronunciation.

Writing

- Explain to pupils that they are going to write five sentences about their school. Elicit from pupils that they can write about where their school is, what it's called, what class they are in, what their favourite subject is, who their favourite teacher is and how many children are in their class.
- Remind pupils to use *and* and *but* where necessary and to proofread their sentences when they have finished.
- You could set this task for homework if you are short of time.

Answers

Pupils' own answers

Extra Task (for early finishers)

See photocopiable material on page 126.

Lesson 2

Objectives

Reading	article – true or false questions
Vocabulary	text-related words; school-related words
Grammar	present simple – negative, question, short answers
Song	school subjects
Listening	ticking the correct boxes
Sounds of English	pronunciation of *oo*

Way in

- Ask pupils to work with a partner and to discuss their school timetables. Tell them to talk about what subjects they have each day and at what time they have them. Then, as a class, ask each pupil about one of their subjects, (*Yiannis, when do you have art*?). If any of your pupils are adults, you can ask them about their English lessons with you.

Reading

- Ask pupils to look at the picture on page 32 and ask them what they think is special about schools in Japan (*Children wear masks, hats and aprons at lunchtime.*).
- Ask pupils to read the text on their own to find out what the differences are between their school and the schools in Japan.
- Give pupils a few minutes to tell you what the differences are.

Suggested answers

- Pupils at my school usually take the school bus / come by car and they don't wear helmets.
- At my school, lessons start at 8 am and finish at 1.50 pm.
- We don't do Japanese lessons.
- We don't eat lunch at school. / We eat lunch at school, but we don't wear masks.
- We never brush our teeth at school.
- We don't clean the classroom.
- We haven't got a karaoke club at school.

Background Information

The children in the picture are pupils at the Rikkyo Primary School on Honshu Island in Tokyo. The children are serving food to their classmates. In Japan, primary education is from age 6 to age 11 to 12.

Comprehension

- Ask pupils to read the sentences so that they know what information to look for when reading the text again.
- Ask them to read the text again to find out if sentences 1 to 5 are true or false and to write *T* or *F* in the boxes provided. Tell them to underline the information in the text that helps them to find the answers.

Answers

1 F (*Japanese pupils usually walk to school…*)
2 F (*In some schools they also wear a uniform.*)
3 F (*Pupils have lunch at school.*)
4 T (*Then they clean their classroom!*)
5 T (*What do Japanese pupils do after school?… Shoko, …, likes the karaoke club at her school.*)

Guess what!

- Ask pupils to read the information in the *Guess what!* feature. Ask them why they think Japanese children wear slippers in class and if they think it's a good idea.
- Ask pupils if there's anything that they wear or do at school that would seem strange to children from other countries.

Vocabulary

- Explain to pupils that the correct answers are in the text. Ask them to look back at the text and to underline the words while they are doing the task.
- Ask pupils to do the task individually, but check the answers as a class.

Answers

1	clean	2	sing	3	finish
4	wear	5	have	6	do

Extra Class Activity

Write the words below on the board and ask pupils to look back at the text to find words that go with them.

wear …, …, …   **have** …, …   **do** …, …

Answers

- **wear** helmets, a uniform, special masks
- **have** lunch, fun
- **do** subjects, (lots of) homework

Grammar

Present Simple

- Ask pupils to underline verbs in the affirmative of the *Present Simple* in the text (Para 1, *walk, wear, wear, start, finish, do, do*; Para 2, *have, eat, carry, wear, eat, brush, clean*; Para 3, *choose, likes, sing, have fun, says*). Ask pupils what the third person singular form of the verbs in plural are (*walks, wears, starts, finishes, does, has, eats, carries, brushes, cleans, sings, has fun*).

- Read the grammar box with the class and ask pupils to say the forms out loud with you. Say the short forms first followed by the long forms. Draw pupils' attention to the word order in the different forms.
- Ask pupils to look back at the text again and to find an example of the *Present Simple* negative form (*Pupils don't only eat Japanese food.*) and of the question form (*What do Japanese pupils do after school*?).
- Ask pupils to do the task individually, but check the answers as a class.

Answers

1b 2a 3b 4b 5a 6a 7b 8b 9b 10b

Song

- Tell pupils that they are going to listen to a song about school and that they should read the song as they listen.
- Play the song and ask pupils who is singing the song (*school pupils*). Play it again and ask the pupils to sing along. Play the song a number of times if the pupils enjoy singing along.
- Ask pupils if they like or, don't like the same things as the pupils in the song.
- Ask pupils to match pictures a to f with the words 1 to 6.

Vocabulary

- Ask pupils to do the task in pairs to encourage discussion, but check the answers as a class.

Answers

1f 2e 3d 4a 5c 6b

Extra Class Activity

Write the sentences below on the board and ask pupils to fill the gaps with the correct words from the Vocabulary task.

1 I always eat lunch in the … .
2 Jane studies in the … .
3 Please put the book in the … .
4 I have got 15 … in my class.
5 We always do sport in the … .
6 Do you wear a … to school?

Answers

1	cafeteria	2	library	3	bookcase
4	classmates	5	playground	6	uniform

Teaching Tip

Give pupils sentences with the new words in, or encourage them to write their own so that they learn the words in context. This will help them to understand how the words are used in English and help them remember new vocabulary.

Listening

- Explain to pupils that they are going to listen to three children talking about what they like and don't like about school. Tell them to look at the table and then ask them what the children's names are (*Eleanor*, *Paola* and *Rashid*). Ask them

what aspects of school they are going to hear about (*English lessons*, *homework*, *teachers*, *uniform*, *school lunch* and *computer lessons*).
- Make sure pupils understand that they only tick the things that the children like. Tell them not to get distracted by the things they say they don't like.
- Play the recording once and ask pupils to work with a partner to discuss their answers. Ask them to justify any answers they have that are different.
- Play the recording again and ask pupils to check their answers and to fill in any missing information.
- Check the answers as a class.

Turn to page 106 for the listening script.

Answers

Eleanor: teachers, school lunch
Paola: English lessons, computer lessons
Rashid: English lessons, homework, uniform, computer lessons

Sounds of English

A
- Ask pupils to work in pairs and to say the words *book* and *school* to each other.
- Play the recording and stop after each word so that pupils can repeat what they have heard.

Answers

The oo in book is pronounced ʊ (*oo*).
The oo in school is pronounced ʊː (*u*).

B
- Ask pupils to work in pairs again to say each of the words to each other and to decide which column each word should go in.
- Play the recording stopping after each word to check the answers.

Answers

1st column	2nd column
cook	cool
good	food
look	moon

Extra Task (for early finishers)

See photocopiable material on page 126.

Lesson 3

Objectives

Reading	letter – missing sentences
Say it like this!	talking about everyday life
Grammar	adverbs of frequency
Writing	word order, writing a paragraph about your perfect school

- Write the tongue twisters below on the board and ask pupils to read them. Correct their pronunciation if necessary.
  - *Who cooks good food for the school?*
  - *Good food, cool food, look, look, look!*
  - *The cook reads a book about food for the moon.*

- Ask the questions below round the class. Ask pupils to reply using short answers. Make sure each pupil answers at least one question.

Suggested questions
- Do you walk to school?
- Does your mum read books?
- Do you speak Spanish?
- Does your science teacher wear a mask?
- Do you watch TV in the library?
- Does your dad eat Japanese food?
- Does your school start at 8.30 am?

Reading

- Ask pupils to look at the picture of the girl and ask them what she might be doing (*reading / writing an email; playing a computer game; surfing the Internet; doing her homework*).
- Ask pupils to skim read the letter to find out what time Anna has dinner (*6.30*). Tell them that they don't need to complete the gaps at this stage.
- Ask pupils why Anna's school is different from most schools (*It's a boarding school and she lives there.*). Ask them if they would like to go to this kind of school.
- Ask pupils to work in pairs and to try to guess what kind of information is missing from each of the gaps. Try to elicit from them that in *1* we need information that explains what a boarding school is and link it to '*I've got a room*'; that in *2* we need information that tells us what Anna and her classmates do after lunch time and before they do their homework; and that in *3* we need information about what happens after dinner at 6.30 and before bedtime at 9.30.

Comprehension

- Ask pupils to read the sentences and complete the letter. Tell them to read back through the letter once they have finished to make sure that they have chosen the correct sentences.
- Ask pupils to do the task individually, but check the answers as a class.
- Explain any vocabulary pupils don't know and correct their pronunciation where necessary.

Extra Class Activity

You can ask the questions below to check pupils have understood the letter.
1. What hasn't Vicky got? (*a computer*)
2. What is a boarding school? (*a school where pupils live*)
3. Who does Anna eat breakfast with? (*other pupils and teachers*)
4. When do lessons start and finish at Anna's school? (*They start at 9 o'clock and finish at 4 o'clock.*)
5. When does Anna write emails to her parents? (*in the evenings*)
6. What time does Anna usually go to sleep? (*10.30*)

Say it like this!

- Read the structures in *Talking about everyday life* to the class. Point out that we use *Present Simple* here.
- Ask pupils to work in pairs and to ask each other about what they do every day.
- As a class, ask each pupil to say what their partner does every day so that they can practise the third person singular form of the *Present Simple*.

Answers
Pupils' own answers

Grammar

Adverbs of Frequency

- Ask pupils what words they used in *Say it like this!* to answer *How often …?* (*every day / week; once / twice / three times a month / year*). Explain that these phrases are *time expressions*. Tell pupils that we can also use *adverbs of frequency* to say how often we do something.
- Read the grammar box to the class and ask pupils to read the example sentences with you. Draw pupils' attention to the order that the adverbs are listed in from left to right. Explain what 100% and 0% of the time mean, and that the order the words are listed in shows the level of frequency.
- Ask pupils to look back at the letter and underline all the adverbs of frequency they can find (*Para 3 always*, *usually*; *Para 4 sometimes*, *usually*).
- Ask pupils to do the task individually, but check the answers as a class.

Suggested answers
Accept any *adverb of frequency* in each sentence, but make sure that pupils realise that these are personal responses.

B
- Ask pupils to do the task individually, but check the answers as a class.
- Alternatively, you could ask pupils to do this task for homework if you are short of time.

Answers
1. Sam always brushes his teeth in the morning.
2. The boys are usually hungry at 12 o'clock.
3. They don't often wear shoes at home.
4. That shop is never open at weekends.

Extra Class Activity

Ask pupils to work in pairs or groups to tell each other things that they always / usually / often / sometimes / never do at the weekends.

Teaching Tip

Encourage pupils to become more active in the learning process by asking them to bring in *magazine* or *newspaper articles*, *books* or *music* in English to share with each other from time to time.

Writing

Word Order

A
- Read the example sentences to the class and ask pupils to use different colours to highlight subjects / subject pronouns (*I, you, Emma, Mr Brown, We, Jim*), auxiliary verbs (*don't, Do, Does*), main verbs (*like, have, Is, wears, are, sing*), time expressions (*once a week, in the evening, at the weekend*) and adverbs of frequency (*usually, sometimes, always, often*).

B

- Tell pupils that they have to use the prompts to make a sentence.
- Ask pupils to do the task individually, but check the answers as a class.

Answers

1 Science is never boring.
2 Do you like maths?
3 I often watch DVDs at the weekends.
4 Is Mrs Hill a good teacher?
5 We don't play computer games every day.

C

- Ask pupils what their idea of a perfect school is. Ask them what subjects the school would have; what subjects it wouldn't have; when school starts and finishes and what other things pupils do at this school.
- Ask pupils to read the paragraph to see if they agree with the writer's idea of a perfect school.
- Ask pupils to do the task individually, but check the answers as a class.

Answers

- We **never have** maths, … .
- We **have sport and computer lessons** every day … !
- We **often listen** to … .
- … and we **never have** tests.
- The teachers **are always** nice … .

Task

D

- Explain to pupils that they are going to write a paragraph about their perfect school.
- Ask pupils to answer the questions in the plan individually, but check the answers as a class. Obviously answers will vary from pupil to pupil, but make sure that the structures are consistent. Once you have discussed their answers, ask pupils to write out their paragraph or ask them to do it for homework.

Suggested answer

In my perfect school, lessons start at 9 o'clock and they finish at 2 o'clock. I have computer lessons and history, but I don't have English and science. I have music and art every day. We have lots of clubs this school! It's cool!

E

- Ask pupils to read back through their answers to check for mistakes in the word order. If you ask them to write the paragraph for homework, then give them a few minutes to do this at the beginning of the next lesson.

Extra Task (for early finishers)

See photocopiable material on page 126.

Project Book

The pupils may do Project 3 now they have completed the unit. The answer key and teacher's notes are on pages 148-152 of this book.

Way in

- Give pupils a few minutes to read each others paragraphs about their perfect school from Unit 3, Lesson 3. They can do this in pairs. Ask them to check that the word order is correct.
- Write *always*, …, …, …, *never* on the board and ask pupils to fill in the missing *adverbs of frequency* in the correct order (*to show the level in frequency from* 100% *of the time to* 0% *of the time.*).
- Ask pupils the following questions at random. Make sure each pupil has the chance to answer at least one question.
  - What do you usually do on Saturdays?
  - Do you sometimes wear jeans to school?
  - Do you often eat in a cafeteria?
  - What do you always do at night?
  - What do you never do in the afternoon?
  - What do you usually do after school?

- Write the word *hobbies* on the board and explain that this is the theme of Unit 4. If necessary, explain that hobbies are things we do in our free time and ask pupils about their hobbies.
- Ask pupils to look at the picture on pages 36 and 37 and to work in pairs to answer the quiz question. Once you have checked the answer as a class, explain the words *riding* and *racing* if necessary and check pronunciation.

Answer
b

Extra Class Activity

Ask pupils if they have ever tried horse riding like the girl in the picture and if so, whether or not they enjoyed it. They may have tried riding other animals such as donkeys or camels or even an elephant. They may have tried riding other animals such as donkeys or camels or even an elephant. If pupils haven't been riding, ask them if they would like to and why or why not.

Lesson 1

Objectives Box

Reading	The Cortuga Mystery
Vocabulary	matching expressions; set phrases
Grammar	question words
Listening	picture matching
Speaking	asking and answering questions about your hobby
Writing	writing sentences about your hobby

The Cortuga Mystery
For teachers using the DVD

- Make sure each pupil has a copy of the DVD Worksheet found on page 115.
- Please follow the instructions in Unit 1, Lesson 1 on pages 12 and 13 for teachers using the DVD.

Before You Watch

Answers
1 a piece of the puzzle
2 in China
3 Ling

While You Watch

Answers
a3 b5 c4 d2 e1

After You Watch

Answers
1T 2F 3T 4F 5T 6F 7F

For teachers using the audio CD

- Begin by asking pupils what the children get at the end of the last episode of *The Cortuga Mystery* (*a piece of the puzzle*). Ask pupils to look at page 38 and to guess where the children are now (*China*). Ask pupils to quickly scan the characters' names to find the name of the new character (*Ling*).
- Tell pupils that they are going to listen to and read the next part of the story. Ask them to look at the pictures and to follow the story as they listen.
- Play the recording once and ask the pupils what kind of competition there is (*a kite competition*). Ask the pupils who makes a kite (*Robbie*).
- Ask pupils to read the story out loud. Assign the roles of Jake, Mandy, Robbie, Kate and Ling to different pupils. If you have a large class, you may have to repeat until all pupils have had a turn.
- Explain any vocabulary pupils don't know and correct their pronunciation where necessary.
- As a class, ask pupils the questions below to check they have understood the episode.
  1 Have the children got any Chinese money? (*no*)
  2 When is the kite competition? (*today*)
  3 What has Ling's uncle got? (*a shop*)
  4 Who makes the kite? (*Robbie*)
  5 Does Ling think the kite is beautiful? (*yes*)
  6 Who wins the competition? (*Ling*)
  7 What is the prize? (*a piece of the puzzle*)

Extra Class Activity

Ask pupils what Robbie's hobby is (*making kites*). Ask them if they know how to make a kite. Give pupils five minutes to draw a kite on a piece of paper and to write their names on the back of the paper. Number and hang the drawings on the wall and ask pupils to look at the kites and decide which one is their favourite. Ask them to make a note of the number of their favourite kite and take a vote to see which kite is the most popular.

Teaching Tip

From time to time, ask pupils to do something creative to take a break from the syllabus. Encourage them to speak to each other in English while doing these kinds of activities so that they get the opportunity to use the language in a relaxed way without being afraid that they will make mistakes.

Vocabulary

A

- Tell pupils that they will have come across similar expressions and replies in the cartoon episode. Make sure they understand that they have to match up the expressions that follow on logically from one another. Tell pupils to draw lines from each expression 1 to 5 to the appropriate reply a to e.
- Ask pupils to do the task individually, but check the answers as a class. Once you have checked the answers ask one pupil to read out an expression from 1 to 5 and another pupil to read out the correct reply from a to e. Ask different pupils to do the same until all the expressions are read out. Correct pupils' pronunciation and intonation where necessary.

Answers

1d **2**e **3**c **4**b **5**a

B

- Write *Let's make a kite!* on the board and underline *make a kite*. Explain to pupils that this is a set phrase. Ask them if they know any other set phrases with the verb *make* (*make lunch, make breakfast*). Ask them what nouns they saw in Unit 3 with the verbs *have* (*lunch, fun*), *wear* (*a uniform, helmet, mask*) and *do* (*homework, subjects*).
- Ask pupils to write the verbs from the wordbank in the gaps to make set phrases about hobbies. Ask pupils to do the task individually, but check the answers as a class.

Answer

1 go **2** watch **3** play **4** collect **5** make

C

- Read the question out to the class.
- Ask pupils to work in pairs to discuss the hobbies in *B*. Ask them to say which hobbies they do, when they do them, how often they do them and where they do them. Ask them to begin like this *In my free time, I like to … .*

Answer

Kite

Grammar

Question Words

- Ask pupils to look back at the cartoon episode on page 38 and to underline all the questions the children ask each other (*Where are we now?, What's your name?, Who are you?, What's the matter?, What do we need?, Who's the winner?*). Ask them which question asks about a place (*Where are we now?*), which questions ask about a person (*Who are you?, Who's the winner?*) and which questions ask about a thing (*What's your name?, What's the matter?, What do we need?*). Elicit that we know this from the words *who, what* and *where*.
- Ask the following questions at random round the class. Hold up a pen and ask...
  - What is this? (*It's a pen.*)
  - What colour is the pen? (*It's blue.*)
  - Put the pen under your desk and ask Where is the pen? (*It's under your desk.*)
  - Whose pen is it? (*It's your pen.*)
  - Point to Ling in your book and ask Who is this? (*It's Ling.*)
  - When do you do your homework? (*in the evening*)

- Read the grammar box with the class and ask pupils to read the example sentences with you. Draw pupils' attention to the note and explain the difference between *Who's* and *Whose*. Write *Whose pen is this?* and *Who's this boy?* on the board as examples. Ask them which question *It's Harry's.* would answer and which one *It's Harry.* would answer.

A

- Make sure they understand that they have to match the questions with the answers that follow on logically from one another. Tell pupils to draw lines from each question 1 to 5 to the appropriate answer a to e.
- Ask pupils to do the task individually, but check the answers as a class. Once you have checked the answers ask a pupil to read out a question from 1 to 5 and another pupil to read out the correct answer from a to e. Ask different pupils to do the same until all the questions and answers have been read out. Correct pupils' pronunciation and intonation where necessary.

Answers

1c **2**a **3**d **4**e **5**b

B

- Get pupils to do the task individually. Before you check the answers as a class, you could ask them to check their answers together. They can then take it in turns to ask and answer the questions and the answers with each other.

Answers

1 What	**4** Where
2 Whose	**5** Who
3 When	

Extra Class Activity

If you feel your pupils need extra practice with *question words*, ask pupils to write two or three questions and answers like the ones in *B*. Ask them to leave the *question word* blank and to swap books with a partner. Ask them to complete each others' questions and then hand them back to their classmates for correction. To finish off, ask each pair to read out one set of questions and answers each.

Listening

- Ask pupils to look at pictures a to e and to tell you what hobbies they show (*reading a comic, collecting stamps, playing the guitar, watching TV and ice-skating*).
- Explain to pupils that they are going to listen to a boy called Adam speaking about his hobbies and that he will talk about which hobby he does each day from Monday to Friday.
- Play the first part of the recording where Adam speaks about Monday and decide as a class what hobby Adam does on that day. Ask pupils to draw a line between Monday and the picture showing Adam playing the guitar (c).
- Play the rest of the recording all the way to the end. Then play the recording a second time and ask them to check their answers or fill in any missing information.
- Check the answers as a class and make sure pupils can justify their answers.

Turn to page 106 for the listening script.

Answers

1c **2**e **3**a **4**b **5**d

Speaking

- Explain to pupils that they are going to talk about their own hobby. Read the questions to the class and explain anything that they don't understand.
- Ask pupils to work in pairs to ask and answer the questions and go round the class monitoring pupils to make sure they are carrying out the task properly. Don't correct any mistakes at this stage, but make a note of any mistakes in structure and pronunciation.
- As a class, ask a pupil all the questions apart from the first one. Ask the other pupils to guess what their classmate's hobby is.
- Write any structural mistakes that pupils make on the board, without saying who made them, and ask them to correct them. Deal with any problems in pronunciation.

Answers
Pupils' own answers

Writing

- Explain to pupils that they are going to write six sentences about their hobby. Tell pupils that they should write down their answers to the questions in the previous speaking exercise.
- Alternatively, you could set this task for homework if you are short of time.

Answers
Pupils' own answers

Extra Task (for early finishers)
See photocopiable material on page 127.

Lesson 2

Objectives

Reading	open-ended questions
Vocabulary	text-related words; words related to free time places
Grammar	can – affirmative, negative, question, short answers
Listening	circle the correct word
Sounds of English	w and h sounds

Optional materials
Magazine pictures of a rollercoaster, a merry-go-round, a ferris wheel, a mirror (preferably a crazy mirror), a slide

Way in
- Ask pupils the following questions at random round the class.
  - What is your hobby?
  - Where do you go swimming?
  - When do you watch TV?
  - Who is your best friend?
  - Whose feet do Emperor penguins' eggs sit on?
- Write go, watch, play, collect and make on the board and ask pupils to write a sentence to talk about a hobby using the words.

Answers
Pupils' own answers

Reading

Background Information
Luna Park first opened in October 1935. It has currently got 14 permanent rides. There have been eight different smiling faces at the entrance since 1935. The face is nine metres wide.

- Write rollercoaster, ferris wheel, merry-go-round, mirror and slide on the board. If you have brought the magazine pictures suggested above to class, show each picture and ask pupils to tell you what they show.
- Ask pupils to read the text on their own to find out where Luna Park is (Sydney, Australia). Explain any words they don't know and correct pronunciation if necessary.
- Ask pupils if they would like to go to Luna Park and what they would like to do there.

Comprehension

- Ask pupils to read the questions before they read the text again so that they know what information to look for.
- Ask pupils to do the task individually, but check the answers as a class. Ask pupils to underline where they get the answer from in the text so they can justify their answers.

Answers
1 a very old and popular amusement park (Read about a fantastic amusement park.)
2 at the entrance (At the entrance there is a huge smiling face.)
3 people of all ages (People of all ages can have fun here.)
4 pizzas, burgers, sandwiches, ice cream (They've got pizzas, burgers and sandwiches.)
5 the rides (…, but you pay for the rides.)

Extra Class Activity
Write the jumbled up words below on the board and ask pupils to unscramble them to find adjectives from the text. When you have checked the answers, ask pupils to write sentences with four of the words.

tcfnasita	(fantastic)
upolapr	(popular)
musafo	(famous)
ynunf	(funny)
cnie	(nice)
eagrt	(great)

Suggested sentences
- The rollercoaster is a fantastic ride.
- The crazy mirrors aren't very popular.
- Are there any famous attractions in your country?
- These sandwiches are great.

Vocabulary

- Tell pupils that the words in the exercise can all be found in the text. Ask pupils to read the definitions and to write in the missing letters. Ask them to check their answers in the text and to pay attention to the number of letters that are missing in each word.

- Ask pupils to do the task individually, but check the answers as a class.

Guess what!

- Ask pupils to read the information in the *Guess what!* feature. If pupils are interested, tell them that the Kingda rollercoaster is in an amusement park called Six Flags Great Adventure in New Jersey, USA. When it opened in May 2005, it was the biggest and fastest rollercoaster in the world.

Grammar

Can

- Ask pupils what you can see from the Ferris wheel in Luna Park (*the amusement park and Sydney harbour*). Then ask the following questions at random round the class. Ask pupils to answer *yes* or *no*.
  - Can you ride a bike?
  - Can parrots swim?
  - Can you play computer games in class?
  - Can your mum speak French?
  - Can your dad play the guitar?
  - Can you walk to school?
  - Can we use mobile phones in class?
- Read the grammar box to the class and ask pupils to read the example sentences with you. Draw pupils' attention to the bare infinitive form of the main verbs in the examples. Read the different forms to the class and ask them to say them out loud after you.
- Write the sentences below on the board and ask pupils to tell you if *can* is used to talk about ability or to ask for or give permission.

  You can use a *Go Wild* pass all day. (*permission*)
  Can I go on the merry-go-round? (*permission*)
  John can't see the huge face. (*ability*)

A

- Ask pupils to do the task individually and explain that in one sentence both *can* and *can't* are possible. Check the answers as a class.
- Once you have checked the answers, ask pupils what *can* talks about in these sentences (*ability*).

Answers

1	can / can't	4	can't
2	can	5	can't
3	can't		

B

- Explain to pupils that they are going to write questions using the prompts given and short answers. Draw their attention to the ticks and crosses in brackets and make sure they understand that they should answer *yes* or *no* accordingly.
- Do the first question together as a class and then ask pupils to do the rest individually, but check the answers as a class.
- Alternatively, if you're short of time, you could assign this task for homework.

Answers

1. Can I play computer games?, Yes, you can.
2. Can we go to bed at 2 am?, No, you can't.
3. Can they use mobile phones at school?, No, they can't.
4. Can she go to the beach?, Yes, she can.
5. Can he have a cat?, No, he can't.

C

- Give pupils a few minutes to think of something to ask you. Then ask each pupil to ask you his or her question. Answer them using short answers.

Suggested answers

- Can I / we play music in the classroom?
- Can I / we bring board games to school?
- Can I / we clean the classroom?
- Can I / we ride my skateboard?
- Can I / we go home early?

Extra Class Activity

Ask pupils to work in pairs to tell each other what they *can* and *can't* do. Encourage them to talk about things that they have the ability to do and things that they are (*not*) allowed to do. Ask pupils to tell the class about one thing they told their partner about.

Teaching Tip

When you ask pupils to do pair work to discuss a subject, make sure that you give them the chance to talk to a different pupil each time. This means that pupils will practise speaking with pupils of different ability and they will get to know their classmates better.

Vocabulary

- Ask pupils to read the words in the wordbank and ask them what they can do in each of these places. Ask them if they go to any of these places and if so, how often.
- Ask pupils to do the task in pairs to encourage discussion, but check the answers as a class. Deal with any problems in pronunciation.

Answers

1	restaurant	4	sports centre
2	Internet café	5	amusement park
3	cinema	6	theatre

Listening

- Explain to pupils that they are going to listen to a conversation between Vicky and Rachel. Ask them to read the sentences and to tell you what they think the girls' conversation is about (*what they are going to do*).
- Play the recording once all the way through. Ask pupils to check their answers with a partner and to justify any answers they have that are different.
- Play the recording again and ask pupils to check their answers and to fill in any missing information.
- Check the answers as a class and ask pupils to justify their answers.

Turn to page 106 for the listening script.

Extra Class Activity

Ask pupils to work in small groups to talk about the things they can do in their free time in their neighbourhood. Ask them to tell each other about places they go to every week and once a month and about a place they never go to. Ask one of the pupils in each group to be the secretary and to take notes on what the other pupils say. At the end of the exercise, the secretary can report to the class about which place is most popular with their class.

Sounds of English

A
- Ask pupils to work in pairs to say the words to each other and to note which words have a *w* sound at the beginning.
- Ask pupils to listen to the recording to see if they were right. Check the answers as a class and ask pupils what sound the other words begin with (*h*).

Answers
who
whose

B
- Do the first example together as a class to make sure that pupils understand that they have to decide whether both words in each pair of words begin with a *wh* or *h* sound.
- Follow the procedure in A.

Answers
1S   **2**D   **3**S   **4**D   **5**S

Extra Task (for early finishers)

See photocopiable material on page 127.

Lesson 3

Objectives

Reading	dialogue – multiple matching
Say it like this!	talking about hobbies
Listening	completing an information sheet
Speaking	talking about pictures
Writing	verb forms; writing a letter to a pen friend

- Ask pupils to tell you what you can do in the places below.
  - a restaurant (*eat dinner*)
  - an amusement park (*go on rides*)
  - a cinema (*see films*)
  - a theatre (*see plays*)
  - a sports centre (*do sports, play basketball*, etc)
  - an Internet café (*send emails, surf the Internet, play computer games*, etc)
- Ask pupils to write two sentences about things they *can do* and two sentences about things they *can't do*.

- Write the tongue twisters below on the board and ask pupils to say them. Correct their pronunciation if necessary.
  - *Who walks in the woods?*
  - *Whose is the house where we do our hobby?*
- If you asked pupils to do *Grammar B* in Lesson 2 for homework, check their answers.

Reading

- Ask pupils to work in pairs to tell each other what they do on Saturdays. Encourage them to tell each other about what they do in the morning, afternoon and evening.
- Ask pupils to look at the pictures and to guess what two hobbies they will read about in the dialogue (*swimming* and *bowling*).
- Ask pupils to quickly read the dialogue to find out who meets his friends on Saturdays (*Eric*). You could extend this by asking them who goes swimming (*Dimitris*) and who goes bowling (*Eric*).

Comprehension

- Explain to pupils that they have to find out which boy does the things mentioned in 1 to 5. Notice that the activities aren't in the order they appear in the dialogue. Tell pupils to underline the information in the text that helps them find the answers.
- Ask pupils to work individually, but check the answers as a class. Explain any words pupils don't know and correct their pronunciation where necessary.

Answers
1 E (*... on Saturday mornings I help in the shop.*)
2 D (*... and then I eat a big meal with my family ...*)
3 E (*I sometimes go to the sports centre with my friends ...*)
4 D (*I often go to the cinema ...*)
5 D (*I often go to the cinema with my parents ...*)

Extra Class Activity

Ask pupils to add another two questions to the comprehension task and then to ask a partner to answer the new questions. To finish off, ask each pupil to ask one of their questions to the class.

Suggested questions

6 goes to an Internet cafe? (*Eric*)
7 doesn't go bowling? (*Dimitris*)

Say it like this!

- Ask pupils the following questions at random round the class.
  - Do you like playing computer games?
  - Are you good at riding a skateboard?
  - Do you like playing the guitar?
  - Are you good at singing?
- Read the notes about *Talking about hobbies* to the class and ask them to read the example sentences with you. Ask them to underline the *–ing* form in the sentences.
- Ask pupils to find an example in the text of *good at + verb + -ing* (*I'm very good at bowling.*) You might also like to point out that Dimitris says *I go swimming* and Eric says *we go bowling*.
- Ask pupils to work in pairs to ask and answer questions about their hobbies. Remind them to use the language they have just seen. To finish off, ask each pupil to tell you about his/her partner's hobbies.

Listening

- Explain to pupils that they are going to listen to a recorded message for a cinema and that they are going to complete the notes. Explain that in some gaps they will write words, in some they will write numbers and in others they will tick boxes. Give pupils a few minutes to read the notes and then ask them what kind of information is missing from each one (1 *word*, 2 *tick*, 3 *numbers/time*, 4 *word*, 5 *tick*, 6 *tick*).
- Play the recording to the end and ask pupils to fill in their answers. Ask them to work with a partner to check their answers and to justify any answers they have that are different.
- Play the recording again and ask pupils to check their answers and to fill in any missing information. Once you have checked the answers, ask pupils which film they would prefer to see and why.

Turn to page 106 for the listening script.

Answers

1	Family	2	funny	3	6.30
4	Winner	5	exciting	6	children

Speaking

- Quickly remind pupils that we use verb + *–ing* with *is/isn't good at*, but the bare infinitive with *can / can't*.
- Ask pupils to work in pairs to take it in turns to say what *Mick is / isn't good at* and what *he can / can't do*. Tell them to use the pictures to help them.

Suggested answers

a
Mick isn't good at ice-skating.
Mick is good at swimming.
Mick is good at computer games.
Mick isn't good at playing tennis.

b
Mick can't ice-skate.
Mick can swim.
Mick can play computer games.
Mick can't play tennis.

Writing

Verb Forms

A
- Ask pupils to read the example sentences and to underline *–ing* forms and the bare infinitive. Elicit which form is used in each sentence (1 *–ing*, 2 *–ing*, 3 *bare infinitive*, 4 *–ing*). Explain that *go* and *like* are verbs that are followed by the *–ing* form and that prepositions are also followed by this form which is why we have *good at making*. Explain that *can* is a modal verb and that modal verbs are followed by the bare infinitive.

B
- Explain to pupils that they have to read the sentences and circle the correct answers.
- Ask pupils to do the task individually, but check the answers as a class.

Answers

1	fly	3	riding
2	reading	4	ice-skating

C
- Ask pupils to read the letter to find out what Liam's brother is called (*Fred*). Tell them not to fill in any gaps yet.
- Ask pupils to use the words in the wordbank to fill in the gaps. Make sure they understand that the form of the word may have to change to fit in grammatically.
- Ask pupils to do the task individually, but check the answers as a class.

Answers

1	collecting	4	swimming
2	playing	5	swim
3	go		

Task

D
- Ask pupils to work in pairs to tell each other which of the two children they will write to. Then ask them to write the name of the person in the gap after *Dear*.
- Ask pupils to work individually to write their answers to the questions. Go round the class reading their answers as they write and help them with any mistakes they make.
- Ask pupils to use their notes in the plan to write a letter on a piece of paper for homework.

Suggested answer

Dear Connie,

My name is Dina Adel and I'm eight years old. I live in Damietta with my mum and my dad and my two brothers Tariq and Sami. In my free time, I like going to the park and playing board games. I also ride my bike every evening. I am good at English, but I can't speak English very often here in Damietta.

Write soon!

Dina

E
- Remind pupils to proofread their letters before they give them to you to check they have used the *–ing* form or the bare infinitive where necessary.

Teacher's Tip

If you teach in a school that has more than one class at each level, arrange with another teacher for your pupils to become pen friends with pupils from another class. You can give their letters to the other teacher to deliver to the pupils in the other class and give your pupils time to read the letters they receive. This way, pupils are given a real reason to write.

Extra Task (for early finishers)

See photocopiable material on page 127.

Project Book

The pupils may do Project 4 now they have completed the unit. The answer key and teacher's notes are on pages 148-152 of this book.

Review 2

Objectives

- To revise vocabulary and grammar from Units 3 and 4.
- Song – What do you do on Saturdays?

Revision

- Explain to pupils that the tasks in *Review 2* are based on the material they saw in Units 3 and 4.
- Remind pupils that they can ask you for help with the exercises or look back at the units if they're not sure about an answer, as the review is not a test.
- Decide how you will carry out the review. You could ask pupils to do one task at a time and then correct it immediately, or ask pupils to do all the tasks and then correct them together at the end. If you do all the tasks together, let pupils know every now and again how much time they have got left to finish the tasks.
- Remind pupils not to leave any answers blank and to try to find any answers they aren't sure about in the units.
- Revise the vocabulary and grammar as a class before pupils do the review.

Vocabulary Revision

- Ask pupils to tell you what school subjects they can remember. They should remember *art*, *English*, *geography*, *history*, *maths*, *music*, *science* and *sport*. Ask them to tell you about their favourite subject and the subject they don't like.
- Write the word *maths* on the board and ask pupils what we do in maths (*sums*) and what we can use to do them (*calculator*).
- Write the words *playground*, *bookcase*, *classmates*, *cafeteria*, *library* and *uniform* on the board and ask pupils to tell you what they mean.
- Ask pupils what the name of the amusement park they read about in Unit 4, Lesson 1 is (*Luna Park*) and where they can see a huge smiling face (*at the entrance to the park*). Elicit that Luna Park is popular with visitors and tourists and that it is near a harbour.
- Put the pupils into two groups and tell them they are going to make a list of words related to amusement parks and having fun. Each group should make their own list and write it on the board so that they can see which group remembered the most words. Make sure pupils revise the words *café*, *ferris wheel*, *merry-go-round*, *crazy mirrors*, *rollercoaster*, *slide*, *theatre*, *cinema*, *ice-skating*, *swimming* and *bowling*.
- Ask pupils what Robbie, in *The Cortuga Mystery*, makes when they go to China (*a kite*). Write *make a kite* on the board and ask pupils to tell you any other expressions with a verb and a noun that they can remember. Ask them to look back at Unit 4 Lesson 1 for a reminder if they need to.

Grammar Revision

- Elicit from pupils that we use *Present Simple* to talk about *general truths*, *things we do regularly* and *permanent states*.
- Check that they remember the third person singular forms of verbs by writing *I eat*, *I give*, *I do*, *I finish*, *I study*, and *I watch* on the board and asking pupils to write he / she / it and the correct form of each verb beside them.

- Check that they remember the negative form of the *Present Simple* by making the verbs they have just written down negative for both *I* and *he/she/it* forms.
- Revise the question form of the *Present Simple* by asking pupils to ask a classmate a question about something he or she does on Saturdays. Remind the other pupil to reply using a short answer. Make sure that all pupils have the chance to ask and answer at least one question.
- Write *sometimes*, *always*, *never*, *usually* and *often* on the board and ask pupils to put them in order beginning with the adverb that shows that we do something all the time. Then ask pupils to use one of these words to tell the class about a thing that they do or don't do.
- Write *Whose in the shop*? and ask pupils to write the correct question (*Who's in the shop*?). Remind pupils that *Whose* asks about possession and that *Who's* means *Who is*. Then ask pupils to write questions beginning with *What*, *Who*, *Where*, *Whose* and *When*. Make sure that they use the question words properly. Tell them to ask a partner their questions and to answer their partner's questions.
- Ask pupils which verb we use to talk about ability and to ask for and give permission (*can*). Then ask pupils to tell the class one thing they *can do* and one thing they *can't do*. Give them an example: *I can ride a bike, but I can't ride a skateboard*.
- Check that they remember the question form of *can* by asking them to ask you a question about your ability or to give them permission to do something. Reply using short answers.

Vocabulary

A

- Ask pupils to say each of the words as a class and then individually. Correct their pronunciation if necessary.
- Ask pupils to go to the first page of stickers at the back of the book and find the stickers for *Review 2*. Tell them to decide which word each sticker shows and to stick it in the correct box.
- Check that pupils have put the correct stickers above each word.

B

- Tell pupils to think about how the words in each group are related to one another so that they can decide which word doesn't belong in the group.
- When checking pupils' answers, ask them to tell you why the words are odd.

Answers

1. library (*We go to the theatre and cinema in our free time, but we go to the library to study or to borrow books.*)
2. sum (*We wear uniforms and jeans, but we do sums in maths lessons.*)
3. shopping (*Ice-skating and swimming are sports, but we go shopping to buy things we need.*)
4. coffee (*We eat sandwiches and pizza, but we drink coffee.*)
5. bowling (*We do science and history lessons at school, but we go bowling in our free time.*)
6. kite (*We pay for things with coins and money, but we fly kites.*)
7. classmate (*Visitors and tourists visit places, but a classmate is someone in our class at school.*)
8. club (*We use a calculator to do our sums in maths lessons, but a club is a place we go to after school.*)

40

C

- Tell pupils to draw lines between verbs 1 to 8 and nouns a to h.
- Ask pupils to tell you which of these things they do at school and which things they do at home.

Answers							
1h	**2**d	**3**a	**4**e	**5**f	**6**b	**7**c	**8**g

Grammar

A

- Remind pupils to check what the subject of the sentence is, whether it is a statement or a question and whether the verb in the sentence is followed by the *–ing* form or the bare infinitive.
- Tell pupils to look back at Unit 3 Lessons 1 and 2 and Unit 4 Lesson 2 grammar boxes and Unit 4 Lesson 3 *Say it like this!* box for a reminder if they need to.

Answers							
1b	**2**b	**3**a	**4**b	**5**b	**6**a	**7**a	**8**b

B

- Explain to pupils that they should use the words to write full sentences and that they should begin with a capital letter and end with a full stop or question mark.
- Tell pupils to look back at Unit 3 Lessons 1 and 3 grammar boxes for a reminder if they need to.

Answers
1 We never go to school on Saturday.
2 I usually write in my diary every day.
3 Geography isn't always boring.
4 Japanese schools sometimes have karaoke clubs.
5 Rollercoasters are often scary.
6 Do you always eat lunch at school?

C

- Explain to pupils that they should change the question words in bold so that the responses to the questions make sense. Tell them to write one word only on the line beside each dialogue.
- Tell pupils to look back at Unit 4 Lesson 1 grammar box for a reminder if they need to.

Answers
1 Whose   4 What
2 Where   5 Who
3 When   6 Whose

D

- Explain to pupils that their answers are personal and that they should reply using short answers with *can*.
- Tell pupils to look back at Unit 4 Lesson 2 grammar box for a reminder if they need to.

Answers
Pupils' own answers

Song

- Tell pupils they are going to listen to a song about things to do on Saturdays. Ask them to read and listen to the song and to find out what the singers don't have on Saturdays (*school*) and when Luna Park is open (*every day*).
- Play the song again and ask pupils to sing along. You could do this verse by verse and then play it all the way through once.
- Ask pupils to tell you what they do on Saturdays and what rides they like to go on in amusement parks.

When checking pupils' answers to the review tasks, make a note of any problem areas in vocabulary and grammar that they still have. Try to do extra work on these areas so that your pupils progress well.

Way in

- Tell pupils to proofread their letter from Unit 4, Lesson 3. Then ask them to swap letters with another pupil and to read each others' work. Alternatively, hang their letters on the wall for them to read when they have time.
- Ask pupils to tell you one thing they are good at and one thing they aren't good at. Then ask them to tell you one thing they *can do* and one thing they *can't do*.

Background Information

The picture shows the annual monkey festival which takes place on the last weekend in November in the town of Lopburi, central Thailand. The town has got about 600 monkeys and they live freely in the town. The festival was started by a local businessman about 20 years ago, as he felt the monkeys helped to develop tourism in the town, even though the monkeys can be a nuisance to tourists and residents at times. During the festival, a large table is set with tonnes of fruit, vegetables, rice and soft drinks for the monkeys. The local people donate the food to the monkeys, as they believe that being kind can make their own lives better.

- Write the word *celebrate* on the board and brainstorm different ways to celebrate special occasions (*parties*, *concerts*, *going out for a meal*, *festivals*).
- Tell pupils to look at the picture on pages 46 and 47 and ask them what kind of celebration they can see (*a festival*) and who they think the festival is for (*the monkeys*).
- Ask pupils to answer the quiz question individually, but check the answers as a class.

Answer
a

Extra Class Activity

Put pupils into small groups and ask them to look at the picture of the monkey festival and to find as many different foods as possible in the picture. Ask one person in each group to write the foods down. Tell them they have two minutes to do the task. When the two minutes are up, ask each group how many things they have found and write the words on the board. The group with the most items wins.

Suggested answers

apple	banana	carrot	corn
grapes	mango	melon	tomatoes
watermelon			

Lesson 1

Objectives

Reading	The Cortuga Mystery
Vocabulary	text-related words; words related to parties
Grammar	imperative; object pronouns; let's
Listening	ticking the correct option
Speaking	making suggestions
Writing	sentences about party preparations

Optional materials
a ball

Reading

The Cortuga Mystery

Background Information

In this episode, the children find themselves in India during the Festival of Colour. This festival is called Holi, which means burning. Holi takes place on the day of the full moon in March and marks the end of the winter. It takes place all over India among people from all levels of society.

For teachers using the DVD

- Make sure each pupil has a copy of the DVD Worksheet found on page 116.
- Please follow the instructions in Unit 1, Lesson 1 on pages 12 and 13 for teachers using the DVD.

Before You Watch

Answers
1 the past and China
2 India

While You Watch

Answers
1	Mandy	2	Robbie	3	Kate
4	Jake	5	Boy	6	Robbie

After You Watch

Answers
1	hot	2	blue	3	paint
4	India	5	fun	6	paint

For teachers using the audio CD

- Begin by asking pupils how many pieces of the puzzle the children have so far (*two*) and where the children were in the previous two episodes (*the past* and *China*). Ask them to look at the episode on page 48 and to guess where they are now (*India*).
- Tell pupils they are going to listen to and read the next part of the story. Ask them to look at the pictures and to follow the story as they listen.
- Play the recording once and ask the pupils what happens to Robbie and Mandy's clothes (*They get paint on them.*).

- Ask pupils to read the story out loud. Assign the roles of Jake, Mandy, Robbie, Kate and the boy to different pupils. If you have a large class, you may have to repeat until all pupils have had a turn.
- As a class, ask pupils the questions below to check they have understood the episode.
  1. Is it cold in India? (*No, it's very hot.*)
  2. What colour paint do Robbie's clothes have on them? (*blue*)
  3. What colour paint do Mandy's clothes have on them? (*red*)
  4. What celebration is there today? (*the Festival of Colour*)
  5. Is the festival fun? (*Yes, it is.*)
  6. Where is the piece of the puzzle? (*in the paint*)

Vocabulary

A
- Explain that the words in the wordbank appear in the cartoon episode. Ask pupils to find the words in the text and underline them. Explain any words they still don't understand.
- Ask pupils to do the task individually, but check the answers as a class. Correct their pronunciation where necessary.

Answers

1	throw	**4**	paint
2	festival	**5**	stall
3	Catch		

Teaching Tip

Encourage pupils to do some research on topics that come up during the lessons. They can search on the Internet or at local libraries. Even if the information they find is in their own language, it will still help to get them interested in what they're doing in English. It also helps them to see that they can learn other things, apart from English, throughout their course.

Grammar

Imperative

- Bring a ball to class and throw it to a pupil and say *Catch!* Then tell the pupil with the ball *Throw the ball to another pupil.* Do this several times and then tell the pupil who has the ball *Don't throw the ball!* Write these three phrases on the board and ask pupils what they notice (*no subject, exclamation mark* and *imperative form*).
- Read the grammar box to the class and ask pupils to read the example sentences with you.
- Ask pupils to look back at the cartoon episode on page 48 and to underline examples of the imperative (*Look at Robbie!, Quick, catch him!, Don't throw paint, please. Look!*).
- Ask pupils to do the task individually, but check the answers as a class.

Answers

1	Don't play	**3**	clean
2	Don't move	**4**	be

Teaching Tip

Give your pupils information about the culture of English-speaking countries where appropriate. For example, you could tell them that in English it is considered polite to say *please* and *thank you* when asking someone to do something or when asking for information. Explain that this can make the difference between sounding rude or not.

Object Pronouns

- Read the grammar box to the class and ask pupils to read the example sentences with you.
- Ask pupils to look at the cartoon episode again and to underline any object pronouns they can find (*There's blue paint on him. Now Mandy's got red paint on her! Quick, catch him!*) Ask pupils what words these pronouns replace in these sentences (*Robbie, Mandy, the boy*).
- Ask pupils to do the task individually, but check the answers as a class.

Answers

1	me	**2**	them	**3**	him	**4**	us

Extra Class Activity

Ask pupils to tell you what words the pronouns in the task above replace in the dialogue (*Claire, the colours, Paul, Sally and Claire*). Then ask pupils to read the dialogue together in pairs.

Let's

- Write *Let's get some paint.* on the board and ask pupils who says this in the cartoon (*Robbie*). Elicit that he says this to suggest something to the other children. Ask pupils to suggest activities that they would like to do now and write them on the board in the infinitive form (*play a game, watch a DVD, go home, have lunch*).
  Ask them how they can suggest these activities to each other using *Let's* (*by putting Let's in front of the bare infinitive*).
- Read the grammar box to the class and ask pupils to read the example sentence with you. Correct their intonation pattern if necessary.
- Ask pupils to do the task individually, but before you check the answers as a class, ask pupils to take turns to read the sentences in pairs.

Answers

1	Let's play.	**4**	Let's swim.
2	Let's dance.	**5**	Let's have.
3	Let's go.		

Vocabulary

- Read the words in the wordbank and ask pupils to say them after you. Correct their pronunciation if necessary. Explain that all the words are things that you need for a party and that they are going to match each word to the correct picture.

Extra Class Activity

Write the words *write*, *make*, *buy*, *wear*, *cut* and *eat* on the board and ask pupils to write as many suggestions as they can using these verbs and the nouns from the previous vocabulary task.

Suggested answers

* Let's write / make (the) invitations.
* Let's buy candles / balloons.
* Let's wear / make party hats.
* Let's eat / make / cut the / a cake.
* Let's write / make the / a card.

Listening

* Explain to pupils that they are going to listen to Jan and Toby planning a party. Elicit that Jan is a girl and Toby is a boy.
* Give pupils time to read the list of things to do before they listen to the recording. Play the first three exchanges on the recording and ask pupils who is having a party (*Jan*) and why (*It's her birthday*).
* Play the rest of the recording to the end and ask pupils to tick the correct boxes. Tell pupils to make sure they don't just tick the person who talks about each of the things on the list, but that they listen to find out who is given each job to do.
* Play the recording again and ask pupils to check their answers and fill in any missing information.

Turn to page 106 for the listening script.

Answers

1	Toby	**4**	Toby
2	Jan	**5**	Jan
3	Jan		

Speaking

* Read the activities in the wordbank to the class and tell them that they are going to suggest doing these things for celebrations 1 to 4. Explain that we say *on my / your birthday*, *at New Year* to talk about things that they can do on this particular day but *for my / your birthday* to talk about preparations that they can do before the day itself. Also teach *during the school holidays / festival*.
* Ask pupils to work in pairs to make suggestions to each other.
* Go round the class to check pupils are doing the task correctly. Correct their pronunciation if necessary.

Answers

Pupils' own answers

Writing

* Ask pupils to imagine that they are planning a birthday party and that they want to leave their brother or sister a note about the preparations. Ask them to write five sentences making suggestions and telling the other person what to do and what not to do.

Suggested answers

* Let's have a party on Friday.
* Please clean the house.
* Don't buy balloons.
* Let's make the cake.
* Let's buy new CDs.

Extra Class Activity

Ask pupils to describe a special festival in their country. Ask them to say when the festival is and what they do during the festival.

Extra Task (for early finishers)

See photocopiable material on page 128.

Lesson 2

Objectives

Reading	circle the correct words
Vocabulary	text-related words; fancy dress
Grammar	countable nouns; uncountable nouns
Listening	matching
Sounds of English	*sh* and *s*

Way in

* Ask pupils to draw *a balloon*, *a cake*, *candles*, *a party hat*, *a birthday card* and *an invitation* and to write the words underneath their pictures. Hang their work on the wall when they have finished.
* Ask one pupil at a time to do the things below.

  * Open / Close the door / window.
  * Clean the board.
  * Stand up.
  * Sit down.
  * Open/Close your books.

* Write the sentences below on the board and ask pupils to correct them. Underline the wrong words if pupils find it difficult.

  * Give it to I! (*me*)
  * Throw paint at she. (*her*)
  * Catch they! (*them*)
  * It's a card from we. (*us*)
  * Let's send he a present. (*him*)

Reading

Background Information

Patras is a small town in the northern Peloponnese region of Greece. The street carnival with floats and parades dates back to 1870 and was originally organised by wealthy residents. It stopped during the Second World War and started again in 1951, but the organisation was taken over by the Municipality of Patras. The carnival begins on 17 January.

* Write *Carnival Crazy* on the board and ask pupils if there are any famous carnivals in their country. Ask where and when the carnivals are and what people do during the carnival.
* Explain that pupils are going to read about a famous carnival and ask them to look at the picture on page 50. Ask pupils if they ever dress up for festivals or special celebrations.

- Ask pupils to read the text on their own to find out what clothes people wear at this carnival (*costumes, funny hats and masks.*).

Comprehension

- Ask pupils to read the sentences so that they know what information to look for on the second read through. Encourage pupils to scan the text to find the answers and to underline the information in the text that helps them find the answer.
- Ask pupils to do the task individually, but check the answers as a class.
- Explain any words pupils don't know and correct pronunciation if necessary. If pupils are interested, give them further information about the Patras Carnival using the Background Information box.

Answers
1 people (*About 40,000 people take part in the carnival …*)
2 make (*At carnival workshops, children make models …*)
3 treasure (*There are also treasure hunts!*)
4 clues (*There are some clues in different places to help them!*)
5 isn't (*It's OK, he isn't a real person!*)

Extra Class Activity

Ask the pupils the questions below about the text to check their understanding.
1 Where do people dance in the Patras Carnival? (*in the streets*)
2 What do children make models out of? (*paper*)
3 Where is the treasure? (*in a secret place*)
4 Who get great prizes? (*the winners of the treasure hunt*)
5 When do people burn the Carnival King? (*on the last night of the carnival*)

Vocabulary

- Explain to pupils that they have to decide which word in the sets of three is different from the other two.
- Ask pupils to work in pairs to encourage discussion, but check the answers as a class. Ask pupils to explain why each word is the odd one out.

Answers
1 clue (*The other words are both types of celebration.*)
2 preparations (*The other words are things you can see at a festival.*)
3 treasure (*The other words are people.*)
4 model (*The other words are places.*)
5 place (*The other words are things you wear.*)

Guess what!

- Ask pupils to read the information in the *Guess what!* feature. Ask them if they know any other famous carnivals (*Rio, Notting Hill, Venice*) and which carnival they would most like to go to and why.

Grammar

Countable Nouns

- Write the words below on the board and ask pupils to write them and the plural form in their notebooks. Ask them to look for the words in the reading text to check their answers.

  - a parade – parades
  - a costume – costumes
  - a hat – hats
  - a mask – masks
  - an adult – adults
  - an event - events
  - a winner – winners
  - a prize – prizes

- Explain that these words are countable nouns and read the grammar box to the class. Ask pupils to read the example sentences with you. Explain to pupils that these words are countable because we can say *one / a parade / costume / hat*, etc as well as *two / three / four parades / costumes / hats*, etc. Remind pupils of the use of *a* and *an*.
- Read the grammar box for uncountable nouns and explain that we can't say *one / a music* or use music in the plural. Some other uncountable nouns that they have seen so far are *food, hair, lemonade, homework* and *paint*.
- Ask pupils to do the task individually, but check the answers as a class. Explain that they should decide if each word is countable or uncountable before filling in each gap and remind them that uncountable words and plural countable words don't need *a* or *an*.

Answers
1 a 2 – 3 an 4 – 5 – 6 a

Vocabulary

- Explain to pupils that they are going to match pictures a to h to words 1 to 8 and that they should write the correct letter in the boxes next to the words. Tell them to look at each word in turn and to find the correct picture.
- Ask pupils to do the task individually, but check the answers as a class.

Answers
1f 2h 3b 4a 5c 6g 7d 8e

Extra Class Activity

If it is traditional in your pupils' culture to celebrate the carnival, ask pupils to tell their partners what they plan to dress up as for this year's carnival or what they have dressed up as in the past.

Listening

- Ask pupils to work with a partner to describe the costumes the five children are wearing. As a class, ask various pupils to describe the costumes. Elicit the following words: *green, mask, lizard, crown, long dress, orange hair, red nose, big shoes, red trousers, black dress, black hat, long grey hair* and *beautiful dress*.
- Ask pupils to read the four names and point out that there are four names but five costumes and make sure that pupils understand that one costume is extra. Tell pupils to listen to each child describing his or her costume and to write the correct costume beside each name.

- Play the first child and decide as a class what costume *Suzy* is wearing. Make sure pupils realise they have to listen to the person asking the question to find out the child's name.
- Play the rest of the recording to the end and give pupils time to write their answers. Play the recording again and ask pupils to check their answers and to fill in any missing information.

Turn to pages 106 and 107 for the listening script.

Turn to pages 106 and 107 for the listening script.

> **Answers**
> 1 Queen   3 Monster
> 2 Witch   4 Clown

Sounds of English

A
- Ask pupils to work in pairs and to say the pairs of words to each other.
- Explain that they are going to hear one of the words in each pair on the recording and that they should circle the word they hear. Play the recording once without stopping then play again, stopping after each word. Ask pupils what word is being said. Write the correct word or ask a pupil to write the correct word on the board to avoid confusion.

> **Answers**
> 1 shoe   2 sea   3 sort   4 show

B
- Play the recording and ask pupils to repeat the tongue twister. If pupils can say it fairly easily, ask them to say it faster. If pupils feel comfortable and confident, ask each one in turn to say the tongue twister.

> **Teaching Tip**
> Remember that we very rarely say words on their own. When teaching pronunciation, say each of the words in a sentence so that pupils can hear how sounds go together.

> **Extra Task (for early finishers)**
> See photocopiable material on page 128.

Lesson 3

Objectives

Reading	article; completing table
Say it like this!	making suggestions
Grammar	some / any
Writing	reference words; writing a paragraph about your birthday

Way in

- Write *countable* and *uncountable* in two columns on the board and ask pupils to come up and write nouns in each column.
- Ask pupils what you can do at the Patras Carnival (*take part in a parade / the treasure hunt, wear costumes, dance in the street, go to a workshop* and *make a model, see fireworks / the Carnival King*).

Reading

> **Background Information**
> The three monuments in the picture are Big Ben in London, the Eiffel Tower in Paris and the Sydney Opera House in Sydney.
> People in Britain celebrate Bonfire Night to remember Guy Fawkes and the Gunpowder Plot. Fawkes tried to blow up the Houses of Parliament during the State Opening on 5 November 1605, as he wanted to change the government. He was caught and parliament was saved.
> People celebrate April Fool's Day in many countries. In France, it lasts all day, but in other countries people only play jokes on each other until 12 noon.
> People celebrate Australia Day to remember the creation of their country and all the good things about it.

- Ask pupils if they remember on which day they burn the Carnival King in Patras (*on the last night of the carnival*). Explain that they are going to read about special days in other countries.
- Ask pupils to read the article on their own and to find out whose pet doesn't like something (*Sophie's cat doesn't like fireworks.*).
- Ask pupils if similar days are celebrated in their own country and to tell you how they celebrate them.

> **Teaching Tip**
> If you are teaching in a foreign country, try to give pupils the chance to tell you about their culture. This will help them to use their English in a more personal way about topics which are familiar to them. It will also put them in the position of being the teacher for a while and you in the position of the learner. This will help you to see things from each others' point of view and you may learn things you didn't know, so you will be able to understand your pupils better.

Comprehension

- Ask pupils to look at the table and then scan each part of the article to fill in the missing words. Encourage pupils to underline the information in the text that helps them to find the answers.
- Ask them to discuss their answers with a partner to encourage discussion. Check the answers as a class.

> **Answers**
> 1 fire   2 fireworks   3 jokes
> 4 April Fish   5 our country   6 barbecue

> **Extra Class Activity**
> Write the sentences below on the board and ask pupils to say if they are true (T) or false (F).
> 1 Bonfire Night is on November 25th.   (F)
> 2 Sophie's family eat salad next to the fire.   (F)
> 3 Pascal's sister is sometimes late for school on 1st April. (T)
> 4 In France, teachers play jokes on the pupils.   (T)
> 5 Ed has a barbecue in the garden.   (F)
> 6 People have parades and parties on Australia Day.   (T)

Say it like this!

Making suggestions

- Read the note about making suggestions to the class and draw pupils' attention to the structure of the question. Ask pupils to say the example question with you and correct pronunciation and intonation pattern if necessary.
- Before pupils work in pairs to make suggestions to each other, brainstorm the kind of things that they can talk about.
- Ask pupils to work in pairs to make suggestions. To finish, ask each pupil to make a suggestion to the class.

Answers
Pupils' own answers

Grammar

Some / any

- Read the grammar box to the class and ask pupils to read the example sentences with you. Draw pupils' attention to the different uses of *some* and *any*. Ask pupils to write questions using the two sentences in *some* (*Have you got any presents?*, *Is there any food on the table?*) and a sentence using the question in *any* (*I've / You've got some paper.*).
- Ask pupils to look back at the picture on pages 46 and 47 and ask the questions below.
  - Are there any watermelons? (*Yes, there are some watermelons.*)
  - Are there any trees? (*No, there aren't any trees.*)
  - Are there any monkeys? (*Yes, there are some monkeys.*)
  - Are there any tourists? (*Yes, there are some tourists.*)
  - Are there any shops? (*No, there aren't any shops.*)

A
- Tell pupils they have to read the sentences and then fill the gaps with *some* or *any*.
- Ask pupils to do the task on their own, but check the answers as a class.

Answers
1 any	**2** some	**3** some	**4** any	**5** any

B
- Ask pupils to read the paragraph quickly to find out why John can't buy balloons (*He hasn't got any money.*). Tell pupils not to fill in the gaps yet.
- Ask pupils to do the task individually, but check the answers as a class.

Answers
1 some	**2** any	**3** some	**4** some
5 any	**6** any	**7** any	**8** some

Writing

Reference Words

A
- Ask pupils to look back at what Sophie says on page 52 and ask what *It's* in the second sentence means (*Bonfire Night*) and what the last word *them* means (*fireworks*). Remind pupils that *it* is a subject pronoun and *them* is an object pronoun.
- Ask pupils to read about reference words on their own. Explain that they make our writing sound better as it helps us avoid repeating the same words again and again.

B
- If necessary, quickly revise all subject and object pronouns.
- Ask pupils to do the task individually, but check the answers as a class. Once you have checked the answers, ask pupils which words are subject pronouns (*they / We*) and which words are object pronouns (*it / her / him*).

Answer
1 it	**2** they	**3** her	**4** We	**5** him

C
- Ask pupils to quickly read the paragraph and to decide what is wrong with it (*There are no reference words so it sounds strange.*).
- Ask pupils to improve the paragraph by using reference words.
- Ask pupils to do the task individually, but check the answers as a class.

Answers
it, we, It, it, they, we

Extra Class Activity
Ask pupils to tell their partners about how they normally spend their birthdays or what they do at family parties.

Task

D
- Read the questions to the class and make sure pupils understand them. Ask pupils to answer the questions on their own. To finish, ask pupils at random round the class one of the questions. Make sure all pupils have the chance to answer at least one question.
- Explain to pupils that they are going to use their answers to write a paragraph like the one in C. You could assign this task for homework.

Suggested answer
Our Eid Party

At Eid we usually have a party. My grandmother invites all my cousins and friends and we have a great time!

We have lots of special food. My grandma makes my favourite sweets and cakes.

We play games and drink coca cola.

Everyone has new clothes for the party and we all have fun!

E
- Ask pupils to read back through their paragraphs and to make sure they use reference words where possible. If you assign this task for homework, then give them a few minutes at the beginning of the next lesson to do this.

Extra Task (for early finishers)
See photocopiable material on page 128.

Project Book

The pupils may do Project 5 now they have completed the unit. The answer key and teacher's notes are on pages 148-152 of this book.

Food!

Way in

- Give pupils a few minutes to read each others paragraphs about their birthday from Unit 5, Lesson 3. They can do this in pairs or you could hang the paragraphs on the wall for them to read when they have time.
- Write the jumbled words below on the board and ask pupils to unscramble them and to write down the words they found in Unit 5, Lesson 3.

  - wrosfkier   (*fireworks*)
  - dlcnea   (*candle*)
  - jeok   (*joke*)
  - sreptne   (*present*)
  - cnpiic   (*picnic*)

- Ask pupils to work in pairs and to discuss an April Fool's joke that they could play on someone. Encourage them to use *some* and *any* where possible when discussing it.

Background Information

The picture shows a Native American Seminole mother and her young child. The mother is giving a baby deer (*fawn*) some milk from a bottle. They are in Florida, an area which has a large Seminole community.

- Ask pupils to look at the title of the unit and the picture on pages 54 and 55. Ask them how the picture relates to the theme of the unit (*The baby deer is drinking milk.*).
- Ask pupils which word best describes the people, scared or relaxed (*relaxed*).
- Ask pupils to do the quiz question in pairs to encourage discussion, but check the answer as a class. Once you have checked the answer, explain that a *doe* is a female deer and a *stag* is a male deer.

Answer
b

Lesson 1

Objectives

Reading	The Cortuga Mystery
Vocabulary	text-related words, food, drink and restaurant related words
Grammar	much, many
Listening	ticking the correct pictures
Speaking	talking about your favourite restaurant or café
Writing	writing sentences about your favourite restaurant or café

The Cortuga Mystery
For teachers using the DVD

- Make sure each pupil has a copy of the DVD Worksheet found on page 117.
- Please follow the instructions in Unit 1, Lesson 1 on pages 12 and 13, for teachers using the DVD.

Before You Watch

Answers
1. India
2. the future

While You Watch

Answers
1. Amazing
2. fast food
3. menu
4. delicious
5. tasty
6. chewing gum

After You Watch

Answers
1. a fast food restaurant
2. a robot
3. pills
4. on a menu
5. They have got chewing gum on them.

For teachers using the audio CD

- Begin by asking pupils how many pieces of the puzzle the children have so far (*three*) and where the children were in the previous episode (*India*). Ask them to look at the episode on page 56 and to guess where they are now (*the future*).
- Tell pupils they are going to listen to and read the next part of the story. Ask them to look at the pictures and to follow the story as they listen.
- Play the recording once and ask the pupils what Robbie gives the robot (*chewing gum*).
- Ask pupils to read the story out loud. Assign the roles of Jake, Mandy, Robbie, Kate and the robot to different pupils. If you have a large class, you may have to repeat until all pupils have had a turn.
- Explain any vocabulary pupils don't know and correct their pronunciation where necessary.
- As a class, ask pupils the questions below to check they have understood the episode.

  1. Where do the children go to eat? (*a fast food restaurant*)
  2. Who helps the children in the restaurant? (*a robot*)
  3. What do people eat in the future? (*pills*)
  4. Where is a piece of the jigsaw? (*on a menu*)
  5. Why can't the waiter move his hands? (*They have got chewing gum on them.*)

Vocabulary

A

- Explain that the words in the task appear in the cartoon episode. Ask pupils to find the words in the text and underline them. Explain any words they don't understand.
- Ask pupils to do the task individually, but check the answers as a class. Correct their pronunciation where necessary.

Answers
1	hungry	4	water
2	orange	5	sandwich
3	Burgers		

Extra Class Activity
Ask pupils to write sentences of their own with the wrong words from the vocabulary task. Ask them to find the words in the cartoon to see how they are used before they write their sentences.

Grammar

Much, Many

- Write the sentences below on the board and ask pupils to find them in the cartoon episode and to correct them.
  - There aren't much things on the menu. (*many*)
  - You don't need many time for preparation. (*much*)
- Read the grammar box to the class and ask pupils to read the example sentences with you. Ask pupils why *There aren't much things* is wrong (*It's in the negative and the noun is countable.*) and why *many time* is wrong (*Time is uncountable.*).
- Draw pupils' attention to the note about *lots of* and *a lot of* and explain that these sound more natural in affirmative sentences than *many* or *much*.
- Ask pupils to do the task individually, but check the answers as a class.

Answers
1	much	4	much
2	many	5	many
3	many		

Extra Class Activity
Ask pupils to work in pairs to talk about things that are/ aren't in the classroom using *much*, *many*, *a lot of* and *lots of*.

Vocabulary

- Explain to pupils that the words in the wordbank are related to food and eating out. Make sure they understand that each sentence describes one of the words.
- Ask pupils to do the task individually, but check the answers as a class.

Answers
1	waiter	2	menu	3	dessert	4	fast food
5	plate	6	bill	7	drink	8	snack

Listening

- Ask pupils to work in pairs and to say what each picture shows. As a class, elicit the words *orange juice*, *food*, *meal*, *burger*, *chips*, *bill*, *dessert*, *sandwich*, *glass of water* and *ice cream*.
- Explain to pupils that they are going to hear five different conversations on the recording and that each one begins with the questions that are written in their books. Give them time to carefully read the questions so they know what information to listen for.
- Play the recording to the end and ask pupils to tick the box next to the picture which answers the question. Ask pupils to discuss their answers with a partner and to justify any answers they have that are different. Play the recording again and ask pupils to check their answers and to fill in any missing information.

Turn to page 107 for the listening script.

Answers
1a 2a 3a 4a 5b

Speaking

- Ask pupils if they remember what food the children order in the cartoon on page 56 (*burgers*, *chips*, *cheese* and *tomato sandwiches*, *ketchup* and *orange juice*). Ask them if they like to eat or drink any of these things. You can also ask them if they like to eat in fast food restaurants and if so, how often.
- Explain to pupils that they are going to work in pairs to discuss their favourite restaurant or café. Read the words in the wordbank to the class. Deal with any words the pupils aren't sure about and correct their pronunciation where necessary.
- As a class, ask pupils to say one thing about their favourite place.

Answers
Pupils' own answers

Teaching Tip
When pupils discuss things that they like or do, try not to judge them. If you make someone feel bad about their diet, for example, they are less likely to speak about themselves in future. Try to cultivate an encouraging atmosphere in the classroom, so that all pupils feel comfortable about speaking.

Writing

- Explain to pupils that they are going to write six sentences about their favourite restaurant or café. Read the questions to the class and make sure pupils understand them. Tell pupils to use their ideas and the vocabulary from the previous speaking task to help them.
- Ask pupils to do the task individually in class or assign the sentences for homework.

Answers
Pupils' own answers

Lesson 2

Objectives

Reading	true or false
Vocabulary	word groups, food
Grammar	a lot of, lots of, a few, a little
Listening	ticking or crossing things on a list
Sounds of English	ch and sh sounds
Song	a song about food

Way in

- Give pupils a few minutes to read each others' sentences from the writing task in Lesson 1.
- Ask pupils to tell you what *plate*, *menu*, *waiter*, *bill*, *snack* and *dessert* are.
- Ask pupils to write sentences using *much*, *many*, *lots of* and *a lot of*. Ask each pupil to read one of their sentences to the rest of class.

Reading

- Ask pupils to quickly read the text to find out which letter means yes (*Y*). Check their understanding by asking how they can see a *Y* (*by cutting a banana in two*).
- Ask pupils if they believe any of these ideas.

Comprehension

- Ask pupils to read the sentences so that they know what information to look for on their second read through. Encourage pupils to scan the text to find their answers and to underline the information that helps them find the answer.
- Ask pupils to do the task individually, but check the answers as a class. Explain any words pupils don't know and correct pronunciation if necessary.

Answers

1 F (*You can't see a 'Y'? Then the answer is no!*)
2 T (*… Swiss cheese. This is the cheese with holes.*)
3 F (*Drink the tea and then look at the tea leaves in the cup.*)
4 F (*… look at the tea leaves …. What do they look like? … a fish means …*)
5 T (*The letter you say when the apple falls is the first letter of your future friend's name.*)

Guess what!

Background Information

The Mount Horeb Mustard Museum in Wisconsin was opened in April 1992 by Barry Levensen. You might like to tell pupils that there is also a salt and pepper shaker museum in Gatlinburg, US, a lunchbox museum in Georgia, US and a vinegar museum in South Dakota, US.

- Ask pupils to read the information in the *Guess what!* feature. Ask them if they would like to visit this museum and why or why not. Ask pupils if there are any strange museums in their country.
- If pupils are interested, give them some further information on the mustard museum by using the Background Information box.

Vocabulary

- Read the words in the wordbank to the class and explain any words they are not sure about.
- Explain to pupils that 1 to 5 have got groups of words that are similar in some way, for example in 1, *fork* and *spoon* are things we use to eat with. Explain that they are going to complete the groups using the words from the wordbank.
- Ask pupils to do the task individually, but check the answers as a class.

Answers

1	knife	**4**	banana
2	cup	**5**	lunch
3	juice		

Grammar

A lot of, Lots of, A few, A little

- Ask pupils to read the extract on cheese again in the Reading section (*page 58*). Ask them which words the writer uses to say how many holes there are in the cheese (*a few* and *a lot of*).
- Read the grammar box to the class and ask the pupils to read the example sentences with you. Explain that *a lot of* and *lots of* mean a large number or amount of something, that *a few* means *some* and *a little* means *a small amount of something*.
- Draw pupils' attention to the use of *a few* with countable nouns and *a little* with uncountable nouns.
- Ask pupils to do the task individually, but check the answers as a class. Tell pupils to decide if the words after the gap are countable or uncountable and to look at the picture to see if there is a large number / amount or a small number / amount of each item.

Answers

1	a lot of	**4**	a lot of
2	a little	**5**	a few
3	a few		

Extra Class Activity

Ask pupils to use *a lot of / lots of* and *a few* to talk about the kinds of restaurants and cafés there are where they live.

Vocabulary

- Ask pupils to work in pairs and for one pupil to cover up words 1 to 8 and pictures e to h with a notebook and the other pupil to cover up pictures a to d and words 1 to 8 with their notebook. Ask pupils to tell each other what food they see in their books. Tell pupils not to worry if there's something they don't know the name of yet.
- Ask pupils to uncover the words and pictures and to write the correct letter in each box.
- Ask pupils to do the task individually, but check the answers as a class.

Teaching Tip

You might like to explain to pupils that all the words in the vocabulary are uncountable, although *chicken* and *chocolate* can also be countable but the meaning changes. Write the sentences below on the board so that they can see the difference.

• I want some chicken. (*uncountable – part of a chicken*)
• I want a chicken. (*countable – a whole chicken or a live chicken*)
• Craig always buys me chocolate. (*uncountable – a bar of chocolate*)
• Craig always buys me chocolates. (*countable – a box or packet with individual chocolates inside*)

Listening

• Ask pupils to read the list and explain that they are going to listen to a boy and a girl making preparations for a picnic. Tell them to put a tick in the boxes next to the things they need to buy for the picnic and a cross in the boxes next to the things they don't need to buy.
• Play the recording all the way to the end and ask pupils to discuss their answers with a partner and to justify any answers they have that are different. Play the recording again and ask pupils to check their answers and to fill in any missing answers.

Turn to page 107 for the listening script

Answers

eggs	✓
bread	✗
apples	✓
bananas	✗
chocolate	✓

Extra Class Activity

Ask pupils to work in pairs to make preparations for a picnic. Encourage them to use *Let's* and *Why don't we* and a *lot of / lots of*, *a few* and *a little* where possible.

Sounds of English

A
• Ask pupils to work in pairs to say the pairs of words to each other. Explain that when they say -*ch* the front part of their tongue touches the roof of their mouth, but that when they say –*sh* they don't touch.

B
• Play the first pair on the recording and ask pupils to tell you which word is said and to tick the correct box. Play the rest of the recording to the end and ask pupils to fill in the rest of their answers.
• Play the recording again, stopping after each pair, and check pupils' answers.

Song

• Explain that pupils are going to listen to a song about food and that they should read the song as they listen.
• Play the song and ask pupils if the singer likes a lot or a little food (*a lot*). Explain the difference between the words *hungry* and *greedy* and ask which word best describes the singer (*greedy*). Play the song again and ask pupils to sing along.
• Ask pupils which foods the singer seems to like best (*chips, sandwiches* and *chocolate*) and which foods from the song they like and which foods they don't like.
• Play the song a number of times if the pupils enjoy singing along.

Extra Class Activity

Ask pupils to say what *there is / are* in the picture that accompanies the song. Encourage them to use *a lot of, lots of*, *a few* and *a little*.

Teaching Tip

Ask pupils to bring in photos from magazines of different foods and make a collage for the wall. Ask pupils to cut out the foods and stick them onto a large sheet of paper and to write the names of each food underneath. Hang the collage in a place where all pupils can see it so that they can refer to it when doing tasks where they need to use food words.

Extra Task (for early finishers)

See photocopiable material on page 129.

Lesson 3

Objectives

Reading	fact sheet, complete sentences
Say it like this!	talking about food
Listening	numbering pictures (*recipe*)
Speaking	dialogue
Writing	time words; writing a recipe

Way in

• Ask pupils to tell you what they have to eat and drink for breakfast, lunch and dinner.
• Point to *a fork*, *a spoon* and *a knife* behind the Reading section on page 60 and ask pupils to tell you their names in English. Also elicit *glass*, *cup* and *plate*.
• Write the headings *A lot of*, *lots of*, *a few* and *A lot of*, *lots of* and *a little* on the board. Ask pupils to make a list of foods underneath each heading.

Suggested answers

A lot of, lots of, a few	A lot of, lots of, a little
apples	bread
bananas	butter
burgers	cheese
cakes	chocolate
chips	ice cream
cups	milk
desserts	orange juice
eggs	rice
forks	spaghetti
glasses	water
knives	
plates	
sandwiches	
spoons	

Reading

- Ask pupils to tell you what the most popular foods are in their country. Ask them what things they need to make these meals and if they eat them hot or cold.
- Ask pupils to read the text on their own to find out which food isn't nice for some people (frog's legs).

Comprehension

- Ask pupils what meals the pictures in the fact sheet show (fish and chips; crepes with chocolate and banana; paella and spaghetti with cheese and tomato sauce). Ask them which is their favourite food out of these four.
- Ask pupils to read the sentences to see what information they need to find when they read it through for the second time. Point out that the words they need are on the fact sheet. Encourage pupils to scan the fact sheet to find the answers and to underline the information in the text so they can justify their answers.
- Ask pupils to do the task individually, but check the answers as a class.

Answers
1 Chinese (There are a lot of Indian and Chinese restaurants.)
2 fast (Fish and chips … It's fast food, …)
3 cheese (A popular snack in France … a pizza with olives, onions and cheese.)
4 rice (… it has got chicken, fish and rice.)
5 fried (Other popular foods are French fries and fried chicken.)

Extra Class Activity
Ask pupils the questions below to check their understanding of the fact sheet.
1 Why do people eat lots of hot food in Scotland? (because it's cold there)
2 What are people in Scotland crazy about? (biscuits)
3 What is France famous for? (croissants and frogs' legs)
4 What dessert do French people love? (crepes with chocolate and banana)
5 Which food is very healthy? (paella)
6 What can you eat in a tapas restaurant? (lots of different snacks)

➡

7 Why is spaghetti popular in the USA? (It's delicious and easy to cook.)

Alternatively, ask pupils to write four or five questions of their own about food around the world and ask them to ask and answer their questions with a partner.

Say it like this!
- Read the language we use to talk about food to the class and ask pupils to read the example sentences with you. Correct their pronunciation and intonation patterns where necessary.
- Ask pupils to work in pairs to do the task using the language shown. To finish, ask pupils to tell you something about food. Make sure all pupils get a chance to speak.

Answers
Pupils' own answers

Listening
- Ask pupils to look at the pictures and to say what the girl is doing (cooking / preparing food). Elicit bread, cheese, meat, butter, tomato and eggs.
- Explain that pupils are going to listen to a woman describing how to make a kind of pizza. Tell pupils to listen to the recording and put the pictures in the correct order so that they show how to make the pizza.
- Play the recording until pupils have heard enough information to enable them to label the first picture. Do this as a class so that they understand exactly what they have to do.
- Play the recording to the end and ask pupils to put the pictures in the correct order. Play the recording again and ask pupils to check their answers and to fill in any missing answers.

Turn to page 107 for the listening script.

Answers
1d 2f 3a 4c 5e 6b

Teaching Tip
Explain to pupils that they don't need to understand every word they hear on a recording in order to do well in listening tasks. They should spend time before they listen trying to work out what the key words are so that they can focus on them as they listen.

Speaking
- Ask pupils to work in pairs and to read the dialogue to each other.
- Explain to pupils that they are going to make their own dialogue. Give them a few minutes to write their new words beside the words in red in the book. Go round the class helping pupils and checking what they have written. Then ask them to practise their dialogues with each other. Both pupils should have the chance to read both Jack and Polly's parts. To finish, ask some pupils to read their dialogues to the class.

Answers
Pupils' own answers

Writing

Time words: order of events

A
- Play the recording for the listening exercise again all the way through and ask pupils to listen out for words that show the order the girl makes the pizza in (*First*, *Then*, *After that*, *Then*, *Finally*).
- Explain that these are called time words and read the sentence about them to the class.

B
- Ask pupils to put numbers 1 to 3 in the correct box to show the order of these words.
- Ask pupils to do the task individually, but check the answers as a class.

Answers
1 first
2 then / after that
3 finally

C
- Ask pupils to quickly read the recipe and to find out what form the verbs are in (*imperative*). Explain that we usually use the imperative in recipes.
- Ask pupils to read the recipe again and to put the time words in the correct gaps.
- Ask pupils to do the task individually, but check the answers as a class.

Answers
1	First	3	After
2	Then	4	Finally

Extra Class Activity
Give pupils a few minutes to think of a recipe for a snack or meal. Ask them to work in pairs to tell each other how to make it using time words. Tell them not to say what the recipe is so that their partner can guess what dish is being described.

Task

D
- Ask pupils to answer the questions about their favourite snack. Explain any verbs that they don't know from the wordbank. Also teach *beat* and *pour* if you think pupils need them for their recipes. Go round the class reading their answers and helping them with any problems.
- Give pupils time to write their recipe like the one in *C* using their answers to the questions. Remind pupils that verbs should be in the imperative.
- Alternatively, you could assign the recipe for homework.

Suggested answer
Ice Cream Dream

You need: strawberry and chocolate ice cream, chocolates and a banana

First you cut the banana into slices. Then put the chocolate and strawberry ice cream into a bowl. After that put the banana slices and chocolates on the ice cream. Finally, eat your Ice Cream Dream!

E
- Give pupils a few minutes to proofread their recipe and to check for time words.
- If you assign this task as homework, give them a few minutes at the beginning of the next lesson to proofread their work before giving it to you or reading it to the class.

Extra Task (for early finishers)
See photocopiable material on page 129.

Project Book
The pupils may do Project 6 now they have completed the unit. The answer key and teacher's notes are on pages 148-152 of this book.

Objectives

- To revise vocabulary and grammar from Units 5 and 6.
- Song – Let's help someone today.

Preparing for the review

- Explain to pupils that the tasks in *Review 3* are based on the material they saw in Units 5 and 6.
- Remind pupils that they can ask you for help with the exercises or look back at the units for a reminder if they're not sure about an answer, as the review is not a test.
- Decide how you will carry out the review. You could ask pupils to do one task at a time and then correct it immediately, or ask pupils to do all the tasks and correct them together at the end. If you do all the tasks together, let pupils know every now and again how much time they have got to finish the tasks.
- Remind pupils not to leave any answers blank and to try to find any answers they aren't sure about in the units.
- Revise the vocabulary and grammar in the review as a class before pupils do the review.

Vocabulary Revision

- Tell pupils to imagine they are going to have a fancy-dress party for a friend's birthday. Ask them to tell you things that they need to buy or prepare for the party. Make sure they revise *balloons, cake, candles, card, invitation* and *party hat*.
- Then ask pupils what costume they are going to wear to the party. Make sure they revise *clown, cowboy, king, magician, mask, monster, pirate* and *queen*. Ask them to tell you two things they need for their costume, *a tall hat, a crown, a red nose*.
- Write c _ _ _ _ _ _ _, f _ _ _ _ _ _ _ _, p _ r _ _ _, c _ _ _ _, p _ i _ _ _ and p _ _ _ _ _ _ _ _ _ _ _ _ on the board and ask pupils to complete the words from Unit 5 Lesson 2 *Reading* (carnival, fireworks, parade, clues, prizes and preparations).
- Write *dessert, tea, apple, egg, glass* and *sandwich* on the board and underline the last letter in each word and the first letter in the following word. Ask pupils what they notice (*The following word begins with the same letter as the last letter in the previous word.*). Then write *breakfast* on the board and ask pupils to work in pairs or small groups to make as long a list as possible like the one above using food words from Unit 6. Try to make sure they revise the words *bill, menu, waiter, restaurant, snack, fast food, biscuits, bread, butter, chewing gum, chicken, meat, knife* and *plate*.

Grammar Revision

- Write *make, not throw, catch, swim, buy* and *not play* in one row on the board and *the ball, a card, in the sea, candles, fireworks, spaghetti, the balloons, water* and *chewing gum* in another row. Ask pupils to write as many sentences as possible with the verbs and nouns using the imperative or *Let's*. If necessary, write a sentence on the board as an example first.
- Make two columns on the board, one with the heading *Subject Pronouns* and the other with the heading *Object Pronouns*. Write *I, you, he, she, it, we, you* and *they* in the first column and ask pupils to copy it in their notebooks and to write in the object pronouns in the second column.

- Write the words *food* and *firework* on the board and elicit from pupils that *food* is uncountable and *firework* is countable. Ask pupils which word can have *a* before it and ask them why it can't have *an* (*firework, because it begins with a consonant*). Ask them to give you examples of countable nouns that have *an* before them (*an apple, an egg, an orange*).
- Ask pupils to write four sentences with *some* and *any*. Elicit from them that we use *some* in affirmative sentences with plural countable and uncountable nouns and *any* in negative sentences or questions.
- Write the nouns below on the board and ask pupils to write *many* or *much* before them.

  cheese
  candles
  invitations
  water
  plates
  rubbish

- Make sure pupils know how to use *a lot of, lots of, a few* and *a little*. Tell them to ask their partner questions using these words and ask the partner to reply.

Vocabulary

A

- Ask pupils to read the words in the wordbank and make sure they understand *costumes, birthday party* and *restaurant*. Tell them to look back at Unit 5 Lessons 1 and 2 and Unit 6 Lesson 1 for a reminder if they need to.
- Accept the correct words in each column in any order when checking pupils' answers.

Answers	
Costumes:	cowboy, pirate, witch
Birthday party:	balloons, candles, invitation
Restaurant:	bill, menu, waiter

B

- Explain to pupils that they should read the whole of the sentence or dialogue so that they understand the context the missing word is in.
- Tell pupils they may need to look back at Unit 5 Lesson 3 and Unit 6 Lesson 1 *Reading* texts for some of the answers as well as the Vocabulary tasks in the two units.

Answers							
1a	**2**b	**3**b	**4**b	**5**b	**6**a	**7**b	**8**a

C

- Ask pupils to say each of the words as a class and then individually. Correct their pronunciation if necessary.
- Ask pupils to go to the first page of stickers at the back of the book and find the stickers for *Review 3*. Tell them to decide which word each sticker shows and to stick it in the correct box.
- Check that pupils have put the correct stickers beside each word.

Grammar

A

- Ask pupils which part of the verb follows *Let's* (the bare infinitive). Remind pupils that this is the form we use for the imperative as well.
- Ask pupils to underline the mistakes in each sentence before they write the correct sentence underneath.
- Tell them to look back at Unit 5 Lesson 1 grammar box for a reminder if they need to.

Answers
1 Let's go to the party!
2 Don't drink that orange juice!
3 Let's have a picnic on Saturday!
4 Don't watch the fireworks!
5 Enjoy her birthday!
6 Don't laugh in the library.

B

- There are no plural countable nouns in this task, so remind pupils to use *a* or *an* for countable nouns and *some* for uncountable nouns.
- Tell them to look back at Unit 5 Lessons 2 and 3 grammar boxes for a reminder if they need to.

Answers
1	a	2	a	3	some	4	an
5	some	6	a	7	a	8	some

C

- Tell pupils to read the sentences carefully and to decide if the words after the options are singular or plural countable nouns or uncountable nouns and to note if it is an ordinary sentence or a question.
- Tell them to look back at Unit 5 Lesson 3 and Unit 6 Lessons 1 and 2 grammar boxes for a reminder if they need to.

Answers
1	any	5	some
2	many	6	a little
3	much	7	a lot of
4	a few	8	many

D

- Explain to pupils that they should change the object pronouns in bold so that the sentences and dialogues make sense. Tell them to write one word only on the line beside each dialogue.
- Tell pupils to look back at Unit 5 Lesson 1 grammar box for a reminder if they need to.

Answers
1	them	5	us
2	him	6	it
3	me	7	her
4	it	8	you

Song

- Tell pupils they are going to listen to a song about helping someone. Ask them to read and listen to the song and to find out what we do every day (*eat*, *sleep*, *work* and *play*) and who we can think of today (*other people*).
- Play the song again and ask pupils to sing along. You could do this verse by verse and then play it once all the way through.
- Ask pupils which idea for helping other people they like.
- To finish, ask pupils to look at the pictures round the song and to find as many things as possible from the song.

When checking pupils' answers to the review tasks, make a note of any problem areas in vocabulary and grammar that they still have. Try to do extra work on these areas so that your pupils progress well.

7 Sport

Way in

- Give pupils a few minutes to proofread their recipes from Unit 6, Lesson 3 to check that they have used time words. Ask them to read each others' recipes or hang them on the wall so they can read them when they have time.
- Ask the following questions at random round the class. Make sure each pupil gets the chance to answer at least one question.
  - What's your favourite food?
  - What about fried chicken / spaghetti / sandwiches / burgers, etc?
  - How often do you eat dessert / chips / pizza / crepes, etc?
  - Is pizza / fish and chips / chocolate, etc healthy?
- Write the word *sport* on the board and ask pupils to write down the names of as many sports as possible.

Suggested answers
basketball, cycling, football, horse riding, ice-skating, swimming, tennis, volleyball

Quiz

Background Information
The picture shows a frozen waterfall in British Columbia, Canada. Low temperatures can cause waterfalls to freeze, creating huge icicles like the ones in the picture. British Columbia is a popular place for winter sports.

- Ask pupils to look at the picture on pages 64 and 65 and ask them what sport the woman is doing (*ice climbing*). Ask them if they would like to do this and to say why or why not.
- Ask pupils to do the quiz question in pairs to encourage discussion, but check the answer as a class.

Answer
a

Lesson 1

Objectives

Reading	The Cortuga Mystery
Vocabulary	text-related words, sports
Grammar	present continuous – affirmative, spelling rules, time expressions
Listening	numbering sports
Speaking	describing a picture
Writing	writing five sentences about a picture

Reading

The Cortuga Mystery
For teachers using the DVD

- Make sure each pupil has a copy of the DVD Worksheet found on page 118.
- Please follow the instructions in Unit 1, Lesson 1 on pages 12 and 13 for teachers using the DVD.

Before you Watch

Answers
1 a robot   2 four   3 in a park

While you Watch

Answers
a6   b4   c1   d5   e3   f2

After you Watch

Answers
1F   2T   3F   4F   5T   6T

For teachers using the audio CD

- Begin by asking pupils how many pieces of the puzzle the children have so far (*four*) and who the children met in the previous episode (*a robot*). Ask them to look at the episode on page 66 and to guess where they are now (*a park*).
- Tell pupils that they are going to listen to and read the next part of the story. Ask them to look at the pictures and to follow the story as they listen.
- Play the recording once and ask the pupils what the prize is (*a trophy with a piece of the puzzle*).
- Ask pupils to read the story out loud. Assign the roles of Jake, Mandy, Robbie, Kate, Simon and the referee to different pupils. If you have a large class, you may have to repeat until all pupils have had a turn.
- Explain any vocabulary pupils don't know and correct their pronunciation where necessary.
- As a class, ask pupils the questions below to check they have understood the episode.
  1 What do the children enter? (*an egg and spoon race*)
  2 Who doesn't enter the race? (*Mandy and Kate*)
  3 What number has Simon got on his T-shirt? (*the number 3*)
  4 Does Jake push Simon? (*No, Simon pushes Jake.*)
  5 What happens to Robbie's egg? (*It falls off his spoon.*)
  6 Who wins the race? (*Jake and Simon*)

Vocabulary

A
- Explain that the words in the wordbank appear in the cartoon episode. Ask pupils to find the words in the text and underline them. Explain any words they still don't understand.
- Ask pupils to do the task individually, but check the answers as a class. Correct their pronunciation where necessary.

Extra Class Activity

Write the words below on the board and ask pupils to make phrases using the verbs in the vocabulary exercise.

1 .... a road   (*cross*)
2 .... a race   (*enter*)
3 .... my bag alone (*leave*)
4 .... a pencil   (*drop*)
5 .... a desk   (*push*)

Grammar

Present Continuous

- Ask pupils the questions below about people in the classroom.
  - *Who is wearing a blue shirt?*
  - *Who is sitting near the door?*
- Write the answers on the board, but in full sentences (*Mary is wearing a blue shirt.* and *George is sitting near the door.*) Ask pupils what the main verbs are (*wear* and *sit*) and tell them that they are in the present continuous tense here. Underline *is* and *wearing* in different colours and explain that in the present continuous we have the verb *be* in the present simple and the main verb in the –*ing* form.
- Read the grammar box to the class down to the spelling rules and ask pupils to read the example sentence and the affirmative forms with you. Read the short forms first and then the long forms.
- Ask pupils to look back at the cartoon episode on page 66 and to underline all the verbs in the affirmative form of the present continuous (*... are having, ... they're playing, ... is running, ... dog's chasing, ... is falling, ... is crossing*)
- Read the spelling rules in the grammar box to the pupils. Explain that verbs with one syllable that end in a vowel and a consonant, like run, double the consonant in the –*ing* form. Tell them that verbs that end in –*e* drop the –*e* in the –*ing* form and that verbs ending in –*ie*. change the –*ie*. to a –*y* in the ing form.
- Read the time expressions and explain that we normally put them at the end of the sentence. Refer pupils back to the example sentence at the top of the grammar box.

A

- Ask pupils to write the verbs in the –*ing* form on the lines provided. Explain that they should look at how each verb ends and refer back to the spelling rules before writing their answers.
- Ask pupils to do the task individually, but check the answers as a class.

Extra Class Activity

If you feel your pupils need further practice, ask them to write the verbs they saw in the vocabulary exercise in the –ing form. ➡

B

- Remind pupils that the verb *to be* in the present continuous is always in the correct person of the verb. Ask them to underline the subject in each sentence so that they know what form of *be* they need. Point out that the main verbs are in brackets after each gap.
- Ask pupils to do the task individually, but check the answers as a class.

Vocabulary

- Explain to pupils that they are going to learn the names of some sports in English. Ask them to look at the pictures of things that are related to each of the sports and to put the correct letter into the boxes beside the name of each sport.
- Ask pupils to do the task in pairs to encourage discussion, but check the answers as a class.

Extra Class Activity

Ask pupils to work in pairs to discuss these sports. Explain that they can tell each other if they like to do these sports or just watch them. Once they have finished, ask each pupil to tell the rest of the class about what their partner said.

Listening

- Ask pupils to read the list of sports and ask them what things they need for these sports. Elicit *horse*, *bike*, *feet* and *boat*. You might also like to pre-teach *helmet* and the expression *Don't look down*.
- Explain to pupils that they are going to hear five conversations about different sports. Tell them that they have to write the numbers 1 to 5 in the boxes beside each sport to show the order they hear them in on the recording. Do the first one together as a class so that pupils know exactly what they have to do.
- Play the rest of the recording to the end and ask pupils to work with a partner to discuss their answers and to justify any answers they have that are different. Play the recording again and ask pupils to check their answers and to fill in any missing information.
- Check the answers as a class and ask pupils which words helped them to choose the correct answers.

Turn to page 107 for the listening script.

Speaking

- Write the verbs below on the board and ask pupils to work in pairs to say what the people in the picture are doing. Remind them to use the present continuous as they are describing what the people are doing now.

chase	push
fall	run
lie	swim
play	wear

- Go round the class monitoring pupils and making sure they are carrying out the task properly. Don't correct any mistakes in structure or pronunciation that you hear at this stage, but make a note of them.
- As a class, ask each pupil to say one thing about the people in the picture.
- On the board, write some of the mistakes in structure that you heard while pupils were doing the task, without saying who made them, and ask pupils to correct them. Deal with any problems in pronunciation.

Suggested answers
- A man is running.
- A boy is falling off a bike.
- A boy is wearing a helmet.
- A woman and a baby are lying under a tree.
- A cat is chasing a dog.
- A girl is pushing a boy.
- A boy is swimming.
- Two boys are playing football.

Writing

- Ask pupils to write five sentences about the picture in the Speaking task. Remind them to look at the spelling rules in the grammar box when writing the –ing form of the main verbs.
- Alternatively, you could assign this task for homework.

Suggested answers
See speaking exercise above.

Teaching Tip
Although you may be under pressure to cover all of the syllabus, try not to rush through the material. Go at the pace of the pupils in each of your classes to make sure they are learning the material and not just getting through it.

Extra Task (for early finishers)
See photocopiable material on page 130.

Lesson 2

Objectives

Reading	article; missing sentences
Vocabulary	text-related words; athletes
Grammar	present continuous – negative, question, short answers
Listening	writing yes or no
Sounds of English	ea, ee and i sounds
Song	song about sport

Way in

- Give pupils a few minutes to read each others' sentences from Unit 7, Lesson 1.
- Write the sentences below on the board and ask pupils to correct them.

1 The mouse is chaseing the cat! (*chasing*)
2 We is playing football in the park. (*are*)
3 Jake is runing really fast. (*running*)
4 They're havving an egg and spoon race. (*having*)
5 Robbie is lieing under the tree. (*lying*)
6 I'm winning at the now. (*at the moment*)

- Ask pupils to tell you one thing each you need for *cycling*, *running*, *sailing*, *diving*, *climbing* and *riding*.

Reading

Background Information
Thai boxing or Muay Thai is a martial art that is practiced in many countries. In Thailand it is the national sport. It is different from other forms of boxing, as boxers can use their hands, arms, elbows, shins, feet and knees when fighting. The knee kick is most powerful and in tests a former champion made an impact on a dummy equal to a 56 kph car crash.

- Ask pupils to look at the pictures on page 68 and ask them what they know about Thai boxing.
- Ask pupils to skim read the article to find out if Manat wins the fight (*No, he doesn't.*). Tell them that they don't need to try to complete the gaps at this stage.
- Ask pupils to work in pairs and to try to guess what kind of information is missing from the gaps. Try to elicit from them that in Q1 we need information about Thai boxing; in Q2 we need information about the training camp; in Q3 we need information about money; in Q4 we need a question about Manat's feelings and in Q5 we need information about the match.

Comprehension

- Ask pupils to read the sentences and to complete the article. Tell them to read back through the article once they have finished to make sure that they have chosen the correct sentences.
- Ask pupils to do the task individually, but check the answers as a class.
- Explain any vocabulary pupils don't know and correct their pronunciation where necessary.

Answers
1b   2e   3d   4a   5c

Guess what!

- Ask pupils to read the information in the *Guess what!* feature. Ask them if this is a healthy thing to do and what things they think people who play sports normally eat and normally don't eat.

Vocabulary

- Explain that the words in the task appear in the text. Ask pupils to find the words in the text and underline them. Explain any words they still don't understand.
- Ask pupils to do the task individually, but check the answers as a class. Correct their pronunciation where necessary.

Grammar

Present Continuous

- Point to the picture of Manat and ask *Is he running?* When pupils say *no* say *No, he isn't running. He's sitting.* Write the forms on the board and elicit that they are the question, negative and affirmative forms of the Present Continuous.
- Read the grammar box to the class and ask pupils to repeat the forms and the example sentences after you.
- Ask the following questions at random round the class and ask pupils to answer using short answers.
  - *Are you reading a comic at the moment?*
  - *Is your partner wearing boots?*
  - *Are the other pupils lying down?*
  - *Is your favourite football / basketball team playing now?*
  - *Is your mum / dad / brother / sister eating lunch / dinner at the moment?*
- Explain to pupils that have to draw lines between each question and its answer and that they should pay attention to the subject in the questions and in the answers. Ask pupils to do the task individually, but check the answers as a class.

Answers

1c   2b   3e   4a   5d

Vocabulary

- Explain to pupils that they should look at each picture and think about what sport each person is doing. Then they should look at the names of the people who do these sports and write the letter of the correct picture in the box.
- Ask pupils to do the task individually, but check the answers as a class.

Answers

1c   2e   3a   4d   5f   6b

Extra Class Activity

Ask pupils to work in pairs to ask and answer what each of the people is doing in the pictures in the vocabulary exercise. To finish, ask each pair to ask and answer about one picture as a class.

Suggested answers

1 What is he doing? He's playing football.
2 Where is he swimming? He's swimming in a swimming pool.
3 What is he doing? He's doing gymnastics.
4 What sport is he playing? He's playing tennis.
5 Why is he wearing gloves? He's boxing.
6 What is he doing? He's cycling.

Teaching Tip

From time to time, bring in large pictures from magazines and newspapers and stick them to the board. Use them to give your pupils extra practice with new language or to revise language from previous lessons. In this lesson, for example, you could use pictures of people doing sports, having fun, eating, writing emails, etc and ask pupils about what they are doing. This way they can practise the grammar in this lesson with vocabulary from previous lessons.

Listening

- Explain to pupils that they are going to listen to two children playing a game called *Who am I?* Tell them that one of the children pretends to be someone famous and the other child asks them questions about himself or herself to which they can only respond *Yes* or *No*. The other child then has to guess who they are pretending to be.
- Ask pupils to read the sentences about the mystery person. Ask them if they have any idea who it might be. Explain that they have to listen to see if the sentences are correct or not and to write *Y* or *N* accordingly.
- Play the recording all the way through until just before the child says who the person is. Stop and ask the class if they know who it is now. Ask pupils to work in pairs to discuss the answers to the questions.
- Play the recording again and ask pupils to check their answers and to fill in any missing information.

Turn to pages 107 and 108 for the listening script.

Answers

1N   2N   3Y   4N   5Y

Extra Class Activity

Put the pupils into small groups and ask them to play *Who am I?* Each pupil should spend a few minutes thinking about their famous person and some well-known facts about his or her life. Decide who the first mystery person will be in each group. Remind pupils that the mystery person can only answer *Yes* or *No*, so all questions must be phrased so that the person can answer them that way. The pupil who guesses who the mystery person is then becomes the mystery person in the next round.

Sounds of English

A

- Ask pupils to read the pairs of words in 1 to 6 and tell them that they are going to hear one of these words on the recording. Ask them to underline the word they hear each time.

Answers

1	live	2	feet	3	Tim
4	it	5	sheep	6	fill

B

- Explain to pupils that these sounds are difficult for learners of English to pronounce and that learning to say them properly can make a big difference to how good they sound when speaking English.
- Ask pupils to say the words to each other in pairs. If you have time, ask them to use each word in a sentence.

Song

- Explain that pupils are going to listen to a song about different sports and that they should read the song as they listen.
- Play the song and ask pupils what sports are mentioned (*training / sailing / climbing / diving / football / swimming*). Play the song again and ask pupils to sing along.
- Play the song a number of times if the pupils enjoy singing along.

Extra Class Activity

Ask pupils to underline the verbs in the present continuous in the song and to write them in the negative form if they are in the affirmative or in the affirmative if they are in the negative.

Extra Task (for early finishers)

See photocopiable material on page 130.

Lesson 3

Objectives

Reading	interview; open-ended questions
Say it like this!	talking about sport
Grammar	present continuous (*for the future*)
Writing	time expressions: word order; writing an email

Way in

- Write the words and phrases below on the board and ask pupils to work in pairs to take it in turns to ask and answer questions about what they are doing. Remind them to use short answers. Go round the class monitoring them and noting down any mistakes they make. Deal with any mistakes once pupils have finished.

  - run
  - climb a tree
  - cycle
  - sit at your desk

Suggested answers

- Are you running?
- Are you climbing a tree?
- Are you cycling?
- Are you sitting in a classroom?

- Ask pupils to write the words below on a piece of paper. To check the spelling, ask one pupil at a time to write one of the words on the board. Then point to the words and ask pupils to say them after you several times. Change the order in which you point to the words each time.

- leave
- fit
- team
- eat
- ship
- feel

Reading

- Tell pupils to work in small groups and give them a few minutes to try to think of as many Olympic sports as possible. Ask a member from each group to write the names of the sports on the board in English and see which group comes up with the most.
- Ask pupils what sport the two people are doing in the picture on page 70 (*ice dancing*) and explain that this is an Olympic sport. Ask them to read the interview with the ice dancers to find out how many times a day they practise (*twice*).
- Tell pupils to look at the subheading again and ask them what Robin and Laura are training for (*a big competition in London*).

Comprehension

- Ask pupils to read the questions before they read the interview again so that they know what information to look for. Ask them to scan the text to find the answers and to underline the information in the interview that helps them find the answer.
- Ask pupils to do the task individually, but check the answers as a class.
- Explain any vocabulary that pupils don't know and correct their pronunciation where necessary.

Answers

1. at 6 / six o'clock (*We get up at six o'clock every morning …*)
2. for three hours (*… we practise for an hour before school. Then after school we practise again for two hours!*)
3. Olympic champions (*We want to be Olympic champions!*)
4. an ice-skating competition (*a big competition in London next week.*)
5. The music they are skating to at the competition. (*What music are you skating to? It's from the film The Lion King.*)

Extra Class Activity

Ask pupils the questions below and ask them to find the answers in the interview.

- Is Laura thirteen? (*No, she's fourteen.*)
- How do Robin and Laura feel about training? (*It's hard work but they love it.*)
- Who is teaching them new things? (*their coach*)
- Why are they excited? (*because young ice skaters from many countries will be at the competition.*)

Say it like this!

Talking about sport

- Read the information in the *Say it like this!* box to the class and ask pupils to say the example sentences with you. You might also like to pre-teach *I don't have a favourite player / team.* and *I don't like sport.* as some pupils may not be interested in team sports.
- Give pupils a few minutes to tell each other about their favourite players and teams. Then ask each pupil to tell the class about their partner's favourite player and team.

Grammar

Present Continuous (for the future)

- Ask pupils to look back at the interview again and to underline the reporter's last question (*What music are you skating to?*). Remind pupils that we use the Present Continuous for things that we are doing now. Explain that we can also use this tense to talk about plans for the future.
- Read the grammar box to the class and ask pupils to read the example sentences with you.
- Ask pupils at random round the class what they are doing using the time expressions in the grammar box (*What are you doing at the weekend? What are you doing at 4 o'clock?*)
- Ask pupils to look at Sally's diary and to use the information to write sentences. Tell them to write the day of the week and that they may have to add articles in some places.

Answers

1   She's / Sally's having a riding lesson on Monday.
2   She's / Sally's watching a basketball match on Tuesday.
3   She's / Sally's going swimming with Jenny on Wednesday.
4   She's / Sally's buying some new trainers on Thursday.
5   She's / Sally's going to a Thai boxing class on Friday.

Extra Class Activity

Ask pupils to work in pairs to ask and answer questions about Sally's week, beginning with *When*.

Suggested Answers

- When is she / Sally watching a basketball match?
  On Tuesday.
- When is she / Sally going to a Thai boxing class?
  On Friday.
- When is she / Sally having a riding lesson?
  On Monday.
- When is she / Sally going swimming with Jenny?
  On Wednesday.
- When is she / Sally buying some new trainers?
  On Thursday.

Writing

Time expressions: word order

A

- Ask pupils to look back at the example sentences in the grammar box and ask them where the time expressions are in each one (*at the end*). Explain that this is the most natural place for time expressions.
- Explain to pupils that they are going to use the prompts to write sentences. Tell them to pay attention to whether or not the prompt has a question mark. Do the first one together as a class so that they understand exactly what to do.
- Let pupils to do the task individually, but check the answers as a class.

Answers

1   Is Mandy coming to the sports centre this evening?
2   Manchester United are playing next week.
3   Are they training at the weekend?
4   We are skating at the moment.
5   Jane is climbing a frozen waterfall on Saturday.

B

- Ask pupils to quickly read the email to find out why Mel is excited. (*He / She's got an extra ticket for a tennis match at Wimbledon.*) Ask pupils what they know about Roger Federer. (*He's a Swiss tennis player and was born in 1981. He won the gold medal for men's doubles at the Beijing Olympics in 2008. He's one of the best tennis players ever.*)
- Ask pupils to read back through the email and to find and correct the three sentences with mistakes in them.

Answers

1   Are you studying tonight?
2   What are you doing on Saturday?
3   Dad and I are leaving my house at two o'clock.

Task

C

- Explain to pupils that they are going to write an email inviting a friend to a sports event. Ask them to look back at the email in *B* and to say how many paragraphs it has (*3*). Explain that each paragraph deals with one main idea.
- Read the plan to the class and make sure pupils understand what they have to write. Give them a few minutes to make some notes before they begin writing.
- Ask them to write their emails individually on a piece of paper. Alternatively, you could assign this task for homework.

Suggested answer

Dear Ben,

How are you? Are you studying tonight? Me too!

What are you doing on Saturday? I'm really excited because I've got an extra ticket for a football match at Wembley. Cristiano Ronaldo is playing and he's my favourite footballer!

Do you want to come? My brother and I are leaving my house at two o' clock.

Bye for now!
Omar

D

- Ask pupils to read back through their emails and to check the word order of time expressions. If you assign this task for homework, then give them a few minutes at the beginning of the next lesson to do this.

Teaching Tip

If your pupils are sports fans, ask them to prepare a short talk on their favourite sport. They can prepare this at home or you could get them to do it during the lesson if you have time. Pupils can tell each other what the sport is called, the names of the famous people who play it, where you can play / watch the sport and what things players need for the sport.

Extra Task (for early finishers)

See photocopiable material on page 130.

Project Book

The pupils may do Project 7 now they have completed the unit. The answer key and teacher's notes are on pages 148-152 of this book.

People and Places

Way in

- Give pupils a few minutes to proofread their emails from Unit 7, Lesson 3. Ask them to read each others' emails or hang them on the wall so they can read them when they have time. You could extend this task by asking them to quickly write a reply to the invitation.
- Ask pupils at random round the class what they are doing this evening / tomorrow / at the weekend / on his / her birthday / next month. Make sure that all pupils have the chance to answer at least one question.
- Write the sentences below on the board and ask pupils to fill in the missing words.

    .... your favourite tennis player? (*Who's*)
    .... is your favourite volleyball team? (*Which*)

- Ask pupils to tell you four things about ice dancing champions, Robin and Laura that they read about in the previous lesson.

Suggested answers

- Laura is fourteen and Robin is thirteen.
- They practise for three hours a day.
- They want to be Olympic champions.
- They are entering a competition in London next week.

Quiz

- Hold open your book at page 72 so that all pupils can see the picture. Ask them to tell you where the picture was taken and if they would like to go there. Ask them why / why not.
- Ask pupils to do the quiz in pairs to encourage discussion, but check the answer as a class.
- Ask pupils what they know about the Great Wall of China and give them further information if they are interested.

Answer

c

Background Information

The picture shows the *Great Wall of China*, which is approximately 6,700 km long. It is actually a series of walls and its construction started 2,500 years ago and continued until the 16th century. The wall was originally built to protect the northern borders of the Chinese Empire, but today it's a popular tourist destination and a symbol of China. If pupils are interested in reading about children their age who have visited the wall, direct them to www.kidsblogs. nationalgeographic.com/globalbros and tell them to search for the *Great Wall of China*.

Extra Class Activity

Put pupils into groups and give each group the name of a famous place (*Eiffel Tower*, *Big Ben*, *Sydney Opera House*, *the Coliseum*, *the Pyramids*) and ask them to prepare some ➡

information on the place to tell the other groups. They can talk about where it is, what kind of building it is, if it is in a town, a city or near the sea. Give the groups any help they may need. Get each group to talk about their place without saying its name and ask the other groups to guess the place.

Lesson 1

Objectives

Reading	The Cortuga Mystery
Vocabulary	text-related words, homes and buildings
Grammar	present simple and present continuous
Listening	completing a table
Speaking	talking about your home
Writing	writing sentences about your home

Reading

The Cortuga Mystery
For teachers using the DVD

- Make sure each pupil has a copy of the DVD Worksheet found on page 119.
- Please follow the instructions in Unit 1, Lesson 1 on pages 12 and 13 for teachers using the DVD.

Before you Watch

Answers
1 the Tower of London
2 a girl called Sally

While you Watch

Answers
a 4 b 3 c 1 d 5 e 2

After you Watch

Answers
1 the River Thames
2 Sally's dad
3 900 years old
4 guards, their families and a few ghosts
5 It's moving.
6 Robbie

For teachers using the audio CD

- Begin by asking pupils to look at the cartoon episode on page 74 and to say where the children are now (*the Tower of London*) and ask them who they meet there (*a girl called Sally*).
- Tell pupils they are going to listen to and read the next part of the story. Ask them to look at the pictures and to follow the story as they listen.

- Play the recording once and ask the pupils what trick Robbie plays this time (*He puts on a knight's costume and scares the other children.*).
- Ask pupils to read the story out loud. Assign the roles of Jake, Mandy, Robbie, Kate and Sally. If you have a large class, you may have to repeat until all pupils have had a turn.
- As a class, ask pupils the questions below to check they have understood the episode.
  1 What can the children see from the Tower of London? (*the River Thames*)
  2 Who works in the Tower of London? (*Sally's dad*)
  3 How old is the Tower of London? (*900 years old*)
  4 Who lives in the Tower of London? (*guards, their families and a few ghosts*)
  5 What is the knight doing? (*It's moving.*)
  6 Who is wearing the knight's costume? (*Robbie*)

Vocabulary

- Explain that the words in the wordbank appear in the cartoon episode. Ask pupils to find the words in the text and underline them. Explain any words they don't understand.
- Ask pupils to do the task individually, but check the answers as a class. Correct their pronunciation where necessary.

Answers
1	ghosts	4	footsteps
2	stairs	5	river
3	view		

Extra Class Activity
Ask pupils to write as many words of three letters or more using the letters from footsteps. Give them a few minutes to write their words and then ask them to shout their words out and make a list on the board. Check their spelling and pronunciation where necessary.

Grammar

Present Simple and Present Continuous

- Read the grammar box to the class and ask pupils to say the example sentences with you.
- Write the sentences below on the board and ask pupils to write them in their notebooks and write if they are *a fact*, *a habit* or *happening now* beside them. Then ask them to tell you what tense is used in each sentence.
  1 A girl is coming up the stairs. (*happening now* – Present Continuous)
  2 My dad works here. (*fact* – Present Simple)
  3 It's moving. (*happening now* – Present Continuous)
  4 Sally often visits the Tower of London. (*habit* – Present Simple)

A
- Quickly revise the affirmative, negative and question forms of both tenses using the verb *hold*.
- Ask pupils to do the task individually, but check the answers as a class. Ask pupils to tell you what use of the tenses we have in each sentence as you check answers.

Answers
1	visit	(*habit*)
2	Does	(*fact*)
3	is having	(*happening now*)
4	touch	(*habit*)
5	are cleaning	(*happening now*)
6	isn't playing	(*happening now*)

B
- Ask pupils to quickly read the dialogue to find out who lives in London (*Bob's aunt's friends*). Tell pupils not to worry about filling in the gaps at this stage.
- Ask pupils to look at the gaps and to tell you which ones need the affirmative, the negative and the question form of the verbs in brackets.
- Ask pupils to do the task individually, but check the answers as a class.
- Alternatively, you could assign this task as homework.

Answers
1	'm / am calling	4	's / is staying
2	visits	5	Are you having
3	doesn't live	6	don't like

Extra Class Activity
Ask pupils to act out the dialogue with a partner. If possible try to pair girls with boys so that they can be Jane or Bob accordingly. Deal with any problems in pronunciation or intonation patterns that arise.

Vocabulary

- Ask children to look at the pictures and to say which place is most like where they live. Ask pupils where they can find each of these places (a *in a village*, b *in a town or city*, c *in a village*, d *on a mountain / by the sea*, e *in Paris*, f *on a river*, g *in the Arctic*, h *in a town or city*).
- Ask pupils to do the task in pairs to encourage discussion, but check the answers as a class.

Answers
1b	**2**h	**3**d	**4**f	**5**a	**6**e	**7**c	**8**g

Listening

- Explain to pupils that they are going to hear three dialogues with children speaking about their homes. Ask them to look at the table to work out which information they need to listen out for. Tell pupils that they will hear each child speaking in the order their names appear on the table and that they should only write one word in each gap. Explain that under *Number of rooms* they can either write the word or the number.
- Play the recording and ask pupils to write in their answers. Ask them to discuss their answers with a partner and to justify any answers they have that are different.
- Play the recording again and ask pupils to check their answers and to fill in any missing information.

Turn to page 108 for the listening script.

63

Answers

1	flat	**6**	river
2	six (6)	**7**	house
3	park	**8**	ten (10)
4	houseboat	**9**	sea
5	four (4)		

Speaking

- Ask pupils which of the houses from the *Listening* they like best and why.
- Explain to pupils that they are going to talk about their own homes with a partner. Read the questions to the class and make sure they understand them. Ask pupils to spend a few minutes preparing what they are going to say before they start talking.
- Go round the class monitoring and making sure they are carrying out the task properly. Don't correct any mistakes you hear in structure or pronunciation at this stage, but make a note of them.
- Ask pupils to tell the class about their homes. Then write some of the mistakes you heard on the board, without saying who made them, and ask pupils to correct them.

Writing

- Ask pupils to write sentences answering the six questions in the *Speaking* task about their homes. Go round the class checking their work and helping them with any problems they have.
- Alternatively, you could assign this task for homework and ask pupils to stick a photograph of their home above their sentences.

Extra Task (for early finishers)

See photocopiable material on page 131.

Lesson 2

Objectives

Reading	article; open-ended questions
Vocabulary	text-related vocabulary; jobs
Grammar	must – affirmative, negative, question, short answers
Listening	numbering the jobs
Sounds of English	rhyming words

Way in

- Give pupils a few minutes to read each others' sentences from Unit 8, Lesson 1.
- Write the letters *F*, *H*, *C*, *H*, *C*, *T*, *H* and *I* on the board one below the other and ask pupils to write the homes and buildings that begin with these letters next to them.
- Write the sentences below on the board and ask pupils to correct them.

1 Do you have fun at the moment? (*Are you having fun at the moment*?)

2 I am often play jokes on my friends. (*I often play jokes on my friends*)

3 Do they visiting Paris this year? (*Are they visiting Paris this year*?)

4 We are never touching the knight's costume. (*We never touch the knight's costume.*)

Reading

- Ask pupils to look at the title of the article and the picture and to guess what the man is doing (*He's probably using a lasso to catch a cow.*). Then ask them to tell you what they know about cowboys.
- Ask pupils to skim read the article to find out how many days a week a cowboy works (*seven days a week*).
- If pupils are interested, give them further information about cowboys using the Background Information box.

Background Information

Cowboys are generally linked to the American West of the late 19th century. It is thought that they originally arrived in the US with the Spanish conquistadors in the 17th century. A cowboy's main job was to round up cattle and to take them to fields to graze. They also lead the cattle across large distances to sell them at markets. This often meant passing through Indian lands. Today, cowboys work on ranches and their main duties involve feeding cattle and treating their injuries. The conditions that they work in can be very tough as they live and work in isolated places. The traditional clothing that cowboys wear is due to the nature of the work that they do, and the conditions that they face.

Comprehension

- Ask pupils to read the questions so that they know what information to look for the second time they read the text. Ask them to scan the article to find the answers and to underline the information that helps them to find the answer.
- Ask pupils to do the task individually, but check the answers as a class.
- Once you have checked the answers, ask pupils if they learnt anything new about cowboys from the article or to tell you if they found anything surprising.

Answers

1 at 5am (*Dan gets up early – at 5am!*)

2 in a tent ('*I sleep in a tent …*')

3 medicine ('*Sometimes the cows get sick and I give them medicine,*'…)

4 He must find new areas with grass. (*Cows eat a lot of grass, so Dan must find new areas with grass for them.*)

5 No, they don't. ('*… we don't make much money,*'…)

Guess what!

- Ask pupils to read the information in the *Guess what!* feature. Ask pupils what other animals they know that sleep in strange positions (*Bats sleep upside down*).

Vocabulary

- Explain to pupils that we use the verbs in the wordbank with the adverbs and nouns in 1 to 5 to make set phrases. Ask them to scan the article to find these words and underline them and the verbs used with them before they fill in their answers.

Answers

1	get up	**4**	make
2	get	**5**	cook
3	get on		

Extra Class Activity

Ask pupils to write questions with each of the phrases from the *Vocabulary* and to leave a space for answers below each question. Go round the class checking their questions and giving them any help they might need. Then ask pupils to give their questions to another pupil to answer. To finish, ask each pupil to read one of the questions and the other pupil's answer to the class.

Grammar

Must

- Read the grammar box to the class and ask pupils to read the example sentences with you. Ask pupils what they notice about the form of *must* (*It stays the same for all persons of the verb*). Draw pupils' attention to the bare infinitive form of the main verb after *must*.
- Ask pupils to look back through the article and to underline examples of *must* (*...he must get on his horse..., Dan must find...*) and *mustn't* (*Dan mustn't stay in the same place...*).
- Ask pupils to do the task individually, but check the answers as a class.

Answers

1	must	**5**	mustn't
2	Must	**6**	mustn't
3	must	**7**	mustn't
4	must	**8**	Must

Extra Class Activity

Write the prompts below on the board and ask pupils to use them to write sentences with *must* and *mustn't*.

Prompts and suggested answers

- you / talk / in the library (*You mustn't talk in the library.*)
- ice dancers / train / very hard (*Ice dancers must train very hard.*)
- Simon / push / Jake (*Simon mustn't push Jake.*)
- we / study / before the lesson (*We must study before the lesson.*)

Vocabulary

- Ask pupils to quickly find four jobs that have been mentioned in the unit so far (*guards, cowboys, teachers* and *waiters*). Ask them to tell you any other jobs they know in English and write them on the board.

- Ask pupils to look at pictures a to h to see if any of the jobs they mentioned are shown there. Ask them to match these pictures with the correct word 1 to 8. Then ask them to match up the rest of the jobs.
- Ask pupils to do the task individually, but check the answers as a class.

Answers

1f	**2**c	**3**e	**4**b	**5**g	**6**a	**7**h	**8**d

Extra Class Activity

Write the words below on the board and ask pupils to match them to each of the jobs from the *Vocabulary* task. You may need to pre teach; *scissors*, *truck* and *plane* as they may not have come across them yet..

- scissors (*hairdresser*)
- TV (*actor*)
- clothes shop (*shop assistant*)
- truck (*firefighter*)
- car (*taxi driver*)
- teeth (*dentist*)
- medicine (*doctor*)
- plane (*pilot*)

Listening

- Explain to pupils that they are going to hear five people talking about their jobs and that they have to write down the order that they speak in.
- If you didn't do the *Extra Class Activity* previously, then ask pupils who might speak about *medicine, TV, a car* and *a clothes shop*.
- Play the recording to the end and ask pupils to work in pairs to discuss their answers and to justify any answers they have that are different. Play the recording again and ask pupils to check their answers and to fill in any missing information.

Turn to page 108 for the listening script.

Answers

a1	**b**4	**c**3	**d**5	**e**2

Sounds of English

A

- Read each of the words in the wordbank and ask pupils to say them after you. Explain that they should use the words to complete the poem and that the words will rhyme with another word in each sentence. Point out that English words can be pronounced in the same way, but we spell them differently.
- Ask pupils to do the task in pairs to encourage them to read the poem and the missing words out loud.

B

- Play the recording and ask pupils to check their own answers, then check them as a class.

Answers

1	wear	**3**	phone
2	school	**4**	sea

Extra Class Activity

Ask pupils if they know any other words that rhyme with the words in Sounds of English.

Suggested answers

phone	bone, tone
school	cool, pool
sea	bee, tree, three, knee
wear	bear, fair

Extra Task (for early finishers)

See photocopiable material on page 131.

Lesson 3

Objectives

Reading	poster; completing sentences
Say it like this!	talking about places
Listening	multiple choice
Speaking	finding the differences between two pictures
Writing	connectors; writing a paragraph

Way in

- Write the prompts below on the board and ask pupils to use them to write some school rules using the verb *must*. Accept *must* or *mustn't* according to what your pupils think the rules should be.
  - *be early for class*
  - *run in the classroom*
  - *do your homework*
  - *listen to the teacher*
  - *throw pens out the window*
- Write the jumbled words below on the board and ask pupils to unscramble them to write the jobs. Then ask them what other jobs they learnt in Lesson 2.
  - hrethgffiire   (*firefighter*)
  - liopt   (*pilot*)
  - catro   (*actor*)
  - tdorco   (*doctor*)
  - posh sitsasnta   (*shop assistant*)
- Write *Scotland* on the board and ask pupils what they know about this country. If any pupils have been to Scotland ask them to tell the class about their visit there. Try to elicit that Edinburgh is the capital city and that Loch Ness is a famous tourist site because of the Loch Ness monster.
- Ask pupils to look at the headlines in the poster and ask them what the poster wants to do (*bring tourists to Scotland*).
- Ask pupils to skim read the poster to find out which place has got two names (*Edinburgh*). Check pupils' pronunciation of Edinburgh (*Edinbura*) and Glamis Castle (*Glamz* – silent –i).

Background Information

Scotland is the most northern part of Great Britain. It is a popular tourist destination due to its natural beauty. As well as the Scottish mainland, there are also over 790 Scottish islands. Edinburgh is the capital city of Scotland and it is famous for its castle, shown in the large photo on the poster on page 78. The Edinburgh Festival, which takes place every August, also attracts many visitors to the capital. Glamis Castle is another famous castle in Scotland. ➡

It dates back to the 16th century and is linked to many legends. It is also where Queen Elizabeth II's mother grew up. Loch Ness is a large freshwater lake with a surface area of 56.5 square kilometres and it is up to 230 metres deep in places. Tourists visit Loch Ness due to the legend of the Loch Ness monster, which people say looks like a dinosaur that lives in the deep waters of the lake.

Comprehension

- Ask pupils to read the sentences to find out what information they need to look for the second time they read it through. Ask them to scan the text to find the missing words.
- Ask pupils to do the task individually, but check the answers as a class.

Answers

1	Nessie	4	plays
2	tourists	5	Athens of the North
3	buildings		

Extra Class Activity

Ask pupils about famous tourist sites in their country. Ask them to tell you where they are and about any unusual stories that are linked to them.

Say it like this!

Talking about places

- Read the *Say it like this!* box to the class and explain to pupils that they are going to talk about their favourite town or city. Give them a few minutes to decide which place they want to speak about and to prepare information on it.
- Ask pupils to work in pairs to ask and answer questions about their favourite places. Remind them to use the language in the *Say it like this!* box. Go round the class monitoring and checking that pupils are carrying out the task properly.
- As a class, ask each pair about one of the places they talked about. Ask one of the pupils where his or her favourite place is and then ask the other pupil what you can do in this place.

Answers

Pupils' own answers

Teaching Tip

When reporting back to the class on speaking tasks always encourage pupils to speak about what their partner said. This means that pupils will make more of an effort to listen to their partners while doing the task.

Listening

- Explain to pupils that they are going to listen to a quiz show with two teams of school pupils. Ask them to quickly read questions 1 to 5 and explain that these are the questions the children answer on the quiz.
- Play the recording all the way to the end and ask pupils to circle the correct answers. Ask them to work with a partner to discuss their answers and to justify any answers they have that are different.
- Play the recording again and ask pupils to check their answers and to fill in any missing information.

Answers

1 b	**2** c	**3** b	**4** a	**5** c

Extra Class Activity

Ask pupils to write two quiz questions each like the ones they heard on the recording. They should be about famous places and they should have a, b, c options and pupils should note the answers. When they have finished, collect all the questions and split the class into two teams. Use the pupils' questions to have your own quiz in class. Give three points for each correct answer and two points when a team gets the answer correct following a wrong answer from the other team.

Speaking

- Ask pupils to work in pairs to find the five differences between the two pictures. Remind them to use the Present Continuous when answering.

Answers

1 In the first picture three children are riding the rollercoaster. In the second picture four children are riding the rollercoaster.
2 In the first picture a boy is eating chocolate. In the second picture a boy is eating an ice cream.
3 In the first picture a girl is wearing a red T-shirt. In the second picture a girl is wearing a blue T-shirt.
4 In the first picture a girl is riding the Loch Ness monster. In the second picture a boy is riding the Loch Ness monster.
5 In the first picture there is a house. In the second picture there is a castle.

Writing

Connectors

A
- Read the information about *because* and *so* to the class and ask pupils to read the example sentences with you. Explain that these words are connectors because they join two clauses together.
- Demonstrate the difference between reason and result further by writing *It's Saturday* and *We can play all day* on the board. Ask pupils to finish the sentences using the words from the example sentences in the book (*It's Saturday, so I'm happy.* and *We can play all day because it's the weekend.*).

B
- Tell pupils to read the sentences and to then fill in the gaps with *because* or *so*.
- Ask pupils to do the task individually, but check the answers as a class.
- If you have time and you want to give pupils extra practice, ask them to write the sentences again beginning with the words after the gaps.

Answers

1 so		**4** because
2 because		**5** because
3 so		

C
- Ask pupils to quickly read the paragraph to find out what the writer doesn't do at the beach (*swim in the sea*) and why (*The sea is very cold.*).
- Ask pupils to do the task individually, but check the answers as a class.

Answers

1 because
2 so
3 because

Task

D
- Tell pupils they are going to write a paragraph about their favourite place like the one in *C*. Ask them to answer the questions before they write their paragraph.
- Ask pupils to tell you something about their favourite place. Pick pupils at random round the class.
- Ask pupils to write their paragraphs on a piece of paper or alternatively, assign the task for homework.

Suggested answer
My Favourite Place

My favourite place in my town is the park. It isn't a beautiful park, but my friends and I play there. We often go there **because** the weather is warm!
We sometimes play basketball in the park. There's also a café **so** we often buy snacks there. The park is great **because** it is near to my house.

E
- Give pupils a few minutes to proofread their paragraphs to make sure they have used *because* and *so* properly. If you assign the paragraph for homework, give pupils time at the beginning of the next lesson to do this.

Extra Task (for early finishers)

See photocopiable material on page 131.

Project Book

The pupils may do Project 8 now they have completed the unit. The answer key and teacher's notes are on pages 148-152 of this book.

Objectives

- To revise vocabulary and grammar from Units 7 and 8
- Song – I want to travel

Revision

- Explain to pupils that the tasks in *Review 4* are based on the material they saw in Units 7 and 8.
- Remind pupils that they can ask you for help with the exercises or look back at the units if they're not sure about an answer, as the review is not a test.
- Decide how you will carry out the review. You could ask pupils to do one task at a time and then correct it immediately, or ask pupils to do all the tasks and then correct them together at the end. If you do all the tasks together, let pupils know every now and again how much time they have got left to finish the tasks.
- Remind pupils not to leave any answers blank and to try to find any answers they aren't sure about in the units.
- Revise the vocabulary and grammar as a class before pupils do the review.

Vocabulary Revision

- Write *Sports* and *Players* on the board. Ask pupils to work in pairs to list as many sports and players as they can. Make sure they revise *cycling, running, sailing, boxing, climbing, diving, ice-skating, riding, boxer* and *footballer* and any other sports related words. Ask them to tell you what their favourite sport is and who their favourite player is.
- Ask pupils what the difference between *practise* and *train* is. Elicit that the players themselves practise a sport and that a coach trains the players. Ask pupils to name any famous sports coaches they know in their country.
- Ask pupils to tell you the different kinds of buildings and houses they know. Make sure they revise *cottage, flat* and *igloo*. Then ask pupils what kind of house they can find on the water (*a houseboat*) and what places with water they know (*river, sea, lake*).
- Revise the adjectives *strong, hard, sad* and *calm* by asking pupils to write a sentence with each word.

Grammar Revision

- Write the verbs *sit, wear, sleep,* and *talk* on the board and ask pupils to use them to write sentences about what is or isn't happening in the classroom at the moment. Tell them to use the Present Continuous affirmative or negative. Drill the forms for each person of the verb if necessary.
- Write the subjects and the verbs below and ask pupils to use them to ask their partners questions using the Present Continuous and any other words they might need. Explain that their partner should answer using short answers.
  - your dad / swim
  - I / cycle
  - the teacher / listen
  - you / study

- Write the sentence below on the board and ask pupils which time expression is correct.
  - *I'm going to the basketball match now / tonight.*

  Elicit that both are correct and remind pupils that we can use the Present Continuous to talk about things that are happening now or for future plans.
- Write the sentences below on the board and ask pupils to tell you which tense the verb is in and why this tense has been used.
  - Karen's living in Manchester now. (*Present Continuous – action happening now*)
  - I love football. (*Present Simple – fact*)
  - Mike usually plays tennis on Saturdays. (*Present Simple – habit*)
- Ask pupils to make a list of rules for playing their favourite sport. The rules could be about things that players *must* and *mustn't* do or wear. Remind them that the bare infinitive follows *must*, that the form of *must* is the same for all persons of the verb and that in the question form *must* comes before the subject, but the main verb comes after the subject.

Vocabulary

A

- Ask pupils to say each of the words as a class and then individually. Correct their pronunciation if necessary.
- Ask pupils to go to the second page of stickers at the back of the book and find the stickers for *Review 4*. Tell them to decide which sport each sticker shows and to stick it in the correct box.
- Check that pupils have put the correct stickers above each word.

B

Ask pupils to read the whole sentence before choosing the correct answer and to read the sentence again to make sure their answer makes sense.

Answers							
1	hard	**2**	doctor	**3**	Leave	**4**	coach
5	trophy	**6**	ghosts	**7**	trains	**8**	calm

C

- Ask pupils to read the words in the wordbank as a class and then individually. Correct their pronunciation if necessary.
- Ask pupils to read the word groups and to decide what the words have in common and to find a similar word in the word bank.

Answers

1. hairdresser (*they are all jobs*)
2. cottage (*they are all buildings*)
3. trophy (*they are all things to do with races*)
4. lake (*they are all types of water*)
5. match (*they are all to do with sport*)
6. kick (*they are all verbs*)

Grammar

A

- Ask pupils to read the sentences first to decide which verb from the wordbank they need in each one. Explain that they should look at the ticks and crosses after each sentence so that they know whether to use the affirmative or negative.
- Tell them to look back at Unit 7 Lessons 1 and 2 grammar boxes for a reminder if they need to.

Answers

1	's / is watching	5	's / is sleeping
2	isn't feeling	6	'm / am not riding
3	are making	7	's / is pushing
4	aren't running	8	isn't eating

B

- Explain to pupils that they need to write questions using the prompts given.
- Tell them to look back at Unit 7 Lesson 2 grammar box for a reminder if they need to.

Answers

1 Are you feeling happy today?
2 Is the cyclist wearing a helmet?
3 Are they having a picnic tomorrow?
4 Is Emma practising for the race?
5 Is the monster swimming in the lake?
6 Are they living in a houseboat?

C

- Tell pupils to pay attention to whether the sentence talks about *a fact, a habit, something happening now* or *a plan for the future*.
- Tell them to look back at Unit 7 Lesson 3 and Unit 8 Lesson 1 grammar boxes for a reminder if they need to.

Answers

1b **2**a **3**a **4**b **5**b **6**b **7**b **8**a

D

- Ask pupils to underline the mistakes in the original sentences first and then to write the correct sentence below. Make sure they focus on changing the words and not the punctuation.
- Tell them to look back at Unit 8 Lesson 2 grammar box for a reminder if they need to.

Answers

1 You mustn't swim in the river!
2 Champions must train hard.
3 Cowboys must sleep in tents.
4 I must cook breakfast today.
5 You must not be sad.
6 Must you get up early every day?
7 She must not get up late.
8 Pupils must do their homework every day.

Song

- Tell pupils they are going to listen to a song about travelling. Ask them to read and listen to the song and to find out where the singer wants to travel to (*around the world*) and which place the singer likes best (*home*).
- Play the song again and ask pupils to sing along. You could do this verse by verse and then play it once all the way through.
- Ask pupils to look at the picture round the song and to name the places and animals in English and to say where you can find them.

When checking pupils' answers to the review tasks, make a note of any problem areas in vocabulary and grammar that they still have. Try to do extra work on these areas so that your pupils progress well.

Holidays and Travel

Way in

- Give pupils a few minutes to proofread their paragraph about their favourite place in their town or city from Unit 8, Lesson 3 to check they've used *because* and *so* correctly. Then ask them to read each others' paragraphs, or hang them on the wall so they can read them when they have time.
- Write the beginning of the sentences below on the board and ask pupils to complete them.
  - *I'm not hungry, so ...*
  - *Jack's seeing the doctor because ...*
  - *I love my town because ...*
  - *There's a beach near here, so ...*
- Ask pupils where the following buildings are: the Pyramids (*Egypt*), the White House (*the USA*), Glamis Castle (*Scotland*) and Big Ben (*London*).
- Write *Holidays and Travel* on the board and tell pupils that this is the theme of Unit 9. Split the pupils into two teams and ask one team to brainstorm as many words to do with holidays as possible, and the other team to brainstorm as many words to do with travel as possible. Make a list of all the words on the board in two columns.

Suggested answers

Holidays	Travel
beach	boat
camping	bike
hotel	bus
sea	car
skiing	passport
sun	plane
swimming	tickets
	train

Quiz

- Ask pupils if they have ever been on holiday to a really cold place. If so, ask them to tell the class about it.
- Ask pupils to look at the picture on page 82 and 83 and ask them if they would like to visit this place.
- Ask them to do the quiz in pairs to encourage discussion, but check the answer as a class.
- Once you have checked the answer, give pupils further information about the glacier if they are interested. Explain that an iceberg floats in the sea, but a glacier forms on a mountain.

Answer
b

Background Information

The picture shows the Medenhall Glacier in Southeast Alaska. The glacier is part of the Tongass National Park, which is actually a rainforest. This area is very popular with tourists due to its spectacular scenery. Visitors to this area ➡️

can also do various activities such as kayaking, camping, hiking, cycling, skiing and skating. Visitors need to keep a safe distance from the glacier, as huge pieces the size of buildings can fall off it at any time. For further information, see www.nationalgeographic.com and search for *Medenhall Glacier*.

Lesson 1

Objectives

Reading	The Cortuga Mystery
Vocabulary	text-related words; holiday equipment
Grammar	past simple – be, affirmative, negative, question, short answers, time expressions
Listening	ticking the correct answer
Speaking	talking about your last holiday
Writing	writing sentences about your last holiday

Reading

The Cortuga Mystery

Background Information

In this episode of the Cortuga Mystery, the children find themselves in the desert in Egypt. They see pyramids and meet the Bedouin there. There are 138 pyramids in Egypt and they were built as tombs for pharaohs. Bedouin are traditionally nomadic people who live in the deserts of Africa and the Middle East. They live in tents and travel across the deserts on camels.

For teachers using the DVD

- Make sure each pupil has a copy of the DVD Worksheet found on page 120.
- Please follow the instructions in Unit 1, Lesson 1 on pages 12 and 13 for teachers using the DVD.

Before you watch

Answers
1 in Egypt / the desert
2 on camels

While you watch

Answers
1	Mandy	4	Asim
2	Bedouin	5	Kate
3	Robbie	6	Jake

After you watch

Answers
1	Kate	4	camel's milk
2	the Bedouin	5	water
3	camels	6	A camel is wearing it.

For teachers using the audio CD

- Begin by asking pupils to look at the cartoon on page 84 and to say where the children are now (*in Egypt / in the desert*) and ask them how they travel in the desert (*on camels*).
- Tell pupils they are going to listen to and read the next part of the story. Ask them to look at the pictures and to follow the story as they listen.
- Play the recording once and ask pupils what it's like in the desert (*There is lots of sand and it's very hot.*).
- Ask pupils to read the story out loud. Assign the roles of Jake, Mandy, Robbie, Kate, the Bedouin and Asim to different pupils. If you have a large class, you may have to repeat until all pupils have had a turn.
- Explain any vocabulary pupils don't know and correct their pronunciation where necessary.
- As a class, ask pupils the questions below to check they have understood the episode.
  1 Who has got some sun cream? (*Kate*)
  2 Whose camp do they go to? (*the Bedouins'*)
  3 What are very tall? (*camels*)
  4 What does Robbie drink? (*camel's milk*)
  5 What does Kate want to drink? (*water*)
  6 Where is the piece of the jigsaw? (*A camel is wearing it.*)

Vocabulary

- Explain to pupils that the missing words appear in the cartoon episode. Ask pupils to read each definition and scan the text to find words beginning with the letters given and underline them.
- Ask pupils to do the task individually, but check the answers as a class. Explain any words they don't understand. Correct their pronunciation where necessary.

Answers

1	pyramids	4	village
2	desert	5	camel
3	sand		

Extra Class Activity

Give pupils a minute to study the words in the *Vocabulary* task. Ask them to close their books and then read out the words one at a time and ask pupils to write them in their notebooks. Check their spelling by asking different pupils to write each of the words on the board.

Grammar

Past Simple – Be

- Write *That was delicious.* on the board and ask pupils why Robbie says this (*He tastes camel's milk and then says this because he likes it.*). Explain to pupils that *was* is the Past Simple form of *is*.
- Read the uses of the Past Simple of *be* in the grammar box to the class and ask pupils to read the example sentences with you. Explain that in the first sentence *was* is used to talk about an event that happened in the past and ask pupils when it happened (*last night*). Explain that in the second sentence *was* is used to talk about a habit in the past and ask pupils how we know this (*because it says 'every day'*).
- Read the rest of the grammar box to the class and ask pupils to say the forms with you. Read the short forms first and then read the long forms. Draw pupils' attention to the note about *There was* and *There were*.
- Ask pupils to quickly read the paragraph to find out where the boy was on holiday (*the Sea of Sand / the Sahara Desert*).

- Ask pupils to do the task individually, but check the answers as a class. Tell pupils that they may have to use capital letters in some places.

Answers

1	were	2	weren't	3	Were	4	wasn't
5	were	6	was	7	was	8	were
9	Was	10	was				

Extra Class Activity

Ask the following questions at random round the class and ask pupils to answer in full sentences or using short answers as appropriate.

- Where were you last night?
- What was your favourite film last year?
- Were you on holiday in June?
- Was it cold two days ago?
- Was the last episode of *The Cortuga Mystery* interesting?
- Was there a piece of the puzzle in the camel's mouth?

Vocabulary

- Explain to pupils that the pictures show things that you may need to take when you go on holiday.
- Ask pupils to do the task in pairs to encourage discussion, but check the answers as a class.
- Once you have checked their answers, ask which things the people who are visiting the glacier on pages 82 and 83 probably need (*a seat – on a train or plane to get there, sun cream – The sun is shining and there'll be glare from the ice, a tent – they're camping, rucksack – to carry all their things.*)

Answers

1a	2b	3c	4f	5d	6e

Listening

- Explain to pupils that they are going to hear three conversations with different people. Ask them to read the three questions and to look at the pictures to guess what the people will speak about (*holidays and preparations for holidays*).
- Ask pupils to work in pairs to describe the three sets of pictures. Explain that they should look for differences between the pictures. Elicit *trees, flowers, view of the sea, on the bed, on the table, in a bag, shorts, sun cream* and *sunglasses*.
- Play the recording all the way to the end and ask pupils to tick the correct boxes. Ask them to discuss their answers with a partner and to justify any answers they have that are different.
- Play the recording again and ask pupils to check their answers and to fill in any missing information.

Turn to pages 108 and 109 for the listening script.

Answers

1a	2a	3c

Speaking

- Ask pupils which conversation in the *Listening* task was about someone who had returned from holiday (*1*). Explain that they are now going to talk about their last holiday.
- Read the questions to the class and make sure that everybody understands them.
- Ask pupils to work in pairs to ask and answer the questions. Go round the class monitoring and checking that pupils are carrying out the task properly. Don't correct any mistakes that you hear in structure and pronunciation at this time, but make a note of them.
- As a class, ask each pupil to tell you one thing about their last holiday.
- Write any mistakes that you heard on the board, without saying who made them, and ask pupils to correct them. Deal with any problems in pronunciation that arose.

Answers

Pupils' own answers

Writing

- Tell pupils that they now have to write five sentences about their last holiday.
- Ask pupils to do the task individually and go round the class checking their writing.
- Alternatively, you could assign this task for homework.

Extra Task (for early finishers)

See photocopiable material on page 132.

Lesson 2

Objectives

Reading	true or false
Vocabulary	text-related words; means of transport
Grammar	past simple (regular verbs) - affirmative and spelling rules
Listening	numbering the places
Sounds of English	*-ed* in past simple
Song	holidays

Way in

- At the beginning of the lesson give pupils a few minutes to read each others' sentences.
- Ask pupils to ask their partner a question using *was* or *were*. Tell the partners to reply with a short answer.
- Ask pupils the questions below about the last episode of *The Cortuga Mystery* and ask them to reply with short answers.

1 Was there a pyramid in the desert? (*Yes, there was.*)
2 Was it cold in the desert? (*No, it wasn't.*)
3 Were there goats in the camp? (*Yes, there were.*)
4 Were the camels very short? (*No, they weren't.*)
5 Was there a piece of the puzzle in Asim's tent? (*No, there wasn't.*)

- Ask pupils to do simple drawings of a *rucksack*, *a seat*, *a suitcase*, *sun cream*, *shorts* and *a tent* and to write the words below them. Check their spelling.

Reading

- Ask pupils to look at the picture on page 86 and ask them how the people are travelling (*by hot air balloon*).
- Ask pupils if they remember what Uncle Oliver in *The Cortuga Mystery* is (*a scientist*). Explain that an inventor is a kind of scientist who makes new things and that these things are called inventions in English.
- Ask pupils to read the text to find out who the first passengers were in a hot air balloon (*a sheep, a duck and a chicken*).
- Give the pupils further information about hot air balloons if they are interested.

Background Information

The Montgolfier brothers first started experimenting with hot air balloons as they wanted to find a way to transport soldiers by air. The first flight using animals took place on 19th September, 1783. Animals were used for safety reasons as it wasn't known how the human body would react to being so high up. A sheep was chosen, as sheep are close to the same weight as a human. A duck was chosen to go along because the brothers wanted to see how the flight would affect a bird that can fly high in the sky. The chicken was chosen to observe what would happen to another kind of bird in the flight, but one that can't fly as high. The animals travelled a distance of 3 km at a height of 460m for 8 minutes.

The first human experiment, with Jean-François Pilatre de Rozier and François Laurent on 21st November 1783, lasted for 25 minutes. They travelled a distance of 9 km at a height of 910m over Paris.

Comprehension

- Ask pupils to read the true or false questions so that they know what information they need to find when they read the text again. Tell pupils to underline the information in the text that gives them the answer.
- Ask pupils to do the task individually, but check the answers as a class.

Answers

1 T (*…they used a sheep, a duck and a chicken for their first flight of their hot air balloon.*)
2 F (*The King of France watched this flight too.*)
3 T (*The hot air balloon … landed in a field.*)
4 F (*Some farmers were scared of the hot air balloon,*)
5 T (*Today hot air balloons are very popular because the view from them is always fantastic.*)

Extra Class Activity

Ask pupils the questions below to check their understanding of the text. ➡

1 What did the Montgolfier brothers use for the hot air balloon? (*smoke from a fire, a silk bag and a basket*)
2 How long did the hot air balloon stay in the air with animals? (*nine minutes*)
3 Who travelled in a hot air balloon for twenty minutes? (*Jean-François Pilatre de Rozier and François Laurent*)
4 What can people do in hot air balloons today? (*go for rides, get married*)

Guess what!

- Ask pupils to read the information in the *Guess what!* feature. Ask them if the word for *pilot* in their language is similar to Pilatre's name.
- Ask pupils if they know who the inventors and pilots of the first aeroplane were (*The Wright Brothers*).

Vocabulary

- Explain to pupils that all the words are in the text. Ask them to underline all the words in the text before they circle the correct words and to pay attention to how each word is used.
- Ask pupils to do the task individually, but check the answers as a class.

Answers
1	smoke	4	landed
2	passengers	5	flight
3	bottle		

Extra Class Activity
Ask pupils to write sentences of their own with the words not selected in the *Vocabulary* task.

Grammar

Past Simple (regular verbs)

- Explain to pupils that most of the text in the *Reading* task tells us about things in the past. Ask them to tell you which paragraphs talk about the past (*1 and 2*) and which paragraph talks about the present (*3*).
- Read the grammar box to the class and ask them to read the example sentence with you. Explain that we usually add –ed to form the past simple, but with verbs that end in e we add –d, with verbs that end in a consonant and –y we drop the –y and add –ied, with verbs that end in a vowel and –y we just add -ed and with verbs that end in a stressed vowel and a consonant we double the final consonant and add –ed, to form the Past Simple.
- Put two columns on the board with the headings *Infinitive* and *Past Simple*. Write the verbs below in the *Infinitive* column and ask pupils to write the Past Simple forms in the other column.

  - clean (cleaned)
  - cook (cooked)
  - fry (fried)
  - listen (listened)
  - live (lived)
  - look (looked)
  - move (moved)
  - study (studied)
  - talk (talked)
  - visit (visited)

- Explain to pupils that the Past Simple form of the verb is the same for all persons of the verb.

A
- Ask pupils to underline all the regular Past Simple verbs, but tell them only to count a verb once if it is used twice in the text.
- Ask pupils to do the task in pairs to encourage discussion, but check the answers as a class. Then ask them what the infinitive form of each verb is.

Answer
eleven (11), filled, tied, wanted, needed, used, stayed, travelled, watched, landed, scared, married

Teaching Tip
When you do vocabulary or grammar tasks that ask pupils to complete a paragraph, always ask them to read the paragraph all the way through before they fill in any gaps. This will allow them to understand the general sense of the paragraph better and see the context that each missing word is in. This will help them to choose their answers more carefully.

B
- Ask pupils to read the paragraph to find out what Jack watched (*a football match*).
- Ask pupils to do the task individually, but check the answers as a class.

Answers
1	lived	5	chased
2	wanted	6	stopped
3	carried	7	watched
4	walked	8	cooked

Vocabulary

A
- Ask pupils to look at the pictures and ask what they all have in common (*They're all means of transport.*). Ask them which means of transport they can use where they live.
- Ask pupils to do the task in pairs to encourage discussion, but check the answers as a class.

Answers
1b	2d	3c	4a

B
- Explain to pupils that the words are related to the places where you can get on or off the means of transport in *A*.
- Ask pupils to do the task individually, but check the answers as a class.

Answers
1	airport	4	port
2	platform	5	stop
3	stations		

Listening

- Explain to pupils that they are going to hear five conversations with people who are in different places. Tell them that they need to listen to decide where the people are and to put the conversation number in the box next to each place.
- Ask pupils to read the places a to e and to tell you what words they expect to hear for each place. Elicit *tickets, passport, flight, platform, station, stop, road, map* and *water*.
- Play the recording to the end of the first conversation and ask pupils to write the number *1* next to the place they think the people are. Make sure that all pupils understand how to carry out the task before continuing.
- Play the rest of the recording and ask pupils to discuss their answers with a partner and to justify any answers they have that are different.
- Play the recording again and ask pupils to check their answers and to fill in any missing information.

Turn to page 109 for the listening script.

Turn to page 109 for the listening script.

> **Answers**
> **a**4   **b**1   **c**2   **d**5   **e**3

Extra Class Activity

Means of transport survey

Tell pupils they are going to ask each other about how they travel. Draw the table below on the board and ask pupils to copy it into their notebooks. Tell pupils to interview their partner about how often he or she uses each means of transport. Then ask them to write sentences about it. For example, the sentences could say *Salma sometimes travels by plane. She never travels by ship.*, etc.

	bus	plane	train	ship	car
always					
usually					
often					
sometimes					
never					

Sounds of English

A

- Ask pupils to work with a partner and to say the words to each other to try to work out how to say –ed in each verb.
- Write *id* and *t* on the board and ask them to listen to the recording and to write these letters next to the word where –ed is said in each of these ways.
- Play the recording to the end and then play a second time stopping after each word and checking the answers as a class.

> **Answers**
> **1** id   **2** t   **3** t

B

- Ask pupils to do the task in pairs to encourage them to say the words out loud, but check the answers as a class.

> **Answers**
> looked   t
> needed   id
> worked   t
> watched   t
> visited   id
> touched   t

- Now ask the pupils to practice the third way to say –ed. Write d on the board to the right of id and t and write *carry* and *live* underneath d. Ask pupils how to form the past simple of these two verbs and change *carry* and *live* on the board to the past simple after pupils have answered you.
- Practise pronouncing these verbs with pupils. Say the verbs and ask the pupils to repeat after you. Contrast the sound with the verbs that end in the id and t sound.
- Using all three sounds, practice with other verbs that have appeared in the unit, such as *camp, travel, tie, try, walk, chase, cook* and *land*, practising both how the past simple is formed and how to pronounce each of them.

Song

- Explain that pupils are going to listen to a song about holidays and that they should read the song as they listen.
- Play the song and ask pupils what the song is about (*holidays*). Play the song again and ask pupils to sing along.
- Ask pupils why the singer says people like holidays (*because they can do what they want to do*) and ask them if they do any of the things mentioned in the song during their holidays.
- Play the song as many times as pupils wish.

Extra Task (for early finishers)

See photocopiable material on page 132.

See photocopiable material on page 132.

Lesson 3

Objectives

Reading	completing the table
Say it like this!	talking about travel
Grammar	past simple (irregular verbs) - affirmative
Writing	adjectives; writing a postcard

Way in

- Write *bus, plane, ship* and *train* on the board and ask pupils to say them after you. Then ask them where we can get on and off these means of transport (*bus stop / station, airport, port, train station / platform*).
- Write the sentences below on the board and ask pupils to correct them.

1 We dancied all afternoon. (*danced*)
2 They stoped at the station. (*stopped*)
3 Anna tryed to make a hot air balloon. (*tried*)
4 They walkt along the platform. (*walked*)

Reading

- Tell pupils they are going to read about two children's holidays and ask them to look at the pictures in the *Reading* task. Ask them where they think the children go on holiday and elicit that the Statue of Liberty (*shown in the illustration beside Rick's photo*) is in New York, USA and that the Eiffel Tower (*shown in the illustration under Holly's picture*) is in Paris, France.
- Ask pupils to read the title of the *Reading* text (*Cool Holidays!*) and ask them if it tells us if Rick and Holly enjoyed their holidays or if they didn't enjoy them (*They enjoyed them.*).
- Ask pupils to skim read the texts to find out what kinds of holidays Rick and Holly went on. Then give them a few minutes to discuss with a partner which holiday they like best and why. As a class, ask which pupils prefer Rick's holiday and why, and which pupils prefer Holly's holiday and why.
- Explain any vocabulary pupils don't know and correct their pronunciation if necessary.

Answer

Pupils' own answers

Comprehension

- Ask pupils to look at the table and ask them where they will find the answers to 1, 3 and 5 (*Rick's writing*) and where they will find the answers to 2, 4 and 6 (*Holly's writing*). Then elicit that beside *Place* they should write the name of a town or country, that beside *Travelled* they should write a means of transport, and that beside *Stayed in* they should write a place where people can sleep.
- Ask pupils to scan the text to find the words to complete the table and ask them to underline the information that helps them to find the answer. Explain that they only need to write one or two words in each space.
- Ask pupils to do the task in pairs to encourage discussion, but check the answers as a class.

Answers

1 New York (*I went on holiday to New York …*)
2 France (*We had a great holiday in France …*)
3 by plane (*We went by plane …*)
4 by car (*We travelled by car, …*)
5 a hotel (*… we stayed in a hotel …*)
6 tents (*We had two tents - …*)

Say it like this!

Talking about travel

- Read the *Say it like this!* box to the pupils and ask them to read the example sentences with you. Draw their attention to the use of *by* and *on* when talking about travel.
- Ask pupils to work in pairs to discuss how they travel to the four places mentioned. Remind them to use the language in *Talking about travel*. Go round the class monitoring and checking that pupils are carrying out the task properly. Don't correct any mistakes in structure or pronunciation that you hear at this time, but make a note of them.
- As a class, ask each pupil how they travel to one of the places. Make sure each pupil has at least one chance to speak and that all the places are discussed. Write any mistakes that you noticed on the board, without saying who made them, and ask pupils to correct them. Deal with any problems in pronunciation that arose.

Grammar

Past Simple (irregular verbs)

- Read the grammar box to the pupils and ask them to read the example sentences with you. Elicit that *went* is the Past Simple of *go* and that *wore* is the Past Simple of *wear*.
- Draw pupils' attention to the list of irregular verbs on page 126. Explain that they should use this list as a reference while doing the rest of the book.
- Ask pupils to underline the irregular verbs in the *Reading* texts and ask them to find the infinitive forms in the irregular verbs list (*Rick – went/go, bought/buy, ate/eat, saw/see; Holly – had/have, took/take, went/go, ate/eat, slept/sleep, told/tell*). Explain that they should use the list in this way whenever they come across an irregular verb.
- Ask pupils to do the task individually, but check the answers as a class. Remind pupils to use the irregular verb list to find and check their answers.

Answers

1	went	4	wore
2	had	5	ate
3	swam	6	bought

Writing

Adjectives

A

- Read the information about adjectives to the class and ask them to read the example sentences with you. Make sure that pupils understand that *beautiful* is an adjective and *beach* is a noun.
- Ask pupils to look back at the *Reading* text to underline adjectives used before a noun and adjectives used after a verb. If you are short of time, assign one text to half of the pupils and the other text to the other half. They should underline the following in Rick's writing: *are great, were very expensive, were cheap, was exciting, famous actor*. They should underline the following in Holly's writing: *great holiday, interesting museums, fantastic restaurants, French food, is delicious, was scared*.
- Write *were expensive, interesting museums* and *fantastic restaurants* on the board and ask pupils what they notice about the adjectives (*They don't agree in number with the verb form or the nouns*.).

B

- Ask pupils to quickly underline the verb *be* in the prompts in 1 to 5 and elicit that the adjective will come after the verb in these sentences. Then ask them to underline the nouns in the other sentences and elicit that the adjective will come before these nouns.
- Ask pupils to do the task individually, but check the answers as a class. Remind pupils to begin each sentence with a capital letter and end with a full stop.

Answers

1 We stayed in a nice hotel.
2 The shops were very expensive.
3 Rome is a fantastic city.
4 The food wasn't very good.
5 We had a delicious meal in the café.

C

- Ask pupils to look at the picture and to read the postcard to find out where Emily is (*Amsterdam*) and what she did yesterday (*She cycled around the city centre*.).
- Read the words in the wordbank to the pupils and ask them to say them after you and correct their pronunciation if necessary.
- Ask pupils to do the task individually, but check the answers as a class.

Answers

1	interesting	4	special
2	beautiful	5	delicious
3	difficult		

D

- Explain to pupils that they are going to write a postcard like the one in C. Ask them to think of a place that they know well enough to write about and give them a few minutes to complete the sentences in the plan. Go round the class checking that pupils are doing the task properly and giving them any help they may need.
- Ask pupils to write out their postcard in full on a piece of paper.
- Alternatively, you could assign this task for homework.

Suggested answer

Dear Penny,
I'm having a great time in Athens! It's a very busy city. The city has got a very interesting history. There are a lot of shops and cafés too in the city centre.

Yesterday, I visited the Acropolis. It was very beautiful. This morning we had breakfast at a café near our hotel. The food was delicious!

See you soon,
Lucy

Teaching Tip

If you are cooperating with another teacher who has a class at this level to exchange your pupils' written work, then this task is a good opportunity for you to swap postcards. Let pupils know you are going to do this before they write and hand in their work. This will make them more careful with their writing and will also give them more reading practice.

E

- Ask pupils to proofread their postcards to make sure that they have used adjectives properly.
- If you assign the postcard for homework, then give them a few minutes to proofread it at the beginning of the next lesson.

Project Book

The pupils may do Project 9 now they have completed the unit. The answer key and teacher's notes are on pages 148-152 of this book.

Fame!

Way in

- Give pupils a few minutes to proofread their postcards from Unit 9, Lesson 3 to check that they have used adjectives properly. Then ask them to read each others' postcards or collect them to give to pupils in another class to read.
- Ask *How do you get to the beach / your friend's house / school / the park / the shops*, etc? at random round the class. Make sure that each pupil has the chance to answer at least once and that pupils use the phrases *by car / bike / bus / train / taxi* and *on foot* properly.
- Write *buy, eat, go, have, see, sleep, swim* and *wear* on the board and ask pupils to write the Past Simple forms.

Background Information

People are fascinated with celebrities and there are many museums or 'halls of fame' dedicated to people who have become famous in the fields of entertainment, sport or more pioneering fields like aviation and space flight. For film stars, there is the Hollywood Walk of Fame. It was created in 1958 as a way to honour entertainment stars. There are over 2,000 pink stars on the Los Angeles pavement called the Walk of Fame and it is a 5.6 km walk. Each pink star has the name of a celebrity or character that is related to TV, theatre, films, radio or music. Under each name there is a sign to show which part of the entertainment industry the person is linked to.

If your class seem interested in the Walk of Fame, tell them to go to http://www.hollywoodusa.co.uk/walkoffame.htm and to search for their favourite celebrities.

- Ask pupils to look at the title of the unit and tell them that *fame* is a noun. Ask them which adjective they know that is similar (*famous*). Ask them what famous people they might read about in Unit 10.

Quiz

- Ask pupils what sort of entertainers become famous. Can they name any stars they admire?
- Ask pupils to do the quiz in pairs to encourage discussion, but check the answer as a class.

Answer

a

Extra Class Activity

Wall of Fame

Tell pupils they are going to make their own wall of fame in the classroom. As a class, brainstorm the names of the famous people pupils think should go on the wall and ask them what they are famous for. Write the names on the board as pupils call them out. Ask pupils to vote for one of the celebrities on the board by writing his or her name on a piece of paper. The five celebrities who get the most votes win a star. Split pupils into groups and give them a piece ➡

of paper to make one of the stars. Tell them to write the person's name and to draw a symbol related to his or her work. Then hang the stars on the wall. You could ask one of the pupils to make a banner saying *Wall of Fame*.

Lesson 1

Objectives

Reading	The Cortuga Mystery
Vocabulary	text-related words; words related to entertainment
Grammar	past simple (regular and irregular verbs) – negative, questions and short answers
Listening	multiple choice
Speaking	playing 'Guess the star'
Writing	writing sentences about a star

Reading

The Cortuga Mystery
For teachers using the DVD

- Make sure each pupil has a copy of the DVD Worksheet found on page 121.
- Please follow the instructions in Unit 1, Lesson 1 on pages 12 and 13 for teachers using the DVD.

Before you watch

Answers
1a   2b

While you watch

Answers
1	film studio	4	talent
2	costume	5	autograph
3	set	6	director

After you watch

Answers
1F   2T   3F   4F   5F   6T

For teachers using the audio CD

- Begin by asking pupils to look at the cartoon episode on page 92 and to say where the children are now (*in a film studio*) and ask them who they speak to there (*the director*).
- Tell pupils they are going to listen to and read the next part of the story. Ask them to look at the pictures and to follow the story as they listen.
- Play the recording once and ask pupils who becomes an actor (*Kate*).
- Ask pupils to read the story out loud. Assign the roles of Jake, Mandy, Robbie, Kate and the director to different pupils. If you have a large class, you may have to repeat until all pupils have had a turn.
- Explain any vocabulary pupils don't know and correct their pronunciation where necessary.

- As a class, ask pupils the questions below to check they have understood the episode.
  1. Do the children see two cameramen? (*No, they see one.*)
  2. Why does the director tell Kate to put a costume on? (*Because she has got a role in the film.*)
  3. Why does Kate say 'Dinner is ready, Sir.'? (*because it is her line in the film*)
  4. What does Jake think Kate has got? (*talent*)
  5. What does the director give Kate? (*a beautiful bag*)
  6. Why can the children go home now? (*because they have got the last piece of the puzzle*)

Vocabulary

- Explain that the words in the wordbank appear in the cartoon episode. Ask pupils to find the words in the text and underline them. Explain any words they don't understand.
- Ask pupils to do the task individually, but check the answers as a class. Correct their pronunciation where necessary.

Answers

1	cameraman	4	autograph
2	role	5	set
3	director		

Grammar

Past Simple (regular and irregular verbs)

- Write *Did you learn your lines*? and *Yes, I did.* on the board and ask pupils who says these lines in the cartoon (*the director and Kate*). Ask them if they are speaking about something that always happens or something that happened in the past (*something that happened in the past*) and ask them how they know this (*from the use of* did). Explain that this is the question and short answer form of the Past Simple. Then ask them to find an example of the negative form of the Past Simple in the cartoon (*She didn't say a lot,...*)
- Read the grammar box to the pupils and ask them to read the example sentences with you. Draw their attention to the use of *did* and bare infinitive in the question form for all persons of the verb and the use of *did / didn't* without a main verb in the short answers.
- Ask pupils to read the dialogue between Steve and Ellie and ask them where they are going (*to a Girlzone concert*).
- Ask pupils to do the task individually, but check the answers as a class. Tell pupils to pay attention to where they need the question and negative forms and that they should use the subject pronouns in the brackets where they appear.

Answers

1	Did you buy	5	Did you speak
2	didn't	6	did
3	didn't have	7	didn't give
4	Did they sell		

Extra Class Activity

Ask pupils to write two questions in the Past Simple about the cartoon on page 92. Then ask them to swap questions with each other and to answer each others' questions with short answers. As a class tell each pair to ask and answer one of their questions in front of the class.

Vocabulary

- Read the words 1 to 6 to the class and ask pupils to say them after you. Correct their pronunciation if necessary.
- Ask pupils to do the task in pairs to encourage discussion, but check the answers as a class.

Answers

1f	2c	3b	4a	5e	6d

Listening

- Ask pupils to do the quiz in pairs and to take it in turns to ask and answer the questions.
- Play the recording all the way to the end and ask pupils to check their answers as they listen. Play the recording a second time if necessary.
- Check the answers as a class.

Turn to page 109 for the listening script

Answers

1a	2b	3c	4b	5a

Speaking

- Explain to pupils that they are going to work in pairs and one of them is going to think of a star. He or she could be a singer, a musician, an actor or a sports star. The other person should ask questions about the star until he or she works out who it is. Then pupils can swap roles so that the person who thought of the star the first time asks the questions the second time.
- As a class, ask each pair to say who their stars were. If you have time, play another round with the whole class. Ask for a volunteer to think of a star and answer the questions.

Writing

- Ask pupils to write five sentences about the star they thought about for the *Speaking* task. Explain that their sentences should answer the questions posed in the *Speaking* task.
- Ask pupils to proofread their sentences. Alternatively, you could assign this task for homework.

Teaching Tip

Try to encourage pupils to use English in a creative way. For example, if they like writing in English encourage them to write their own songs or short plays that they can perform in class.

Extra Task (for early finishers)

See photocopiable material on page 133.

Lesson 2

Objectives

Reading	missing sentences
Vocabulary	text-related vocabulary; films
Grammar	*wh-* questions in the past simple
Listening	ticking the correct film
Sounds of English	*c, g, s* and *y* sounds

Way in

- Give pupils a few minutes to proofread their sentences from Unit 10, Lesson 1. Then ask them to swap sentences with another pupil and to read theirs.
- Write the pairs of words below on the board and ask pupils to write sentences with both the words from each pair in them.

  director - role, audience - concert, singer - autograph, cameraman - set

- Ask pupils the following questions about the previous episode of *The Cortuga Mystery* at random round the class and encourage pupils to use short answers.

  - Did the children go to a concert? (*No, they didn't.*)
  - Did Kate put on a costume? (*Yes, she did.*)
  - Did Kate forget her lines? (*No, she didn't.*)
  - Did Robbie, Mandy and Jake like Kate's acting? (*Yes, they did.*)
  - Did the director give Kate his autograph? (*No, he didn't.*)
  - Did the children find the last piece of the puzzle? (*Yes, they did.*)

Background Information

Walt Disney was born in 1901 and died in 1966. He was a film producer, director, animator and voice actor amongst other things. He was the co-founder of Walt Disney Productions, one of the most successful film studios in the world. He created many characters during his career, of which Mickey Mouse is probably the most famous.

Disney, who won 26 Oscars in his lifetime, has a star on the Hollywood Walk of Fame. Mickey Mouse became the first cartoon character and Disneyland became the first company to receive stars on the Hollywood Walk of Fame.

Reading

- Ask pupils to look at the title of the text and the picture beside it and ask them what they know about Walt Disney. Ask them who the characters in the picture are (*From top left to bottom right: Alice in Wonderland, Peter Pan, Goofy, Dopey the Dwarf and Snow White, Mickey Mouse, Pinocchio, Bambi, Chip and Dale, Donald Duck, Pluto and Jiminy Cricket*).
- Ask pupils to read the text quietly to themselves to find out what Walt Disney's dream was. Explain that they shouldn't worry about the gaps at this point. If pupils are interested, give them some further information about Walt Disney.
- Ask pupils to work in pairs and to try to guess what kind of information is missing from the gaps. Try to elicit from them that in 1 we need information about the pictures he drew; that in 2 we need information introducing his brother; that in 3 we need information about the films Walt and his brother made; that in 4 we need information about his dream amusement park and that in 5 we need information about Walt's amusement parks in other parts of the world.

Answer

To open his own amusement park.

Comprehension

- Ask pupils to read the sentences and complete the text. Once they have finished, tell them to read back through the text to make sure that they have chosen the correct sentences.
- Ask pupils to do the task individually, but check the answers as a class.
- Explain any vocabulary pupils don't know and correct their pronunciation where necessary.

Answers

1c	**2**e	**3**b	**4**a	**5**d

Teaching Tip

When pupils are doing missing sentence tasks, point out that they need to look for clues in the missing sentences. In particular, they should look for subject and object pronouns, for example, in sentence *b* in the previous *Comprehension* task. Pupils need to put this sentence after a sentence which speaks about two or more people. Also, connectors are important as they show us the sequence that events happened in. For example, pupils should pay attention to words like *first*, *then*, *after that* and *finally*.

- Ask pupils to read the information in the *Guess what!*

Guess what!

feature. Ask them if they have heard of Mortimer Mouse. If they have, ask them who he is. If they haven't, explain that the name Mortimer was later given to another mouse in the Mickey Mouse comics.

Vocabulary

- Explain that the missing words appear in the text. Ask pupils to read each definition and to scan the text to find words beginning with the letters given and underline them.
- Ask pupils to do the task individually, but check the answers as a class. Explain any words they don't understand. Correct their pronunciation where necessary.

Answers

1	character	**4**	neighbours
2	dream	**5**	poor
3	garage		

Extra Class Activity

Write the names below on the board and ask pupils to guess which are the names of the Seven Dwarfs. The ticks in brackets show the real names.

Bashful	(✓)	Grumpy	(✓)
Daffy		Happy	(✓)
Dippy		Sleepy	(✓)
Doc	(✓)	Sneezy	(✓)
Dopey	(✓)	Snoopy	
Goofy		Tinky	

Grammar

Wh- questions in the Past Simple

- Ask pupils to find three questions in the text about Walt Disney (*What do we know about his early life?*, *How did he start making films?* and *When did Disneyland® open?*) and explain that *What*, *How* and *When* are question words. Elicit that *what* asks about things, *how* asks about the way to do something and *when* asks about time.
- Read the grammar box to the class and ask pupils to read the example questions with you. Correct their intonation patterns if necessary.
- Draw pupils' attention to the question form and the use of *did* as an auxiliary verb in questions in the Past Simple. Then read the note and elicit that there is no auxiliary verb when the question word asks about the subject.
- Write the answers below on the board and ask pupils to write them in the grammar box next to the question that they could answer.

  – an amusement park
  – Because he wanted my autograph.
  – My aunt.
  – The director's.
  – Cameron Diaz
  – last week
  – That he liked the film.
  – Very excited.

A

- Explain to pupils that they have to use the words to make questions.
- Ask pupils to do the task individually, but check the answers as a class. Remind pupils that we don't use the question form when the question word asks about the subject.

Answers

1 When did your neighbours go to Disneyland
2 Where did you buy that Mickey Mouse T-shirt
3 What did Jim Carrey say in the interview
4 Which film did they see last night
5 Why did Nancy give him the tickets
6 Who did the reporter interview in the film

Extra Class Activity

If you have time, ask pupils to write answers to the questions in *A*.

B

- Ask pupils to look at the sentence in 1 and ask them which question word can ask about Jack and his sister (*who*). Then ask them what question they could ask here using *who*.
- Ask pupils to work in pairs to decide which question word should replace the underlined words in 2 to 6. Then ask them to write the questions individually, but check the answers as a class.

Answers

1 Who came to the studio
2 When did you get the singer's autograph
3 How did the film star arrive
4 Where did he see me / you
5 What did they have
6 Whose interview was that on TV

Vocabulary

- Explain to pupils that the pictures show different types of films. Ask them which of these films they would prefer to watch and why.
- Ask pupils to do task in pairs to encourage discussion, but check the answers as a class.

Answers

1b	2f	3d	4c	5e	6a

Extra Class Activity

Ask pupils to make a table in their notebooks with six columns and to write the names of the different kinds of films they learnt in the *Vocabulary* task as headings. Tell them they have five minutes to write the names of as many films as possible under each heading. Then make a list of all the pupils' films on the board and make sure they go under the correct heading. If they are unsure about the name of a film in English, ask pupils to find it out as part of their homework.

Listening

- Write the words and names below on the board and ask pupils which of the films from 1 to 5 they might be linked to.

  - Jim Carrey (*comedy*),
  - singing and dancing (*musical*),
  - Mission Impossible 3 (*adventure film*),
  - The Green Mile (*drama*),
  - Keanu Reaves (*science fiction*)

- Explain to pupils they are going to listen to a boy and a girl talking about which DVDs to rent and that they should tick the ones that they choose.
- Play the recording all the way through and ask pupils to work in pairs to discuss their answers and to justify any answers they have that are different. Elicit that the children are going to choose two DVDs before you play the recording again.
- Play the recording again and ask pupils to check their answers or to fill in any missing information.

Turn to page 109 for the listening script.

Answers

Pupils should tick 3 and 5.

Extra Class Activity

Ask pupils to work in groups to talk about their favourite films. They can tell each other what the film is called, who the actors are and why they like the film. Then you could hold a class discussion about their favourite films.

Sounds of English

- Ask pupils to work in pairs and to say the words to each other. Go round the class listening to their pronunciation, but don't correct them at this stage.
- Play the recording and stop after each pair and ask pupils to say the words and discuss the difference in sound between the coloured letters.

B

- Ask pupils to look at the words 1 to 8 and ask them to guess what the missing letters are. Then play the recording and ask them to write in the missing letters.
- Play the recording again, stopping after each word and checking pupils' answers. Then ask pupils to say each of the words.

Extra Task (for early finishers)

See photocopiable material on page 133.

Lesson 3

Objectives

Reading	interview; open-ended questions
Say it like this!	talking about stars
Listening	completing a table
Speaking	practising a dialogue
Writing	using paragraphs; film review

Way in

- Ask pupils to work in pairs to ask and answer questions using *which, who, where, when, why, what, how* and *whose* in the Past Simple.
- Say the words *character, dream, garage, neighbours* and *poor* and ask pupils to write them down. As a class, check the spelling and write the words on the board for pupils to check against their answers.
- Write the words below on the board. Point to one word at a time and ask pupils to say them. Repeat several times, but change the order that you point to the words in.

comedy	sleep
dance	stage
go	was
piece	young
scary	

Reading

- Write the word *audition* on the board and elicit that it is like a test for actors, singers, dancers, etc to see if they are good enough to work in the theatre, a film, get into a school, etc. Ask pupils if they have ever had an audition for something. If so, ask them to tell the rest of the class what they did at the audition, what it was for and how they felt before and after the audition.
- Ask pupils to read the title of the text and to guess what the text is going to be about.
- Ask pupils to skim read the interview to themselves to find out what Zoe did at the audition.

Comprehension

- Ask pupils to read the questions so they know what information to look for the second time they read the text. Tell them to scan the interview to find the answers and to underline the information that helps them to find the answers.
- Ask pupils to do the task individually, but check the answers as a class.

Say it like this!

Talking about stars

- Read the *Say it like this!* box to the class and explain to pupils that they are going to talk about their favourite stars. Give them a few minutes to decide which person or people they want to speak about.
- Ask pupils to work in pairs to ask and answer questions about their favourite stars. Remind them to use the language in the *Say it like this!* box. Go round the class monitoring and checking that pupils are carrying out the task properly.
- As a class, ask each pair about one of the stars they talked about.

Listening

- Ask pupils to look at the picture and ask them what they think it shows (*an audition*) and ask them who are on the stage (*a boy and a girl*).
- Explain to pupils that the boy's name is *Damian* and the girl's name is *Amber* and that they are auditioning for a place on a talent show called *Young Stars*. Ask pupils to look at the table to see what kind of information they need to listen for. Elicit that the use of *talent* here means what they do at the audition, for example, *singing, dancing, acting*, etc.
- Play the recording and ask pupils to complete the table. Ask them to work with a partner to discuss their answers and to justify any answers that are different.
- Play the recording again and ask pupils to check their answers and to fill in any missing information.

Turn to page 110 for the listening script.

Speaking

- Ask pupils to work in pairs and to read the dialogue to each other. Go round the class monitoring and making a note of mistakes in pronunciation. Deal with any problems in pronunciation before they do the next part of the task.
- Give pupils a few minutes to prepare their dialogue and make sure they understand what information they need to change. Explain that words like *he* and *him* won't change if their favourite actor is a boy or a man and that they can speak about a film that they liked or disliked. Brainstorm adjectives that they can use, for example, *good*, *bad*, *boring*, *interesting*, *exciting*, *fantastic*, *amazing*, etc.
- Ask pupils to take turns reading the parts of Amy and Jack using their own words.
- As a class, ask pupils what films and actors they spoke about. Ask some pairs to read their dialogue out to the rest of the class.

Teaching Tip

If pupils feel too shy to talk about who they like or think the other pupils will laugh at them, tell them that they don't always have to say who they really like. They can pick any famous person they want and talk about that person. Alternatively, they can talk about who someone they know likes.

Writing

Using paragraphs

A

- Write the paragraph below on the board. Then ask pupils how many sentences it has got (*three*) and what the subject of the paragraph is (*the film Pirates of the Caribbean*).

    I saw the film Pirates of the Caribbean last night. It is a great film. The pirates have lots of adventures in the film.

- Read the information about paragraphs to the class and explain that the topic of a paragraph is its main idea. At the beginning of most paragraphs you will find a topic sentence which sets the tone for the rest of the paragraph. Ask pupils what the topic of the paragraph on the board is (*the film Pirates of the Caribbean*) and explain that the other two sentences tell us more things about the film.

B

- Elicit that a *film review* tells us what someone thinks about a film and that it can either be good or bad. Ask pupils to put the sentences in the correct order to make a paragraph. Tell them to read the paragraph again once they have decided which order they go in.
- Ask pupils to do the task in pairs to encourage discussion, but check the answers as a class.

Answers

My parents enjoyed it too.	3
It was a cartoon, but it wasn't just for children.	2
The film *Shrek* was fantastic.	1

C

- Ask pupils to read the rest of the film review and then discuss the topic of each paragraph in pairs. Remind pupils that the topic is always written about in the first sentence.

Answers

Paragraph 2	the story
Paragraph 3	Shrek's character

Extra Class Activity

If you have time, ask pupils to underline all the words that show the writer of the review on *Shrek* liked the film. Then ask them to imagine that they didn't like the film and to replace these words.

Suggested answers

- fantastic—boring
- but it wasn't just for children—but it was for really young children
- enjoyed—hated
- great—silly
- I also liked—I also didn't like
- funny—stupid

Task

D

- Give the pupils time to make notes for their review by answering the questions about each paragraph. Go round the class monitoring and checking that they are doing the task properly. Give them any help they need at this stage.
- Ask pupils to write their reviews on a piece of paper and point out that they should leave a gap between each paragraph. Ask them to proofread their reviews before giving them to you, or to another pupil to read.
- Alternatively, you could assign this task as homework.

Suggested answer

Kung Fu Panda

The film *Kung Fu Panda* was amazing. It was a cartoon, but it wasn't just for children. My parents enjoyed it too.

The story was about a lazy panda, called Po, and a nasty Snow Leopard, Tai Lung. Po must learn to be a Kung Fu master.

The character of Po was great and I also liked his friends, Tigress and Crane. The film was very funny.

Extra Task (for early finishers)

See photocopiable material on page 133.

Project Book

The pupils may do Project 10 now they have completed the unit. The answer key and teacher's notes are on pages 148-152 of this book.

Objectives

- To revise vocabulary and grammar from Units 9 and 10
- Song – Fame

Revision

- Explain to pupils that the tasks in *Review 5* are based on the material they saw in Units 9 and 10.
- Remind pupils that they can ask you for help with the exercises or look back at the units if they're not sure about an answer as the review is not a test.
- Decide how you will carry out the review. You could ask pupils to do one task at a time and then correct it immediately, or ask pupils to do all the tasks and correct them together at the end. If you do all the tasks together, let pupils know every now and again how much time they have got to finish the tasks.
- Remind pupils not to leave any answers blank and to try to find any answers they aren't sure about in the units.
- Revise the vocabulary and grammar as a class before pupils do the review.

Vocabulary Revision

- Ask pupils to imagine they are going camping in a hot country. Tell them to make a list of all the things they need to take with them. Make sure they revise *sun cream*, *passport*, *tickets*, *suitcase*, and *tent, etc.*
- Ask pupils what we call the hot place that the children in *The Cortuga Mystery* went to in Lesson 9 (*the desert*). Ask them what animal they rode on there (*a camel*) and what Robbie drank (*camel's milk*). Ask them what other animals they know in English that give us milk. Make sure they revise *goat* and *sheep*.
- As a class, ask pupils what the unusual means of transport that they read about in Unit 10 was (*a hot air balloon*) and where it landed (*in a field*). Then ask one pupil to say the name of another means of transport and ask another pupil to say where you can get on or off it. Make sure they revise *bus – bus stop, train – station/platform, ship – port, plane – airport*. Then ask pupils what we call the place where people put their cars at home (*garage*).
- Ask pupils to tell you the different kinds of films they know (*adventure, cartoon, comedy, drama, musical, science fiction*). Then ask them to tell you other words they can remember related to entertainment. Make sure they revise *dressing room, director, actor, star, concert, stage, audience, autograph* and *fan*.
- Ask pupils to write sentences using the words; *poor, nervous, expensive* and *interesting*.

Grammar Revision

- Write the dialogue below on the board and ask pupils to change it so that it talks about last week.

    Tim: Are you on holiday?
    Rea: Yes, I am.
    Tim: You are lucky! We aren't. We're at school this week.

Answers

Tim: Were you on holiday?
Rea: Yes, I was.
Tim: You were lucky! We weren't. We were at school last week.

- Write *I land, you use, we carry* and *they stop* on the board and ask pupils to tell you their Past Simple forms (*I landed, you used, we carried* and *they stopped*). Remind pupils of the spelling rules if necessary. Then ask pupils what the negative form of these verbs in the Past Simple are (*I didn't land, you didn't use, we didn't carry* and *they didn't stop*) and what the question form is (*Didn't I land, Didn't you use, Didn't we carry* and *Didn't they stop*).
- Write *I eat, you ride, we go,* and *they buy* on the board and use the same procedure as above to revise the affirmative, negative and question forms.
- Ask pupils to work in pairs to ask and answer questions using the Past Simple. Tell them to answer the questions using short answers. As a class, ask each pair to ask and answer one question each. Correct any mistakes the pupils make.
- Write *Which, Who, Where, When, Why, What, How* and *Whose* on the board and ask pupils to work in pairs to write questions to ask another pair. As a class, ask the pairs of pupils to take turns to ask another pair one of their questions. Tell each pair which question word to use in their question to make sure all the words are practised.

Vocabulary

A
Tell pupils to draw lines between the words 1 to 6 and the nouns a to f.

Answers

1c	**2**f	**3**a	**4**e	**5**b	**6**d

B
- Tell pupils to think about how the words in each group are related to one another so that they can decide which word doesn't belong in the group.
- When checking pupils' answers, ask them to tell you why the words are odd.

Answers

1. passenger (*The other two are people who work in the entertainment industry, but a passenger is someone who rides a bus, train, plane,* etc.)
2. seat (*The other two are types of films, but a seat is something you sit on.*)
3. director (*The other two are forms of entertainment, but a director is a person. You could also accept 'concert' as the odd one out here, as directors work on films.*)
4. hotel (*The other two are means of transport, but a hotel is a place where you can stay.*)
5. camp (*The other two are animals, but a camp is a place where you can put up a tent.*)

C

- Ask pupils to say each of the words as a class and then individually. Correct their pronunciation if necessary.
- Ask pupils to go to the second page of stickers at the back of the book and find the stickers for *Review 5*. Tell them to decide which word each sticker shows and to stick it in the correct box.
- Check that pupils have put the correct stickers above each word.

D

Ask pupils to read the whole sentence before circling the correct answer, and to read the sentence again to make sure their answer makes sense.

Answers

1	poor	4	autograph
2	interesting	5	neighbour
3	planes	6	tickets

Grammar

A

- Ask pupils to read the postcard without filling in the gaps to find out what Stacey's favourite food is (*pizza*).
- Ask pupils to read back through the postcard once they have written their answers to make sure it makes sense.
- Tell them to look back at Unit 9 Lessons 1, 2 and 3 grammar boxes for a reminder if they need to.

Answers

1	arrived	5	were
2	was	6	ate
3	went	7	spoke
4	had	8	looked

B

- Explain to pupils that they should only change the form of the verbs.
- Tell them to look back at Unit 10 Lesson 1 grammar box for a reminder if they need to.

Answers

1 The hot air balloon wasn't / was not expensive.
2 The hotel didn't / did not have a swimming pool.
3 We didn't / did not like the concert.
4 The brothers weren't / were not inventors.
5 The baby didn't / did not eat my ice cream.
6 I didn't / did not wear my new T-shirt at the beach.

C

- Explain to pupils that they will need to add other words to make their questions.
- Tell them to look back at Unit 10 Lesson 1 grammar box for a reminder if they need to.

Answers

1 Did Cindy go to Paris?, she did
2 Did Mark and Chris buy a new tent?, they didn't
3 Did you ride a camel in the desert?, I / we did
4 Did your dad meet a famous actor?, he didn't
5 Did you and Jane get a role in the play?, we did

D

- Explain to pupils that they should write only one word in each question and that they should pay attention to the responses before deciding which word goes in each space.
- Tell them to look back at Unit 10 Lesson 2 grammar box for a reminder if they need to.

Answers

1	When	4	How
2	Which	5	Why
3	Where	6	Whose

Song

- Tell pupils they are going to listen to a song about *fame*. Ask them to read and listen to the song and to find out who is singing the song (*a superstar*) and where the singer is working (*in the studio*).
- Play the song again and ask pupils to sing along. You could do this verse by verse and then play it once all the way through.
- To finish, ask pupils to look at the picture round the song and to point to the superstar, people who want her autograph, people who want an interview with her and people who want to take her picture.

When checking pupils' answers to the review tasks, make a note of any problem areas in vocabulary and grammar that they still have. Try to do extra work on these areas so that your pupils progress well.

Way in

- If you assigned Unit 10, Lesson 3 Writing Task D for homework, then give pupils a few minutes to proofread their reviews before giving them to you or another pupil to read.
- Ask each pupil at random round the class who his or her favourite singer or actor is.
- Ask pupils to write sentences using the words *audition*, *nervous*, *musical* and *acting*.

Background Information

The picture shows a mother cheetah and her cubs. Cheetahs are mammals that live on the African plains. Cheetahs are the fastest mammals in the world and can run at up to 70 miles per hour in short bursts. Their brown and black spotted fur is used for camouflage in the African bush. Cheetah cubs stay with their mother until they are between 12 and 20 months old. For further information, go to www.nationalgeographic.com and follow the link for *animals*.

- Ask pupils which animals they have talked about in the previous units of *Wonderful World 3* (*scarlet macaws*, *chimpanzees*, *Emperor penguins*, *fish*, *monkeys*, *deer*, *horses*, *camels* and *dogs*).
- Ask them if they remember what we call a baby deer (*a fawn*). Then ask them to look at the picture on pages 100 and 101 and ask them if they like the animal in the picture.
- Ask pupils to do the quiz in pairs to encourage discussion, but check the answer as a class. Once you have checked the answer, elicit that a puppy is a baby dog and that a teddy bear is a toy.

Answer
c

Extra Class Activity

Write the names of the *animals* below on the board in one column and the names of the *young* in another column in the incorrect order as shown below and ask pupils to match them. Draw a line between the *animal* and its *young* when pupils match the pair correctly.

Animals	Young
cat	calf
cow	cub
lion	kitten
sheep	lamb

Answers
cat – kitten, cow – calf, lion – cub, sheep – lamb

Lesson 1

Objectives

Reading	The Cortuga Mystery
Vocabulary	text-related words; wild animals
Grammar	comparative – short adjectives, long adjectives, irregular adjectives
Listening	completing a fact sheet
Speaking	comparing animals
Writing	writing sentences about your favourite animal

Reading

The Cortuga Mystery
For teachers using the DVD

- Make sure each pupil has a copy of the DVD Worksheet found on page 122.
- Please follow the instructions in Unit 1, Lesson 1 on pages 12 and 13 for teachers using the DVD.

Before You Watch

Answers
1 8 / eight
2 in her rucksack

While You Watch

Answers
a2   b4   c1   d6   e3   f5

After You Watch

Answers
1 Henry, the lizard   4 Jake
2 Mandy   5 Robbie
3 Kate   6 Mandy

For teachers using the audio CD

- Begin by asking pupils to look at the cartoon episode on page 102 and ask them how many pieces of the puzzle they have got now (*eight*) and ask them where Kate is putting a torch and binoculars (*in her rucksack*).
- Tell pupils they are going to listen to and read the next part of the story. Ask them to look at the pictures and to follow the story as they listen.
- Play the recording once and ask pupils what the puzzle is (*a map*).
- Ask pupils to read the story out loud. Assign the roles of Jake, Mandy, Robbie and Kate to different pupils for each part of the story. If you have a large class, you may have to repeat until all pupils have had a turn.
- Explain any vocabulary pupils don't know and correct their pronunciation where necessary.

- As a class, ask pupils the questions below to check they have understood the episode.
  1 Who is still in the same place in the hut? (*Henry, the lizard*)
  2 Who is good at puzzles? (*Mandy*)
  3 Who doesn't like bats? (*Kate*)
  4 Who wants to make some sandwiches? (*Jake*)
  5 Who gives the lizard food? (*Robbie*)
  6 Who is tired? (*Mandy*)

Teaching Tip

Use *The Cortuga Mystery* cartoon episodes in different ways. For example, you could ask pupils to cover up the dialogues and write their own dialogues based on the pictures before they read the story. They could do this in groups and you could assign different parts to each group.

Vocabulary

- Explain that the words in the wordbank appear in the cartoon episode. Ask pupils to find the words in the text and underline them. Explain any words they don't understand.
- Ask pupils to do the task individually, but check the answers as a class. Correct their pronunciation where necessary.

Answers

1	a torch	4	insects
2	Bats	5	tired
3	caves		

Grammar

Comparative

- Read the use of the comparative and short adjectives in the grammar box to the class and ask pupils to say the example sentence and the forms with you. Explain to pupils that we add –er to most short adjectives. Point out that we just add –r to adjectives that end in –e, that we double the last consonant and add –er to adjectives that have one syllable and end in a vowel and a consonant, and that we drop the –y and add –ier to adjectives that end in –y.
- Read the long adjectives and irregular adjectives to the class and ask pupils to say the forms with you. Draw pupils' attention to the use of *more* with adjectives which have three or more syllables and that we don't add –er to these adjectives. Also explain to pupils that they should make a note of irregular adjectives in their basic form and in the comparative when they meet them.
- Ask pupils to look back at *The Cortuga Mystery* on page 102 and ask them to find one example each of the comparative form of short adjectives (*nicer than*), long adjectives (*more dangerous than*) and irregular adjectives (*better than*).
- Ask pupils to do the task individually, but check the answers as a class. Remind pupils to check the ending of each of the adjectives in brackets and to refer back to the grammar box if they need to.

Answers

1	uglier	4	taller
2	smaller	5	more dangerous
3	better		

Vocabulary

- Ask pupils to work in pairs and tell one pupil to cover up the pictures a to c and the words 1 to 6 and the other pupil to cover up the words 1 to 6 and the pictures d to f. Ask them to try to name the three animals that they can see in their own books.
- Ask pupils to do the task in pairs to encourage discussion, but check the answers as a class.

Answers

1f	2b	3d	4a	5c	6e

Extra Class Activity

Ask pupils to three write sentences about the animals in the *Vocabulary* task using the comparative.

Suggested answers
- Swans are prettier than eagles.
- Leopards are bigger than worms.
- Whales are more dangerous than dolphins.

Listening

- Ask pupils to read the fact sheet and to try to guess what kind of information is missing. Ask which gaps need numbers (*1 and 6*), which ones need the names of animals (*2 and 3*), and which ones need the names of places (*4 and 5*).
- Play the recording and ask pupils to complete the fact sheet. Then ask them to discuss their answers in pairs and to justify any answers they have that are different.
- Play the recording again and ask pupils to check their answers and to fill in any missing information. When you have checked the answers, ask pupils if they find any of the crocodile facts interesting and if so, which ones.

Turn to page 110 for the listening script.

Answers

1	6 / six	2	fish	3	lions
4	Australia	5	rivers	6	60 / sixty

Speaking

- Ask pupils to say the words in the wordbank and point to each of the animals in the pictures and ask pupils to say what they are. Correct their pronunciation if necessary.
- Ask pupils to work in pairs and to take turns describing the animals with the words given. Go round the class monitoring, making sure that they are carrying out the task properly. Don't correct any mistakes in structure and pronunciation that you hear at this stage, but make a note of them.
- As a class, ask each pair to compare two animals.
- Write any mistakes that you heard on the board, without saying who made them, and ask pupils to correct them. Deal with any problems that arose with pronunciation.

Suggested answers
- The dolphin is more beautiful than the whale.
- The lion is more dangerous than the camel.
- The butterfly is smaller than the eagle.
- The whale is cleverer than the camel.
- The eagle is uglier than the lion.
- The camel is taller than the eagle.

Writing

- Ask pupils to read the questions and to think about their favourite animal. Make sure they understand each of the questions and give them any help they might need. Elicit that *What can it do?* means if it can *fly*, *swim*, *run fast*, etc.
- Ask pupils to write their sentences and then give them to another pupil to read.

> **Answers**
> Pupils' own answers

> **Extra Task (for early finishers)**
> See photocopiable material on page 134.

Lesson 2

Objectives

Reading	circling the correct words
Vocabulary	text-related words; domestic animals
Grammar	superlative – short adjectives, long adjectives, irregular adjectives
Listening	true or false
Sounds of English	*a* and *u* sounds
Song	Susie the pet dog

Way in

- Say the adjectives below and ask pupils to tell you their comparative form. Then ask which word always follows the comparative (*than*).

  - bad   (*worse*)
  - cold   (*colder*)
  - dangerous   (*more dangerous*)
  - good   (*better*)
  - hot   (*hotter*)
  - hungry   (*hungrier*)
  - tall   (*taller*)

- Write the letters *d*, *e*, *l*, *s*, *w* and *w* on the board and ask pupils to write the names of the animals that they learnt in Lesson 1 next to each one.

Reading

> **Background Information**
>
> It is traditional for US presidents to keep pets during their time in office. Warren Harding was the 29th president and served from March 1921 to August 1923. Theodore Roosevelt was the 26th president and served from September 1901 to March 1909. John F. Kennedy was the 35th president and served from January 1961 to November 1963. The herd of elephants mentioned in the text was given to the 15th president, James Buchanan, from the King of Siam (now Thailand). For further information on presidents and their pets go to: http://kids.nationalgeographic.com/Stories/History/Uspresidentialpets
> The sculpture at Mount Rushmore is a National Memorial and is part of a national park in South Dakota. In order to make the sculpture, 450,000 tonnes of rock were removed from the mountain face using dynamite. For further information visit www.nps.gov/moru.

- Elicit from pupils that Uncle Oliver has got a pet lizard. Ask pupils if they have got any pets and if so, what kind of animals they are.
- Ask them to name as many presidents of the United States as they can and ask if they know about any pets the presidents had.
- Ask pupils to skim read the text to themselves to find out how a pony got up to Archie Roosevelt's bedroom.

> **Answer**
> His brother Quentin put it in the lift.

Comprehension

- Ask pupils to read the sentences so that they know what information to look for the second time they read the text. Ask them to scan the text to find the answers and to underline the information that gives them the correct answers.
- Ask pupils to do the task individually, but check the answers as a class.

> **Answers**
> 1 dog (*The President had a birthday party for his dog.*)
> 2 Quentin (*Quentin brought him a visitor – his pet pony!*)
> 3 Macaroni (*… a pony called Macaroni. … it got letters from fans!*)
> 4 the President's (*Another time Quentin also put some snakes on his father's desk!*)
> 5 got (*Sometimes presidents get presents…*)

Guess what!

- Tell pupils to read the information in the *Guess what!* feature. Ask them what the most popular pet in their country is.

Vocabulary

- Explain that the words in the wordbank appear in the text. Ask pupils to find the words in the text and underline them. Explain any words they don't understand.
- Ask pupils to do the task individually, but check the answers as a class. Correct their pronunciation where necessary.

> **Answers**
> 1 popular   4 important
> 2 lift   5 unusual
> 3 president

Grammar

Superlative

- Read the grammar box to the class and ask pupils to read the example sentence and the forms with you. Point out the spelling rules for short adjectives and the use of *the* before adjectives.
- Ask pupils to look back at the *Reading* text to find examples of the superlative of short adjectives (*the luckiest*), long adjectives (*the most popular*, *the most unusual*) and irregular adjectives (*the most*, *the worst*) in the superlative.
- Explain to pupils that they are going to write sentences about the animals in the pictures using the prompts given. Tell them to use the superlative form of the adjectives and to add any articles that are necessary.

- Ask pupils to do the task individually, but check the answers as a class.

Extra Class Activity

Write *Who's the tallest person in your family?* and *My cousin Ted is the tallest person in my family.* on the board. Ask pupils to work in pairs and to ask and answer similar questions using the superlative. To finish, ask each pupil to tell the rest of the class one thing their partner told them.

Vocabulary

- Ask pupils to quickly look at the pictures a to f and ask them which of these pets they read about in the *Reading* text (*pony*, *dog*).
- Read the words to the class and ask them to say them after you. Elicit that a kitten is a young cat and a puppy is a young dog.
- Ask pupils to do the task in pairs to encourage discussion, but check the answers as a class. When you have checked their answers, ask pupils which animals they find the prettiest / the most interesting / the most horrible, etc.

Answers

1e   2b   3f   4a   5d   6c

Listening

- Ask pupils which animal they would choose if they were to get a new pet and ask them to say why they would choose this pet. Ask them about which animals they wouldn't like as pets and ask them to say why they wouldn't like them.
- Explain to pupils that they are going to listen to a girl and her dad talking about which pet to buy. Ask them to read sentences 1 to 5 and ask them to underline the kinds of pets they are going to hear about.
- Play the recording all the way to the end and ask pupils to write their answers. Ask them to discuss their answers with a partner and to justify any answers they have that are different.
- Play the recording again and ask pupils to check their answers or fill in any missing information.

Turn to page 110 for the listening script.

Answers

1F   2T   3F   4T   5F

Extra Class Activity

Animal charades

Split the class into two teams and tell pupils they are going to play animal charades. Decide which team will go first and ask each team to decide who will act out the first animal. Whisper or write down the name of an animal to the player of the first team. The player should try to pretend to be the animal so that the other team members can guess what kind of animal they are supposed to be. ➡

If they get it correct, give them two points, if they get it wrong, offer it to the other team for one point. Then play another round with the other team. Play until all pupils who want to act out an animal get a chance to do so. The team with the most points at the end is the winner.

Teaching Tip

If you have an odd number of pupils in your class or there is a pupil who doesn't want to take part in games, make him or her the scorekeeper. This means that he or she won't be sitting doing nothing during the game, and you don't have to make the pupil do something that will make him or her feel uncomfortable.

Sounds of English

A

- Ask pupils to work in pairs to read the words out loud. Write *a* (æ) and *o/u* (ʌ) on the board and ask them to use these sounds to talk about the coloured letters in each of the words.

Answers

1 a (æ)   2 u (ʌ)   3 a (æ)
4 o (ʌ)   5 a (æ)   6 u (ʌ)

B

- Ask pupils to work in pairs to decide which column the words should go in. Then play the recording and ask them to check their answers.

Answers

1 fun   2 love   3 puppy
4 animal   5 bat   6 parrot

Song

- Explain to pupils that they are going to listen to a song about a dog called Susie and that they should read the song as they listen.
- Play the song and ask pupils what Susie is doing in the pictures (*eating her food, going for a walk, playing in her basket, chasing butterflies*).
- Play the song again and ask pupils to sing along.
- If pupils enjoy singing along, play the song again.

Extra Task (for early finishers)

See photocopiable material on page 134.

Lesson 3

Objectives

Reading	completing the table
Say it like this!	talking about animals
Grammar	comparative and superlative
Writing	spelling; writing an advert

Way in

- Ask pupils to write three sentences talking about an animal using the superlative. Tell them to write one with a short adjective, one with a long adjective and one with an irregular adjective.
- Give pupils two minutes to write down as many animals as they can remember.
- Write the words below on the board and ask pupils to say them.
    - animal
    - bat
    - fun
    - love
    - monkey
    - puppy
    - rabbit

Reading

- Ask pupils to look at the title of the text and the pictures and to say what clever things they think these animals might do.
- Ask pupils to skim read the texts to themselves and then discuss with a partner which animal they think is the cleverest.

Answer
Pupils' own answers

Comprehension

- Ask pupils to look at the table and ask them where they will find the answers to 1, 2 and 3 (*in Lynn's writing*), where they will find the answers to 4, 5 and 6 (*in Helen's writing*), and where they will find the answers to 7, 8 and 9 (*in Alvin's writing*). Then elicit that beside *Name* they should write the name of a pet, that beside *Animal* they should write a kind of animal, and that beside *Can* they should write things that the animals can do.
- Ask pupils to scan the text to find the words to complete the table and ask them to underline the information that helps them to get the answer. Explain that they only need to write a word or a short phrase in each space and that *3* has got two answers.
- Ask pupils to do the task individually, but check the answers as a class.

Answers

1	Arthur	**6**	sleep on the sofa
2	parrot	**7**	Mattie
3	talk, count to five	**8**	dog
4	Nelly	**9**	do tricks
5	cat		

Say it like this!

Talking about animals

- Read the *Say it like this!* box to the class and ask them to say the example sentence with you. Correct their intonation pattern if necessary. Draw their attention to the position of the adjective between the article and the noun and to the fact that there is no verb.
- Ask pupils to work in pairs to talk about the animals in the pictures. Elicit that they are *a dog*, *a parrot* and *a mouse*. Remind pupils to practise the language shown.
- Ask pupils at random round the class to talk about one of the animals. Make sure that all pupils have the chance to speak and ask pupils to use different adjectives each time.

Teaching Tip

Try to make time in your lessons for extra revision as you approach the end of the book. Ask pupils questions about the grammar and some of the vocabulary they have learnt in earlier units. This will help you to see where pupils need extra practice or remedial work.

Grammar

Comparative and Superlative

- Read the grammar box to the class and ask them to read the example sentences with you.
- Ask pupils to read the paragraph to find out what kind of animal a *Komodo dragon* is (*a lizard*) and where it lives (*on some islands in Indonesia and in zoos*).
- Ask pupils to do the task individually, but check the answers as a class. Remind pupils that they should use the comparative before the word *than*, and that they should use *the* with the superlative.

Answers

1	the scariest	**4**	faster
2	bigger	**5**	most popular
3	more dangerous		

Extra Class Activity

Ask pupils to write two sentences using the comparative and two sentences using the superlative to compare the animals in the *Say it like this!* box.

Suggested answers

- The dog is uglier than the mouse.
- The parrot is cleverer than the dog.
- The mouse is the smallest animal.
- The parrot is the most beautiful animal.

Writing

Spelling

A

- Ask pupils to do the task individually, but check the answers as a class. Ask individual pupils to spell out each of the words and write them on the board so that pupils can compare them with their answers.

Project Book

The pupils may do Project 11 now they have completed the unit. The answer key and teacher's notes are on pages 148-152 of this book.

B

- Ask pupils to read the advert and to underline the five spelling mistakes. Check that they have underlined the correct words.
- Ask pupils to do the task individually, but check the answers as a class. When you have checked the answers, ask pupils if they would like to have these kittens as pets and to say why or why not.

Task

C

- Ask pupils to work in pairs to discuss which animal they are going to write about and to say why.
- Read the questions to the class and make sure pupils understand them. Explain that for *What do they look like*? they can talk about the animal's size and colour and that *What do they need?* means what food and care they must have.
- Ask pupils to use the answers to the questions to write an advert like the one in *B*. They can decorate their advert to make it more attractive and stick on photos of the animal or draw a picture of it.
- Alternatively, you could assign this task as homework.

D

- Ask pupils to proofread their adverts and to pay attention to their spelling.
- Hang pupils' adverts on the wall and ask them to read each others' when they have time. If you assign this task as homework, then give pupils a few minutes at the beginning of the next lesson to proofread their adverts.

Extra Class Activity

Say the words below and ask pupils to write them down. Then ask different pupils to write them on the board to check their spelling.

- chase
- colour
- favourite
- metre
- naughty
- neighbourhood
- taught
- trick

Extra Task (for early finishers)

See photocopiable material on page 134.

 **Weather and Nature**

Way in

- If you assigned Unit 11, Lesson 3 Writing Task C for homework, then give pupils a few minutes to proofread their adverts to check their spelling.
- Ask pupils at random round the class to say one sentence each using either the comparative or the superlative to talk about things in the classroom or other pupils in the class. If they get stuck, help them out by giving them an adjective to use.
- Ask pupils to quickly look at Unit 11, Lesson 3 to find the cleverest bird in the world (*Arthur*, *the parrot*), one of the scariest animals in the world (*the Komodo dragon*), the best pet in the world (*Mattie*, *the dog*), an animal that's nicer and cleverer than a dog (*Nelly*, *the cat*) and the most beautiful kittens in the world (*Robbie, Ray and Wilf*).

Background Information

The picture shows a storm with forked lightning striking an open field. Lightning is the effect that we see when electricity in the air is disturbed during a storm. The noise that we hear during a storm is called thunder. Lightning can be very beautiful but if it hits the earth, it can also be dangerous. You can find out more about lightning by visiting http://environment.nationalgeographic.com/environment/natural-disasters/lightning-profile.html.

Quiz

- Write *Weather* and *Nature* on the board and ask pupils to say the words after you. Correct their pronunciation if necessary. Ask pupils whether they have ever seen the effect shown in the picture (lightning).
- Ask pupils to do the quiz in pairs to encourage discussion, but check the answers as a class. Once you have checked the answer, ask pupils what they know about lightning. (The light is caused by electricity in the air during a rain storm. It can be dangerous and cause fires.).

Answer
b

Lesson 1

Objectives

Reading	The Cortuga Mystery
Vocabulary	text-related words; weather
Grammar	be going to – affirmative, negative, questions, short answers, time expressions
Listening	numbering pictures
Speaking	talking about plans for the weekend
Writing	writing sentences about plans for the weekend

Reading

The Cortuga Mystery
For teachers using the DVD

- Make sure each pupil has a copy of the DVD Worksheet found on page 123.
- Please follow the instructions in Unit 1, Lesson 1 on pages 12 and 13 for teachers using the DVD.

Before you watch

Answers
1 a cave near Eagle Point
2 pupils' own answers

While you watch

Answers
1 clouds
2 switch on
3 box
4 medallion
5 rainbow

After you watch

Answers
1 because they haven't got raincoats
2 in the cave
3 Uncle Oliver
4 he saw the puzzle
5 the lost medallion of Sethenca
6 have a great summer

For teachers using the audio CD

- Begin by asking pupils to look at the cartoon episode on page 110 and ask them where the children are going now (*to a cave near Eagle Point*) and ask them what they think happens at the end of *The Cortuga Mystery* (*Pupils' own answers*).
- Tell pupils they are going to listen to and read the next part of the story. Ask them to look at the pictures and to follow the story as they listen.
- Play the recording once and ask pupils what the puzzle is   (*a map*).
- Ask pupils to read the story out loud. Assign the roles of Jake, Mandy, Robbie, Kate and Uncle Oliver to different pupils for each part of the story. If you have a large class, you may have to repeat until all pupils have had a turn.
- As a class, ask pupils the questions below to check they have understood the episode.
  1 Why doesn't Mandy want it to rain? (*because they haven't got raincoats*)
  2 Where is the gold box? (*in the cave*)
  3 Who is also in the cave? (*Uncle Oliver*)
  4 How did Uncle Oliver find the children? (*he saw the puzzle*)
  5 What is inside the gold box? (*the lost medallion of Sethenca*)
  6 What are the children going to do now? (*have a good summer*)

Vocabulary

- Explain that the words in the wordbank appear in the cartoon episode. Ask pupils to find the words in the text and underline them. Explain any words they don't understand.
- Ask pupils to do the task individually, but check as a class. Correct their pronunciation where necessary.

Answers

1	rainbow	4	rocks
2	switch on	5	looking
3	raincoat		

Grammar

Be going to

- Ask pupils if it's raining at the beginning of the last episode of *The Cortuga Mystery* (*no*) and how they know this (*Kate says it's going to rain.*). Explain that we use *be going to* for the future.
- Read the uses of *be going to* in the grammar box to the class and ask them to say the example sentences with you. Explain what *intentions*, *predict* and *proof* mean if necessary.
- Ask pupils to find an example in the cartoon episode on page 110 of *be going to* for future plans and intentions (*We're going to have a great summer now*) and two examples of it being used to predict something (*It's going to rain.* and *We're going to get wet.*).
- Read the forms of *be going to* in the grammar box and ask pupils to read them with you. Read the short forms first and then the long forms.
- Ask pupils to read the dialogue to find out what Mark, his friends and his dad are going to make (*a tree house*).
- Ask pupils to do the task individually, but check the answers as a class.

Answers

1 Are, going to go
2 'm / am not
3 'm / am going to stay
4 are, going to do
5 are going to make
6 's / is going to help
7 're / are going to invite

1 What are you doing tomorrow?
2 Where are you going this weekend?
3 Is it going to rain today?
4 Are your favourite football team going to win the cup this year?
5 Are we going to finish the book this month?
6 When are you going to go on holiday this summer?

Vocabulary

- Elicit that all the pictures are related to the weather in some way.
- Read each of the words to the class and ask them to say them after you. Correct their pronunciation if necessary. Point out to pupils that we use these words with *It's*.
- Ask pupils to do the task in pairs to encourage discussion, but check the answers as a class. Once you have checked the answers, ask pupils which weather they like best.

Answers

1d	2f	3b	4c	5a	6e

Listening

- Ask pupils to work in pairs to work out what weather symbols a to e might show. Explain that there is one that isn't used in the listening task.
- Explain to pupils that they are going to listen to four different conversations about the weather and that they have to put the weather symbols in the order they hear the conversations in.
- Play the recording and ask pupils to number the symbols, then ask them to work in pairs to discuss their answers and to justify any answers they have that are different. Establish that *d* isn't used.
- Play the recording again and ask pupils to check their answers and fill in any missing information.

Turn to page 110 for the listening script.

Answers

a4	b2	c3	d-	e1

Speaking

- Read the questions to the pupils and make sure that they understand them.
- Ask pupils to work in pairs to take turns asking and answering the questions.
- Go round the class monitoring and checking that pupils are carrying out the task properly. Don't correct any mistakes in structure or pronunciation that you hear at this stage, but make a note of them.

- As a class, ask each pupil one of the questions about his or her partner. Write any mistakes you heard on the board, without saying who made them, and ask pupils to correct them. Deal with any problems in pronunciation that arose.

Answers
Pupils' own answers

Writing

- Ask pupils to write five sentences about their plans for the weekend by answering the questions in the *Speaking* task. Ask them to proofread their sentences once they have finished to check that they have used *be going to* properly.
- Alternatively, you could assign this task for homework. Give pupils time at the beginning of the next lesson to proofread their sentences.

Extra Task (for early finishers)
See photocopiable material on page 135.

Lesson 2

Objectives

Reading	open-ended questions
Vocabulary	text-related vocabulary; landscapes
Grammar	future simple – affirmative, negative, questions, short answers, time expressions
Listening	completing notes
Sounds of English	*a* sounds

Way in

- Draw a *sun*, *clouds*, *clouds with rain*, *snowflakes* and a *tree blowing in the wind* on the board. Ask pupils to copy them and write what weather symbols they are below them.
- Ask pupils to write three sentences with *be going to* using the affirmative, negative, question form and a short answer in reply to their question.

Reading

Background Information
The text is about a group of scientists lead by Dr Michael Fay who is an American ecologist and conservationist. The journey described in the text took place in 1997 and Fay and his team walked 2,000 kilometres across Africa in 455 days. During their journey, the scientists studied trees, wildlife and the negative effects that humans have had on the rainforest. The study resulted in the government of Gabon making 28,500 square kilometres into 13 national parks.
The pictures show Michael Fay during an expedition and the part of the rainforest where the journey ended at the Atlantic Ocean. Congo and Gabon, the parts of Africa that they travelled across, are marked in red on the map of Africa in the picture.

- Ask pupils what we sleep in when we go camping (*a tent*) and what we call a bag that we carry on our back (*a rucksack*). Explain that the man in the picture needed these things on his journey through Africa. Then ask pupils to skim read the text to themselves to find out where his journey finishes.

Answer
At the Atlantic Ocean

- Ask pupils to look back at the title of the text and ask them why nature is in danger (*Because companies want to cut down parts of the rainforest and this will be bad for animals and plants.*).
- Explain any vocabulary that pupils don't know.

Comprehension

- Ask pupils to read the questions to see what information they need to find the second time they read the text. Ask them to scan the text to find the answers and to underline the information that gives them the answers.
- Ask pupils to do the task individually, but check the answers as a class.

Answers
1 thousands of kinds of plants and animals (*This is the second largest rainforest… there are thousands of kinds of plants and animals there.*)
2 on foot (*The scientists will travel on foot…*)
3 cut down the trees (*Companies want to cut down the trees so they can sell them as wood.*)
4 the leader of the group (*…says the leader of the group, Dr Michael Fay.*)
5 more than a year (*More than a year later, the team arrives at the Atlantic Ocean.*)

Extra Class Activity
Write the sentences below on the board and ask pupils to decide if they are *true* or *false*.

1	The rainforest in Africa is the largest in the world.	(F)
2	The scientists will take their own tents with them.	(T)
3	The scientists will walk because they haven't got cars.	(F)
4	The rainforest is wild.	(T)
5	One scientist didn't finish the journey.	(F)

Guess what!

- Ask pupils to read the information in the *Guess what!* feature. Ask them where they think the medicines come from (*plants*).
- Ask pupils if they know any other ways that humans use the rainforests (*tourism, farming*).
- Explain that the words in the wordbank appear in the text.

Vocabulary

- Ask pupils to find the words in the text and underline them. Explain any words they don't understand.
- Ask pupils to do the task individually, but check the answers as a class. Correct their pronunciation where necessary.

Answers
1	survive	4	arrive
2	destroy	5	carry
3	cut down		

Grammar

Future Simple

- Read the uses of the Future Simple in the grammar box to the pupils and ask them to read the example sentence with you. Ask them which word is the bare infinitive (*cut*).
- Read the forms of the Future Simple and ask pupils to read them with you. Ask them what they notice about the form of the Future Simple (*It's the same for all persons of the verb.*).
- Ask pupils to look back at the *Reading* text and to underline examples of the Future Simple affirmative (*will travel, will carry, will be*) and question form (*What will they find, Will they survive, Will the rainforests survive*). Draw pupils' attention to the word order in the ordinary question form and in *wh–* questions. Remind pupils that when we have a *wh–* question that asks about the subject of a sentence, the word order is the same as the affirmative, for example, *Who will arrive first?*

A

- Explain to pupils that they should put the verbs into the affirmative if there is a tick at the end of the sentence, or into the negative if there is a cross at the end.
- Ask pupils to do the task individually, but check the answers as a class.

Answers

1	will follow	4	won't rain
2	won't drive	5	won't be
3	will be		

B

- Ask pupils to look at the picture of Jim and explain that he's thinking about the future. Ask them to work in pairs to decide which picture each question asks about and whether Jim's answer will begin with *yes* or *no*.
- Read the verbs in the wordbank to the pupils and explain that they should use these verbs to complete the sentences and that they will use the verb *be* in two sentences.
- Ask pupils to do the task individually, but check the answers as a class.

Answers

1 Will, drive, No, they won't.
2 Will, be, Yes, it will.
3 Will, have, No, we won't.
4 Will, be, No, there won't.
5 Will, live, Yes, they will.
6 Will, do, Yes, they will.

Extra Class Activity

Put pupils into small groups, give each group different years (*2020, 2050, 2100*, etc) and explain that they are going to decide what the future will be like in that particular year. Ask them to think of five things that will be different in their year. Then ask each group to tell the other groups about their year.

Vocabulary

- Ask pupils to look at the pictures of different landscapes and ask them which ones they can find in their country. Then ask them which one is their favourite.
- Read words 1 to 6 to the class and ask pupils to say them after you. Correct their pronunciation if necessary.
- Ask pupils to do the task in pairs to encourage discussion, but check the answers as a class.

Answers

1d	**2**f	**3**c	**4**a	**5**b	**6**e

Extra Class Activity

Ask pupils to write sentences with the words from the *Vocabulary* task.

Listening

- Explain to pupils that they are going to listen to an advert for holiday centres. Ask them to read the advert to decide what kind of information they need to find to complete the notes. Elicit that they need a number in 1, a place in 2 and leisure activities in 3, 4 and 5.
- Play the recording once and ask pupils to work in pairs to discuss their answers and to justify any answers that are different.
- Play the recording again and ask pupils to check their answers and to fill in any missing information. When you have checked the answers, ask pupils if they would like to go to a nature park for a holiday and to say why or why not.

Turn to page 111 for the listening script.

Answers

1	5 / five	4	mountain
2	a lake	5	tennis
3	cycling		

Sounds of English

A

- Say each of the words and ask pupils to say them after you. Point out that all the words have got –a in them, but that it doesn't sound the same in all the words.
- Play the recording and ask pupils to listen carefully to how the words are said and to decide which words sound alike in the pairs (*have/can* and *save/danger*).

Answer

The –*a* in *have* and *can* is pronounced æ, but in *save* and *danger* it is pronounced ɛɪ.

B

- Ask pupils to work in pairs and to say the words in the wordbank to each other. Then ask them to decide together which column each word goes in.
- Play the recording and ask pupils to check their answers. Stop after each word and ask pupils to say them.

Answers

1	black	4	lake
2	map	5	nature
3	natural	6	place

Extra Class Activity

Ask pupils to add any other words they can think of to the columns in *Sounds of English B*.

Teaching Tip

Try to recognise which areas of pronunciation your pupils have problems with in English. Do remedial work from time to time to stop them from developing bad habits.

Extra Task (for early finishers)

See photocopiable material on page 135.

Lesson 3

Objectives

Reading	interview; completing the sentences
Say it like this!	talking about the weather
Listening	numbering the pictures
Speaking	making predictions
Writing	checking for mistakes; writing a letter to a friend

Way in

- Write the sentences below on the board and ask pupils to say them as a class and then individually.
  - *A man gave me a map of a black lake.*
  - *Nature's in danger, but we can save this place.*
- Ask pupils to write sentences in the Future Simple with the verbs *arrive*, *carry*, *cut down*, *destroy* and *survive*.
- Write c _ _ _ _ _, c _ _ _ _, f _ _ _ _ _, m _ _ _ _ _ _ _, o _ _ _ _ and w _ _ _ _ _ _ _ _ on the board and ask pupils to complete with the different landscapes from Lesson 2.

Reading

- Ask pupils if they know any strange hobbies. Then ask them to look at the title of the text and to then read the sentences before the interview to find out who has an unusual hobby and what it is (*Brett Jarvis*, *watching tornados*). Make sure that pupils pronounce *tornado* properly and explain that the –a is pronounced ɛɪ like in *save*.
- Write the adjectives below on the board and ask pupils which one(s) they think best describe this hobby.

  amazing
  boring
  dangerous
  exciting
  scary
  stupid

- Ask pupils to skim read the interview to themselves to find out when tornados usually happen.

Answers

In spring

Comprehension

- Ask pupils to read the sentences to find out what information they need to find the second time they read the text. Ask them to scan the text to find the missing words.
- Ask pupils to do the task individually, but check the answers as a class.

Answers

1	cloud	**4**	photographs
2	about 750	**5**	spring
3	lift		

Extra Class Activity

Ask pupils the questions below to further check their understanding of the text.

1. Why can tornados move very fast in the west of the USA? (*because there aren't many mountains*)
2. What do tornados destroy? (*everything near them*)
3. What is exciting for Brett? (*getting close to tornados*)
4. How does Brett feel when a tornado comes towards him? (*scared*)
5. What is Brett going to follow? (*the next tornado in his area*)

Say it like this!

Talking about the weather

- Read the information in the *Say it like this!* box to the pupils and ask them to read the example sentences with you. Revise the four seasons of the year and weather-related words and phrases if necessary. Draw pupils' attention to the use of *in* with the seasons.
- Ask pupils to work in pairs to talk about the weather at different times of the year in their country. Tell them to take turns talking about one of the four seasons and to use the language they have just seen.
- Go round the class monitoring and checking that they are carrying out the task properly. Don't correct any mistakes in structure and pronunciation that you hear at this stage, but make a note of them.
- As a class ask individual pupils to tell the rest of the class about the weather during one of the seasons. Then write any mistakes in structure you heard on the board, without saying who made them, and ask pupils to correct them. Deal with any problems that arose in pronunciation.

Listening

- Explain to pupils that they are going to listen to a story about the sun and the wind. Ask them to close their books,then play the recording once and ask pupils just to listen to the story. Ask them what the sun and the wind are trying to see (*who is the strongest and can make the man take off his hat*) and who manages to do it (*the sun*).
- Ask pupils to open their books at page 115 and ask them to work in pairs and to decide what each picture shows.
- Play the recording again and ask pupils to write numbers 1 to 6 in the correct box beside pictures a to f. Then ask them to discuss their answers with a partner and to justify any answers they have that are different.
- Play the recording again and ask pupils to check their answers or fill in any missing information. When you have checked their answers, ask pupils what they liked about the story.

Turn to page 111 for the listening script.

Teaching Tip

When listening tasks require pupils to match pictures to what is said on the recording, give pupils time to study the pictures and to talk about what's happening in each one before they listen. Encourage them to look at the small differences between the pictures, as these will be important in getting the answer correct.

Speaking

- Ask pupils to look at the four pictures and as a class decide which verbs will be used with each one.
- Ask pupils to work in pairs to predict what is going to happen in each picture. Remind them to use the correct form of *be going to*.

Suggested answers
- They're going to get wet.
- He's going to drop his ice cream.
- The dog is going to run away.
- He's going to fall off his bike.

Writing

Checking for mistakes

A
- Write the sentences below on the board, then read the information in *A* to the class. Elicit from the pupils what kind of mistake is in each sentence and what the sentence should read.

  1   What a tornado is? (*word order, What is a tornado?*)
  2   She are going to fall. (*grammar, She's going to fall.*)
  3   There are usualy more tornados in spring. (*spelling, There are usually more tornados in spring.*)
  4   What's Bretts hobby? (*punctuation, What's Brett's hobby?*)

B
- Ask pupils to read the sentences and to decide which ones are correct and which ones have got a mistake in them. Tell them to put a tick in the box if the sentence is correct and a cross if the sentence is incorrect. Tell them not to correct the mistakes yet.
- Check that pupils have put ticks or crosses in the correct boxes, then ask them to correct the incorrect sentences in their notebooks.

Answers
1   (✗)   *There are some eagles on that rock.*
2   (✗)   *Tornados are often dangerous.*
3   (✓)
4   (✗)   *I'm going to visit my cousins this summer.*
5   (✗)   *Have you got an umbrella?*
6   (✓)

C
- Ask pupils to read Nigel's letter to find out what Juan needs to take with him to England (*a raincoat*).

- Ask pupils to work in pairs to find and underline the eight mistakes in Nigel's letter. Tell them not to correct the mistakes just yet.
- Check that pupils have underlined all the mistakes, then ask them to correct them individually, but check the answers as a class.

Answers
1st paragraph	redy (*ready*)
2nd paragraph	Ive (*I've*), We going (*We're / We are going*), their (*there*), I'm going take (*I'm going to take*), It be (*It'll be*)
3rd paragraph	sometimes but it (*but it sometimes*), rain (*rains*)

Task

D
- Explain to pupils that they are going to write a letter like the one in *C*. Ask them to read the plan so that they know what they will write in each paragraph.
- Ask pupils to write their letters individually using the plan given.
- Alternatively, assign the letter for homework.

Suggested answer

Dear Ahmed,

How are you? Are you ready for your trip to Egypt? You'll be here in one week!

I've got lots of plans for your holiday. We're going to go camping in the desert. The sea is terrific in the summer, so we're going to go to the beach too. It'll be great!

The weather in June will be sunny, but sometimes it is very hot. Bring sun cream with you!

See you soon!

Khalid

E
- Ask pupils to proofread their letters to check for mistakes in punctuation, grammar, spelling and word order. Alternatively, you could ask pupils to proofread each other's letters and give each other feedback.
- If you assign the letter for homework, give pupils a few minutes at the beginning of the next lesson to proofread their own or a partner's letter.

Extra Task (for early finishers)

See photocopiable material on page 135.

Project Book

The pupils may do Project 12 now they have completed the unit. The answer key and teacher's notes are on pages 148-152 of this book.

Review 6

Objectives
- To revise vocabulary and grammar from Units 11 and 12
- Song – English weather

Revision
- Explain to pupils that the tasks in *Review 6* are based on the material they saw in Units 11 and 12.
- Remind pupils that they can ask you for help with the exercises or look back at the units if they're not sure about an answer, as the review is not a test.
- Decide how you will carry out the review. You could ask pupils to do one task at a time and then correct it immediately, or ask pupils to do all the tasks and correct them together at the end. If you do all the tasks together, let pupils know every now and again how much time they have got to finish the tasks.
- Remind pupils not to leave any answers blank and to try to find any answers they aren't sure about in the units.
- Revise the vocabulary and grammar as a class before pupils do the review.

Vocabulary Revision
- Write the words; *worms, dolphin, parrot, kitten, crocodile, snake, swan* and *leopard* on the board and ask pupils to work in pairs to describe them.
- Write the verbs below on the board in one column and the nouns opposite them in another column. Ask pupils to match the verbs to the correct nouns. Explain that they can only use each verb once.

carry	a bag
cut down	a forest
look for	a tornado
show	a television
survive	treasure
switch on	someone a cave

Answers
- carry a bag
- cut down a forest
- look for treasure
- show someone a cave
- survive a tornado
- switch on a television

- Write weather on the board and ask pupils to tell you the different kinds of weather they know. Make sure they revise *cloudy, windy* and *rainy*. Then ask them what you need to wear when it's raining (*a raincoat*) and what you can see when the sun comes out after it has been raining (*a rainbow*).
- Ask pupils what a *waterfall* is and then ask them to write down other landscapes that they know. Make sure they revise *cliff, cave* and *rainforest*.
- Write the following jumbled words on the board and ask pupils to unscramble them to find words from Units 11 and 12.

ulaoppr	(*popular*)
filt	(*lift*)
incblasrou	(*binoculars*)
rocth	(*torch*)
ulasunu	(*unusual*)
tranpoitm	(*important*)
tnlpa	(*plant*)
onildemla	(*medallion*)

Grammar Revision
- Write the adjectives below on the board and ask pupils to write their comparative and superlative forms.

small	(*smaller, the smallest*)
big	(*bigger, the biggest*)
tasty	(*tastier, the tastiest*)
horrible	(*more horrible, the most horrible*)
good	(*better, best*)
bad	(*worse, the worst*)
many / much	(*more, the most*)

- Ask pupils to write two sentences using the comparative and the superlative. Make sure they use *than* in the comparative.
- Ask pupils to work in pairs to ask and answer four questions using *be going to*. Then ask each pupil to ask one of his or her questions to someone else in the class.
- Ask pupils when we use *be going to* (*to talk about future plans and intentions and to predict something when we have proof or information*) and when we use the Future Simple (*to make predictions about the future*).
- Revise the affirmative, negative, question and short answer forms of the future simple as a class.

Vocabulary

A

Tell pupils to read the definitions of each animal, look at the first letter of each word carefully and pay attention to the number of letters missing.

Answers

1	worms	5	crocodile
2	dolphin	6	snake
3	parrot	7	swan
4	kitten	8	leopard

B
- Ask pupils to say each of the words in the wordbank as a class and then individually. Correct their pronunciation if necessary.
- Explain to pupils that they don't have to change the form of the verbs in the sentences, but sometimes they may need a capital letter.

Answers

1	Switch on	4	show
2	carry	5	cut down
3	survive	6	look for

C

- Explain to pupils that they should read the whole of the sentence so that they understand the context the missing word is in.
- Remind pupils to read the sentence again once they have chosen their answer to make sure it makes sense.

> **Answers**
>
> **1**b   **2**c   **3**a   **4**c   **5**a

D

- Ask pupils to say each of the words as a class and then individually. Correct their pronunciation if necessary.
- Ask pupils to go to the second page of stickers at the back of the book and find the stickers for *Review 6*. Tell them to decide which word each sticker shows and to stick it in the correct box.
- Check that pupils have put the correct stickers above each word.

Grammar

A

- Explain to pupils that they should only write one word to replace the word in bold.
- Tell them to look back at Unit 11 Lessons 1, 2 and 3 grammar boxes for a reminder if they need to.

> **Answers**
>
> | **1** friendlier | **2** hottest | **3** more |
> |---|---|---|
> | **4** biggest | **5** than | **6** most |

B

- Ask pupils to read the words in the wordbank and then look at the pictures 1 to 6 to decide which verb goes with each picture.
- Ask them to read the sentences and explain that the sentences talk about the pictures with the same numbers. Tell them to fill the gaps using the verbs either in the affirmative if there is a tick after the sentence or in the negative if there is a cross after the sentence.
- Tell them to look back at Unit 12 Lesson 1 grammar box for a reminder if they need to.

> **Answers**
>
> **1** 's / is going to fall
> **2** aren't going to swim
> **3** isn't going to rain
> **4** 's / is going to go
> **5** aren't going to catch
> **6** 's / is going to destroy

C

- Explain to pupils that the answers here are their own personal opinions.
- Tell them to look back at Unit 12 Lesson 2 grammar box for a reminder if they need to.

> **Answer**
>
> Pupils' own answers

Song

- Tell pupils they are going to listen to a song about the weather. Ask them to read and listen to the song and to find out why the singer went into a shop (*because it started raining and he didn't have an umbrella*) and why he says 'Thank you, rainy weather (*because the rain brought him and Suzanne together*).
- Play the song again and ask pupils to sing along. You could do this verse by verse and then play it once all the way through.
- To finish, ask pupils to think about all the songs they have heard in *Wonderful World 3* and ask them which one was their favourite.

When checking pupils' answers to the review tasks, make a note of any problem areas in vocabulary and grammar that they still have. Try to do extra work on these areas so that your pupils progress well.

National Geographic DVD Worksheets

General Note

The National Geographic videos can be used as an interesting way to introduce your pupils to other cultures. They are authentic National Geographic videos, and it is not necessary for pupils to understand everything they hear to benefit from them. Some of the tasks focus on the visual aspects of the videos, so pupils can concentrate more on what they see than on what they hear. They are also a good way to encourage your pupils to watch TV programmes and films in English so that they can get used to the sound of the language. The more pupils are exposed to English, the easier it will be for them to pick up the language.

Video 1
The Young Riders of Mongolia

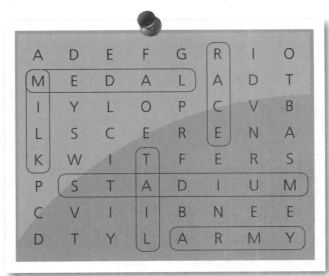

Background Information

The story in the video takes place in Ulan Bator, the capital of Mongolia. Mongolia is a republic situated between China and Russia. On 11th July each year, a three-day festival begins in Ulan Bator. The festival is called Naadam and involves wrestling, horse racing and dancing. The main festival events take place over three days in Ulan Bator, but the festival continues all month throughout Mongolia. For further information go to www.nationalgeographic.com and search for Naadam.

Before you watch

A

- Ask pupils to read the title and look at the pictures. Ask them what kind of riders it talks about (*horse riders*).
- Explain to pupils that they are going to see a video about a festival in Mongolia and that horse racing is an important part of this festival.
- Ask pupils to work in pairs to answer the questions with a partner. Then as a class use the questions to have an open discussion about horses.

Answers
Pupils' own answers

The story

- Read the information about Ulan Bator to the pupils and draw their attention to its position on the map. Explain that it's between China and Russia. Ask pupils to say Mongolia several times and correct their pronunciation if necessary.
- Explain to pupils what capital city means by giving them examples of well-known capitals, for example, *London*, *Paris*, *Rome*, *Madrid*, etc. Ask pupils what the capital city is in their country.

Words to know

- Ask pupils to look at the pictures and the words on the right. Explain that they will hear these words when they watch the video. Say the words to the class and ask pupils to say them after you as a class and then individually. Correct their pronunciation if necessary.
- Ask pupils to do the word search individually, but check the answers as a class.

While you watch

A

- Ask pupils to read the sentences before they watch the video so that they know what information to listen for while they watch. Explain any words that the pupils have difficulty with.
- Make sure pupils realise that they should put the numbers 1 to 6 in the boxes provided to show the order the sentences should go in. Play the video until you hear the information about the riders preparing for the race and elicit that sentence 6 should be number 1.
- Play the rest of the video and ask pupils to number the rest of the sentences. Then ask them to discuss their answers with a partner and to justify any answers they have that are different.
- Check the answers as a class. See the times in the brackets after the answers below if you want to show pupils the part of the video that gives them the answer again.

Answers

1	2	(0:01:36)
2	4	(0:02:40)
3	5	(0:03:02)
4	3	(0:01:55)
5	6	(0:03:06)
6	1	(0:01:04)

B

- Ask pupils to read the sentences before they watch the video again. Ask them if they know any of the answers at this stage and to underline them if they do.
- Play the video again and ask pupils to listen carefully and to circle the words they hear.
- Ask pupils to do the task individually, but check the answers as a class.

Answers

1	July	(0:00:39)
2	twelve	(0:01:00)
3	parents	(0:01:35)
4	horses	(0:02:06)
5	thirty	(0:02:34)
6	year	(0:03:08)

After you watch

A

- Ask pupils to read the whole sentence before they choose their answer and then to read the sentence again with their answer to make sure it is correct.
- Ask pupils to do the task individually, but check the answers as a class.

Answers

1a   2b   3b   4c

B

- Revise the question words by writing *When, Where, Who, What* and *Whose* in one column on the board and *Harry's, Spain, Margaret, in December* and *a festival* in another. Ask pupils to match the question words to the correct word or words in the second column (*When – in December, Where – Spain, Who – Margaret, What – a festival, Whose – Harry's*).
- Ask pupils to do the task individually, but check the answers as a class.

Answers

1	When	4	What
2	Who	5	Whose
3	Where		

Project

- Explain to pupils that they are going to do a project about a festival.
- Read the instructions and the example poster to the pupils. Ask them the following questions.
  1. What kind of festival is the poster for? (*a strawberry festival*)
  2. When can you visit the strawberry festival? (*every June*)
  3. What can you do at the festival? (*eat strawberries and have fun*)
- Ask pupils to find a word that means good to eat (*yummy*). Then ask them to make a list of adjectives that show that something is good. Make a list on the board of the adjectives found in the book so far.

amazing	good
beautiful	great
cool	happy
exciting	magic
fantastic	nice
fast	perfect
favourite	popular
funny	special

- Ask pupils to underline *Come, Visit* and *Don't miss* on the poster. Ask them what they notice (*the subject is missing*). Explain that they can use this form in their project to persuade people to go to their festival.
- Ask pupils to work in pairs or small groups. Tell them to spend some time thinking about what kind of project they want to plan. Help them with any vocabulary they might need.

- Ask pupils to make a poster telling people what the festival is, when it is, what you can do there and where it is. Ask pupils to bring in photos from magazines or newspapers to decorate their posters.
- Once they have finished their posters, hang them on the wall.

Video 2
Monkey Party

Background Information

See Teacher's Book page 42 for background information on the Lopburi Monkey Party.

Before you watch

A

- Ask pupils to read the title and look at the pictures. Ask them what they remember about the monkey festival they saw in the *Quiz* in Unit 5.
- Explain to pupils that they are now going to see a video about the monkey festival in Thailand.
- Ask pupils to work in pairs to answer the questions with a partner. Then as a class use the questions to have an open discussion about monkeys.

Answers

Pupils' own answers

The story

- Read the information about Lopburi to the pupils and draw their attention to its position on the map. Explain that it's close to Bangkok, the capital of Thailand. Ask pupils to say Thailand several times and correct their pronunciation if necessary.
- Ask pupils where else they think wild monkeys might live (*Africa, Central and South America* and *Asia*).

Words to know

- Read the words in the wordbank to the class and ask them to say them after you as a class and then individually. Correct their pronunciation if necessary.
- Ask pupils to do the task individually, but check the answers as a class.

Answers

1	monkey	4	cake
2	festival	5	banquet
3	street		

While you watch

A

- Ask pupils to read the sentences before they watch the video so that they know what information to look and listen for while they watch. Explain any words that the pupils have difficulty with and explain that they should choose their answers based on what they see in the video.
- Play the video until the street scene with the monkeys ends and elicit that the monkeys don't sit on a blue car so 1 is false.
- Play the rest of the video and ask pupils to do the rest of the task. Then ask them to discuss their answers with a partner and to justify any answers they have that are different.

- Check the answers as a class. See the times in the brackets after the answers below if you want to show pupils the part of the video that gives them the answer again.

Answers

1 F (0:00:16)
2 T (0:00:30)
3 T (0:00:44)
4 F (0:01:17)
5 F (0:01:39)
6 T (0:02:18)

B

- Ask pupils to read the sentences before they watch to the video again. Ask them if they know any of the answers at this stage and to underline them if they do.
- Play the video again and ask pupils to listen and to circle the correct words.
- Ask pupils to do the task individually, but check the answers as a class.

Answers

1	town	(0:00.00)
2	trouble	(0:00.27)
3	animals	(0:00.49)
4	food	(0:01:18)
5	banquet	(0:01:39)
6	cake	(0:02:15)

After you watch

A

- Ask pupils to read the whole sentence before they choose their answer and then to read the sentence again with their answer to make sure it is correct.
- Ask pupils to do the task individually, but check the answers as a class.

Answers

1a 2c 3c 4c

B

- Write *fruit, flower, car, food* on the board and ask pupils which two are countable (*flower* and *car*), and which two are uncountable (*fruit* and *food*).
- Ask pupils to write sentences with these words and *some / any*, *much / many* and *a lot of / a few*. Ask pupils to read one of their sentences to the class and revise the use of the quantifiers further if necessary.
- Ask pupils to do the task individually, but check the answers as a class.

Answers

1	a lot of	4	some
2	any	5	much
3	Many		

Project

- Explain to pupils that their project is to write a recipe for a *Monkey Party Cake*.
- Read the instructions and the ingredients to the pupils. Ask pupils to work in groups to brainstorm the kind of ingredients that they could use in the cake and make a list on the board like the one below.

eggs
milk
butter
sugar
chocolate
bananas

- Ask pupils to decide in their groups how they can make the cake and then to write the recipe and draw the picture of the cake.
- Tell pupils to look back at Unit 6, Lesson 3 Writing C for help with the recipe.
- Once they have finished their recipes, hang them on the wall.

Video 3
Alaskan Ice Climbing

Background Information

The Matanuska glacier is the largest glacier in Alaska that is accessible by car. For this reason, it is very popular with visitors and is open to the public for winter and summer holidays. Once they reach Matanuska, visitors must hike for 15-20 minutes to reach the glacier. The glacier is active and moves 30 cm per day. This activity is due to the pull of gravity.

Before you watch

A

- Ask pupils to read the title and remind them of the picture in the *Quiz* in Unit 7. Ask them what the woman was climbing (*a frozen waterfall*).
- Explain to pupils that they are going to see a video about ice climbing in Alaska.
- Ask pupils to work in pairs to answer the questions with a partner. Then as a class use the questions to have an open discussion about Alaska.

Answers

Pupils' own answers

The story

- Read the information about Alaska to the pupils and draw their attention to its position on the map. Explain that it's the most northern state in the USA. Ask pupils to say *Alaska* several times and correct their pronunciation if necessary.

Words to know

- Read the words in the word bank to the class and ask them to say them after you as a class and then individually. Correct their pronunciation if necessary.
- Ask pupils to do the task individually, but check the answers as a class.

Answers

| 1 | skiing | 2 | climbing | 3 | hiking |

D

- Ask pupils to look at the pictures and the words on the right. Explain that they will hear these words when they watch the video. Say the words to the class and ask pupils to say them after you as a class and then individually. Correct their pronunciation if necessary.
- Ask pupils to do the word search individually, but check the answers as a class.

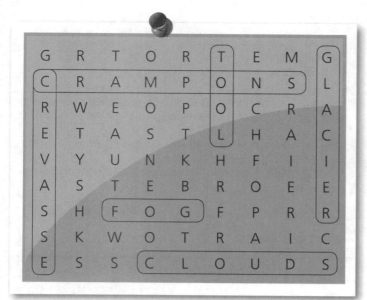

The word search grid:

G	R	T	O	R	T	E	M	G
C	R	A	M	P	O	N	S	L
R	W	E	O	P	O	C	R	A
E	T	A	S	T	L	H	A	C
V	Y	U	N	K	H	F	I	I
A	S	T	E	B	R	O	E	E
S	K	F	O	G	F	P	R	R
S	K	W	O	T	R	A	I	C
E	S	S	C	L	O	U	D	S

While you watch

A

- Ask pupils to read the sentences before they watch the video so that they know what information to look out for while they watch. Explain any words that the pupils have difficulty with.
- Make sure pupils realise that they should put the numbers 1 to 6 in the boxes provided to show the order the sentences should go in. Play the video until you see the people arriving at the school and elicit that sentence 3 should be number 1.
- Play the rest of the video and ask pupils to number the rest of the sentences. Then ask them to discuss their answers with a partner and to justify any answers they have that are different.
- Check the answers as a class. See the times in the brackets after the answers below if you want to show pupils the part of the video that gives them the answer again.

Answers

1	4	(0:02:08)
2	5	(0:02:37)
3	1	(0:00:26)
4	6	(0:03:57)
5	2	(0:01:21)
6	3	(0:01:31)

B

- Ask pupils to read the sentences before they watch the video again. Ask them if they know any of the answers at this stage and to underline them if they do.
- Play the video again and ask pupils to listen and to circle the correct words.
- Ask pupils to do the task individually, but check the answers as a class.

Answers

1	mountains	(0:01:08)
2	climb	(0:01:57)
3	beautiful	(0:02:37)
4	air	(0:03:31)
5	easy	(0:04:07)
6	people	(0:04:35)

After you watch

A

- Ask pupils to read the whole sentence before they choose their answer and then to read the sentence again with their answer to make sure it is correct.
- Ask pupils to do the task on their own, but check the answers as a class.

Answers

1 a   **2** b   **3** a   **4** c

B

- Revise the *comparative* and *superlative* by writing the adjectives *old*, *white*, *good* and *many / much* on the board and asking pupils to tell you their comparative and superlative forms (*older – oldest, whiter – whitest, better – best* and *more – most*).
- Ask pupils to do the task individually, but check the answers as a class.

Answers

1	highest	4	best
2	largest	5	more
3	colder		

Project

- Explain to pupils that they are going to make a holiday advert.
- Read the instructions and the example posters to the pupils. Ask them the questions below.
  1. What kind of holidays are the posters for? (*a cruise and a mountain climbing course*)
  2. What can you see on the cruise? (*glaciers and mountains*)
  3. How long is the mountain climbing course? (*two weeks*)
- Ask pupils to work in pairs or small groups. Tell them to spend some time thinking about what kind of holiday they want to make a poster for. Help them with any vocabulary they might need.
- Ask pupils to make a poster telling people where the holiday is to, how you can get there and what you can do there. Ask pupils to bring in photos from magazines or newspapers to decorate their posters.
- Once they have finished their posters, hang them on the wall.

Notes on the Play - Surprise!

Introduction

The play in *Wonderful World 3 Pupil's Book* has been designed to give pupils the chance to use the English they have learnt throughout the year creatively. The play contains grammar, vocabulary and functional language from the whole of the Pupil's Book, so it is designed to be performed at the end of the school year. It can be found on pages 124 and 125 of the Pupil's Book.

Cast

The main characters from the Cortuga Mystery (*Jake, Kate, Mandy* and *Robbie*) star in the play as well as their friends and Kate's mum and dad.

Encourage all pupils to get involved in the play, but be sensitive to pupils who feel too shy to take on a speaking role. These pupils can play Kate's friends or be more active in preparing props and costumes. Allocate the roles according to pupils' confidence levels and ability. Develop a positive and fun atmosphere during rehearsals and allow scope for pupils' creativity. At this level, it's more important that they enjoy performing than be word perfect.

Give pupils positive feedback during rehearsals so that they feel more confident and proud of their achievements.

Rehearsals

Decide on a date at the end of the year that is convenient for the performance and schedule at least two rehearsals before then. Rehearsals can take place during class time or, if possible, you can arrange extra lessons for rehearsals.

Before allocating roles, allow pupils to listen to the play on the recording all the way through and to follow the script in their books at the same time. Ask pupils why the play is called *Surprise!* (*because Kate's family and friends throw a surprise birthday party for her*) Ask them how Kate feels in Scene 1 (*sad*) and how she feels in Scene 2 (*happy*).

Play the recording again in sections and ask pupils to take turns to read different parts of the script. Do this several times so that pupils become familiar with the script and make a note of any vocabulary and structures that they have problems with. Do remedial work on these points before the performance or adapt them to your class's ability if you think they are too challenging, but make sure pupils make a note of any changes you make to the script.

Allocate the roles and ask pupils to practise their lines at home before the next rehearsal. Suggest that they practise in front of a mirror, a friend or a member of their family so that they can develop their confidence.

During the second rehearsal, put the characters into their positions and give them directions about where to stand and what to do while they say their lines. Ask pupils to pay attention to how their character is feeling in each section and to act it out. Once pupils have practised their lines in position a few times, encourage them to learn each section by heart. Tell pupils to highlight their lines on the script to help them to do this.

The story

It's Saturday morning and it's Kate's birthday. She speaks to Jake on the phone and is disappointed that he doesn't remember it's her birthday. Then she realises that Robbie and her dad don't remember it's her birthday and she feels very sad. Her dad tells her to go to her grandma's house, as this is what she always does on Saturday afternoons. Kate does what her dad tells her to do, but she feels very, very sad. Nobody wishes her 'happy birthday' and she doesn't get any presents. While Kate is at her grandma's, her family and friends prepare a surprise party for her. When she comes home from her grandma's she finds everyone at her house and everything ready for the party. They wish her 'happy birthday' and give her presents. Kate is very happy.

Characters

Kate
Jake
Mandy
Robbie
Kate's dad
Kate's mum
Friends

Props and materials

- 2 telephones
- a chair
- a pair of trainers for Robbie
- a toy dog
- a table with a colourful table cloth, drinks and party cups
- party hats, balloons, decorations, presents
- a birthday cake

Preparing the set and the props

The set and props for the play are simple and shouldn't require a lot of preparation or expense. Pupils can make party hats by cutting out cones from cardboard, colouring them and stapling the ends together. Presents can be made by wrapping empty boxes with colourful paper and sticking bows and ribbons on them. Decorations can be made by cutting triangles out of coloured paper and stapling them to string to hang on the walls. A birthday cake can either be made out of coloured cardboard or you could ask one of the parents to make a real cake so that the cast can eat it after the performance. The table cloth, cups and drinks can be brought from home by yourself or various pupils.

Scene 1

In Scene 1, the story takes place in two different places – Kate's living room and Jake's living room. It's not necessary to have two separate rooms on stage. The characters can be at different ends of the stage or can be fairly close to each other but not facing each other, to give the impression that they're speaking on the phone and not directly to each other. There should be a small table in each living room for the telephones. Use mobile phones if you can't provide ordinary house phones.

There should be at least one chair in Kate's living room for Robbie to come and sit down on and his trainers should be behind this chair from the beginning. The table that will be used for the party can also be there from the beginning, but there shouldn't be anything for the party on it.

Scene 2

As soon as Kate leaves for her grandma's, the rest of the cast and any pupils who don't want to have a speaking role can come on stage and prepare Kate's living room for the party. The audience can see these preparations happening.

Costumes

The play doesn't require any special costumes to be made. Kate can wear casual clothes throughout the play and shouldn't have a costume change. Jake, Mandy, Robbie and Kate's dad can wear casual clothes in Scene 1, but can change into party clothes for Scene 2. Pupils can provide their own clothes, but you might like to suggest that the pupil who plays Kate's dad wears a tie so that it's clear that he's an adult.

Promotion

Pupils who don't want to perform can also be responsible for promoting the play. They can design and make posters to hang up on the school walls to inform fellow pupils when and where the play will take place. They can also design invitations to give to pupils' family and friends.

Listening script

Introduction
The Alphabet
B
1. B-O-Y
2. C-A-R
3. D-E-S-K
4. H-O-R-S-E
5. P-E-N-C-I-L
6. S-C-H-O-O-L

Colours

On Planet Od, the trees are purple and the flowers are yellow. There is a pink duck. The sun is red and the sky is grey. The dogs are green and white and the birds are orange. The car is brown. Ziggy and Bleck live on Planet Od. Ziggy is blue and Bleck is red.

Unit 1
Lesson 1

This is a picture of my friends. Becky is twelve. She's tall with fair hair and she's very nice. The other girl is Jane. She's thirteen. She's short with dark hair. Jane is very clever! Jack and Sam are cousins. Jack is fourteen years old. He's the tall boy with the dark hair. And this is Sam. He's very young. He's 6 years old and he's short with fair hair. He's funny! Oh, and that's Rocky! He's my dog and he's my friend too.

Lesson 2

Uncle Peter is my mum's brother. He's thirty five years old. He's tall. His hair is dark and his eyes are blue. He's very nice to me and my sister. He can do funny tricks too!

Aunt Jenny is his wife. She's young – she's twenty-eight years old. She's short with fair hair. Aunt Jenny is very clever. She's a scientist.

Tina is their daughter and of course, she's my cousin. She's very young. She's only 3 years old.

Unit 2
Lesson 1

1
Boy I've got all my toys in here. Look Vicky! This is my teddy bear.
Girl Has it got a name?
Boy Of course! It's Bruno.

2
Girl Is he very old Robin?
Boy Yes, he's ten years old!
Girl But … you're ten years old too! Are you very old?
Boy Oh, very funny. No, I'm not!

3
Girl OK. Sorry! What have you got in that box?
Boy Oh, just three board games. I don't play those now.
Girl Why not?
Boy They aren't my favourite things now. I've got lots of new computer games. They're great!

4
Boy This is my new skateboard.
Girl Wow! It's cool. I've got one too.
Boy Really? That's amazing!

5
Girl But what's your favourite thing?
Boy My favourite thing is in the garden.
Girl What is it?
Boy It's red and it's very fast!
Girl Ha! Ha! OK. It's your bike!
Boy That's right!

Lesson 2

Helen It's my brother's birthday on Friday.
Oliver Really?
Helen This is Tom's birthday present.
Oliver What is it?
Helen Guess!
Oliver It's a CD.
Helen No! It's a book.
Oliver A book? Not a very exciting present.
Helen Yes, it is! It's a book of tricks. It's really funny.
Oliver OK, OK. Where's it from?
Helen There's a new toy shop near my house. It's got books and computer games too.
Oliver Has it got DVDs?
Helen Yes, but Tom's got lots of DVDs.
Oliver Has he got the DVD of 'Shrek 3'?
Helen Er … no. That's a good idea!
Oliver So where is this shop …?

Lesson 3

1
Boy 1 Come on Becky. It's my turn!
Girl 1 OK, OK.
Boy 1 Look, Becky.
Girl 1 Wow! – 260. That's great!

2
Girl 1 Can I have a go on that?
Boy 1 Well er …
Girl 1 It's OK, I'm really good.
Boy 1 Hey, slow down! Oh no. Are you OK?

3
Boy 2 It's your turn now, John.
Boy 1 OK. Six! One, two, three, four, five, six.
Boy 2 Oh … you're in front now.
Boy 1 Yes, I'm good at this.

4
Girl 1 Ready, Jane?
Girl 2 Yes.
Girl 1 Catch! Well done!
Girl 2 Now it's your turn, Kim.
Girl 1 Oh no!
Man Hey! Who ….?
Girl 2 Sorry!

Unit 3
Lesson 1

Lesson 1

Teacher	Where is Italy? Does anyone know? Yes, Helen?
Girl 1	It's next to France, Miss.
Teacher	That's right. Where is it on the map?
Girl 1	Here, Miss Brown.
Teacher	Well done!

Lesson 2

Boy 1	This is really difficult.
Girl 2	No, it isn't!
Boy 1	OK, what's the answer?
Girl 2	12 x 6 + 27 − 9 = 90.
Boy 1	Yeah, very clever. You've got a calculator!

Lesson 3

Boy 2	What's that in your picture?
Girl 1	It's a beach. That's the sea.
Boy 2	Where?
Girl 1	There.
Boy 2	But that's red.
Girl 1	Yes.
Boy 2	Why red?
Girl 1	Because I don't like the colour blue!

Lesson 4

Boy 1	I don't like this game. And I never have the ball.
Boy 2	Yeah. And it's cold! What time is it?
Boy 1	Three o'clock. Ouch!
Teacher	Jones! Are you OK?
Boy 1	Er, yes Sir. I think so.

Lesson 2

My name's Eleanor and I'm from England. What do I like about school? Well, I like my teachers. They're all very nice. I like school lunches too – some children don't like the food. But I don't like my school uniform. It's grey and white and it isn't very nice!

I'm Paola and I'm from Mexico. School … well, I like computer lessons, but I don't like maths. I also like English lessons, but I don't like tests! And I don't like homework! Of course I do my homework every day. Well, not every day.

I'm Rashid and I'm from India. I like lots of things about my school! I like my school uniform. It's blue and white and it's cool. I like my lessons and I also like homework because then I don't do boring jobs at home. Oh! There's one bad thing about school! Tests!

Unit 4
Lesson 1

Have I got any hobbies? Well, I play the guitar but I'm not very good at it! On Mondays I have a music lesson with my teacher Mr Pane. On Tuesdays I go ice-skating with my friends. It's cold there, but it's fun! On Wednesdays I don't go out. I stay at home and read my comics. Asterix is my favourite because it's very funny! On Thursdays I go to my friend's house. Jim and I look at his stamps. He's got some amazing stamps. He collects stamps from different countries. And on Fridays? On Fridays I stay at home and I watch TV!

Lesson 2

Vicky	Hey, Rachel. Let's go to the amusement park today.
Rachel	Oh, I don't like those parks. I'm always scared on the rides!
Vicky	Well let's go to the cinema then.
Rachel	Is there a good film on?
Vicky	Yes. There's a new film with Tom Cruise. It's really exciting.
Rachel	Oh no. Not Tom Cruise!
Vicky	Why don't you like him?
Rachel	His films are always boring. I know, Vicky. We can watch a DVD here.
Vicky	But I want to go out!
Rachel	OK then, we can go to the park.
Vicky	It's cold there Rachel!
Vicky	That's my mobile phone. I've got a message from Emma.
Rachel	Is she at home.?
Vicky	No, she's at the Internet café near the school. She's with Jane. Great! I can go out with my friends now.
Rachel	But what am I …?
Vicky	Have fun with your DVD Rachel! Bye!

Lesson 3

Welcome to Star Cinemas. Saturday 16th June.
In Star Cinema 1: 'My Crazy Family' with Robbie Williams and Jennifer Lopez. A very funny film about a very strange family! For all the family.
Times: 6.30 pm and 9 pm

In Star Cinema 2: 'The Winner' with Daniel Allen. Mike is good at one thing and he wants to be a winner. Can he win the swimming competition? An exciting new film for children.
Times: 4pm and 7pm

Ring 0800 224675 for more information

Unit 5
Lesson 1

Jan	It's my birthday on Saturday.
Toby	I know!
Jan	Let's have a party!
Toby	Really? That's fantastic! I can help you.
Jan	OK. Great! Can you make some invitations on your computer?
Toby	Yes, of course. Do we need a lot?
Jan	No, only about 20.
Toby	I can bring some of my CDs for music.
Jan	No, don't need any. I've got lots of CDs here.
Toby	All right. I can bring my camera then.
Jan	No, it's OK. I've got a new camera.
Toby	OK. Have you got any balloons?
Jan	No, I haven't. Good idea!
Toby	I can buy lots of balloons and birthday hats.
Jan	Oh thanks a lot.
Toby	And a cake! Let's buy a big cake!
Jan	Why? I can make one!
Toby	Wow! OK. Do we need anything else?

Lesson 2

1

Woman	What's your costume, Suzy?
Girl	I've got a beautiful long dress and my husband is a king.

2

Woman Is your costume good, Nicky?

Girl Yes, it is. <u>I've got black clothes and a big black hat.</u> <u>My hair is long and grey. I can do magic but I'm not</u> <u>a magician.</u>

3

Woman Mel, have you got a good costume?

Boy Yes, it's great. <u>I've got a mask and my body is green.</u> I'm not a lizard but <u>little children are scared of me!</u>

4

Woman Sam, tell me about your costume.

Boy <u>I've got a big red nose and orange hair. I've also got</u> <u>funny clothes and very big shoes!</u>

Unit 6

Lesson 1

1 **What is delicious?**

Girl Mmm. <u>This is delicious!</u>

Boy What? The food?

Girl <u>No, the orange juice.</u>

2 **What does the boy want?**

Waiter What would you like?

Boy <u>A burger, please.</u>

Waiter <u>Do you want chips with it?</u>

Boy <u>No</u>, thanks.

3 **What does the waiter bring?**

Waiter Would you like some dessert?

Woman <u>No, but can we have the bill</u>, please?

Waiter <u>Yes, of course. Here you are.</u>

Woman Thank you. That's 25 euros.

Waiter That's right. Thank you.

4 **What does the woman want?**

Boy I'm hungry. Let's go to 'Freddie's' for a meal.

Woman I'm not very hungry. <u>I just want a snack.</u>

Boy OK, <u>you can have a sandwich there</u>. Is that OK?

Woman That's fine.

5 **What does the girl want?**

Man Do you want a dessert?

Girl <u>Yes, I'd like some ice cream</u>. What about you?

Man No, I just want a glass of water.

Lesson 2

Boy What do we need for the picnic?

Girl Let's make a list.

Boy OK. I want some egg sandwiches. Have we got any eggs?

Girl We've only got a few. <u>Buy some eggs.</u>

Boy OK. Do we need any bread?

Girl No, we've got a lot of bread. <u>But we haven't got many</u> <u>apples.</u>

Boy <u>OK, apples. How many do we need?</u>

Girl Er, four or five.

Boy OK. What about bananas?

Girl No, we've got a lot of bananas, so don't buy any.

Boy OK. Is that all?

Girl Yes! Well, ... er. <u>I want some chocolate!</u>

Boy <u>OK, chocolate.</u>

Girl That's all I think.

Lesson 3

Fast Pizza

This is a great recipe for a delicious pizza. It's quick and easy. Try it and surprise your friends and family. For this recipe you need four eggs, 10 slices of bread, 10 slices of cheese, 10 slices of meat, two tomatoes, and some butter. You also need an oven pan, so ask your mum for one. <u>First you put the butter all over</u> <u>the bottom of the pan.</u> <u>Then you put the slices of bread in the</u> <u>pan.</u> These go one next to the other. <u>After that you put the slices</u> <u>of meat on top of the bread</u> and <u>then the slices of cheese.</u> <u>Then</u> <u>you cut the tomatoes into slices and put them on top of the</u> <u>cheese.</u> <u>Beat the eggs and pour the mixture over the pizza.</u> Ask your mum for help with the oven. Finally, put the pan in the oven and wait 15 minutes. The pizza is then ready.

Unit 7

Lesson 1

1

Girl Wow! <u>Look at the horses!</u>

Boy Yes. They're very fast.

Girl Oh, no! That girl's falling off. Is she OK?

2

Boy Here they come! That man's winning.

Girl Who? <u>The man on the red bike?</u>

Boy Yes. <u>He's also wearing a black helmet</u>.

3

Boy <u>Ouch! My feet!</u>

Girl <u>We're nearly there</u>. Are you OK?

Boy Not really but can I have some water?

Girl Yes, here you are.

4

Boy It's a fantastic day today.

Girl Yes. <u>The sea is beautiful</u>.

Boy <u>Can you see the boats?</u>

Girl Yes, and look! <u>Dad's boat is winning!</u>

5

Girl <u>I'm scared! I don't want to fall!</u>

M <u>Don't look down! Put your foot here</u> ... that's it. Well done.

Girl Phew!

Lesson 2

Boy Remember I can only answer 'yes' or 'no' to your questions.

Girl OK.

Boy I'm ready.

Girl OK, my first question. <u>Are you a woman?</u>

Boy <u>No.</u>

Girl OK, that means you're a man. Are you a singer?

Boy No.

Girl Are you a sports person?

Boy Yes!

Girl OK, a sports person. <u>Are you a tennis player?</u>

Boy <u>No.</u>

Girl Are you a footballer?

Boy Yes.

Girl <u>Are you English?</u>

Boy <u>Yes.</u>

Girl	OK. You're an English footballer. <u>Are you living in England now?</u>
Boy	<u>No.</u>
Girl	<u>Is your wife a famous singer?</u>
Boy	<u>Yes.</u>
Girl	I know! You're David Beckham!

Unit 8
Lesson 1

1

Man	<u>Tell me about your home, Jill.</u>
Jill	Well, my home is really nice. <u>It's a flat</u> near the city centre.
Man	Is it a big flat?
Jill	<u>Yes, it's got six rooms.</u>
Man	Has it got a nice view?
Jill	Well, er … it's on a big street, but <u>we also have a nice view of a small park.</u> I often go and play with my dog there.

2

Man	<u>Do you like your home, Carl?</u>
Carl	Yes, it's great.
Man	Is it a flat or a house?
Carl	No, it isn't a flat or a house. <u>I live in a houseboat on the River Thames!</u>
Man	Really? How many rooms has it got?
Carl	It's small – <u>there are only four rooms.</u>
Man	And has it got a good view?
Carl	Of course it has. <u>It's got a great view of the river!</u> It's also next to a great park.

3

Man	<u>What's your home like, Eve?</u>
Eve	<u>It's a house near a nice beach.</u>
Man	Is it big?
Eve	Yes, <u>it's got ten rooms.</u> There is also a swimming pool behind the house.
Man	You're a lucky girl. And has it got a nice view?
Eve	Yes, it has. <u>From all the bedrooms you can see the sea.</u>

Lesson 2

1

My job is very difficult. I am scared sometimes. <u>I need lots of water for my job.</u> <u>I wear red clothes and a helmet.</u> <u>I also drive a big red truck.</u>

2

<u>I'm in my car for many hours every day.</u> <u>I take people to different places in the city.</u> I meet many different people in my job. Some of them are nice and friendly, but some aren't!

3

<u>People come to me when they're sick.</u> They <u>tell me what the problem is and I give them some medicine.</u> I sometimes go to sick people's houses.

4

I'm very lucky because I've got a great job. <u>You know my face because I'm often on TV.</u> <u>I've got a lot of fans</u> and I make a lot of money!

5

<u>I work in a clothes shop.</u> I like my job because I love clothes but I must stand up all day and this is bad for my feet. The shop is very busy on Saturdays.

Lesson 3

Presenter	Hello and welcome to 'What do you know?' Our two teams today are from Layton School in Nottingham …
1st group of children	Hello.
Presenter	And St John's School in Brighton.
2nd group of children	Hello.
Presenter	So, you know the rules. Let's start with the first question. <u>Where are the Pyramids?</u> Are they a in India, b … Amy, from St John's School.
Girl 1	<u>In Egypt.</u>
Presenter	Correct, Amy. That's three points for St John's. Question number 2. This is an easy one. <u>In which city is Euro Disney?</u> Darren from Layton School.
Boy	<u>It's in Paris.</u>
Presenter	Correct! Euro Disney is in Paris. Three points to Layton School. Question 3 now. <u>Where is the White House?</u> Is it a in Scotland, b in the USA or … Helen from Layton School.
Girl 2	It's in Scotland.
Presenter	Wrong! St John's School, can you answer the question for two points?
Boy 2	<u>Yes, it's in the USA.</u>
Presenter	Correct, that's two points for St John's. Question 4. <u>Which city is the capital of Germany?</u> Is it a Berlin, b Frankfurt or c Bonn? Harry from St John's School.
Boy 3	The capital of Germany is Bonn.
Presenter:	I'm sorry, Harry, it isn't. Layton School, can you answer the question?
Girl 3	<u>Yes, it's Berlin.</u>
Presenter	Correct! Two points to Layton School. The score at the moment is St John's School 5 points, Layton School 5 points! And this is the last question! Ready everyone? <u>What tells the time in London?</u> Is it a Little John, b Big Brother or c. Lucy, Layton School.
Girl 1	<u>Big Ben.</u>
Presenter	Correct! Big Ben is a clock! 3 points to Layton School! And Layton School are the winners. Congratulations! That's all we've got time for now ….

Unit 9
Lesson 1

1   **Which picture shows the hotel?**

Boy	Was your holiday good?
Girl	Yes, it was great.
Boy	Where was the hotel?
Girl	It <u>was next to the beach and there was a great view of the sea.</u> <u>There weren't any trees, but there were lots of flowers.</u>

2   **Where is the passport?**

Woman	<u>Where's my passport?</u> It isn't in my bag.
Man	It was on the table a few minutes ago.
Woman	Well, it's not there now.
Man	Well, have a look in your bedroom.
Woman	It's OK, I've got it. <u>It's on the bed.</u>

3 **What does the girl's mother want to buy?**

Mother Let's go shopping. I need a new swimsuit for my holiday.

Girl Have you got any sunglasses?

Mother No, I want to buy some sunglasses too.

Girl Me too Mum, but I also want some sun cream.

Unit 9

Lesson 2

1

M Tickets, please. Thank you.

Girl Which platform do I need for Victoria station?

M Platform 6.

Girl Thanks. Is Victoria the first station?

M No, it isn't. There are two stops before that.

Girl Thanks.

2

W I think this is the wrong road.

M Me too.

W Can I see the map?

M Yes, here you are. I think we're here.

W Let's ask that man over there.

M Excuse me! Where is Amber Road?

3

Girl We're moving!

Boy Mmm. Look at all the people down there.

Girl Yeah, and look at the water! We've got a great view up here.

4

W Can I see your passport and ticket please?

M Yes, here you are.

W I'm sorry but your flight is leaving at 6.30 and not 6.00.

M Oh, no!

W And how many suitcases have you got?

M Two, and this bag. Can I take it with me?

W Yes, but you must put it above or under your seat.

5

Boy I'm cold.

Girl Me too.

Boy What time is it?

Girl Quarter to nine.

Boy Where is it?

Girl It's late!

Boy Let's take a taxi.

Girl No, we haven't got much money. We can walk.

Boy No! I hate walking. Let's wait.

Unit 10

Lesson 1

G1 Let's do the pop quiz in this magazine.

G2 OK.

G1 Right, first question. Where is Kylie Minogue from? Australia, England or the USA?

G2 That's easy. Australia!

G1 Correct. I didn't know that. Now let's see the next question. It's about Robbie Williams.

G2 Oh, I don't know much about him. What's the question?

G1 Which pop group did he sing in? 'Boyzone', 'Take That' or 'Steps'?

G2 Er ….

G1 Guess!

G2 OK, 'Steps'.

G1 Wrong! It was 'Take That'. I knew that because my sister has all their CDs. OK, question 3. Who sang the song 'Baby one more time'?

G2 Oh, what's her name? I know that song. Er …

G1 Was it Madonna …

G2 No, it wasn't her.

G1 … Christina Aguilera or Britney Spears.

G2 The last one! Britney Spears!

G1 Yes! It was Britney Spears. Question 4. Did Greece win the Eurovision Song Contest in 2004, 2005 or 2006?

G2 I can't remember. I think it was 2006.

G1 No! It was 2005!

G2 Oh, OK. What's the last question?

G1 Which singer was in the pop group 'Destiny's Child'? Avril Lavigne, Beyonce or Shakira?

G2 Well it wasn't Shakira. I think it was Beyonce.

G1 Well done! You scored 3 out of 5 correct. Not bad!

G2 Thanks. Now it's my turn.

Lesson 2

Boy Let's go to the DVD Club and get some films out tonight.

Girl OK. That's a good idea. We can watch them at the weekend.

Later, in the DVD Club.

Boy Look! This is a good film.

Girl What's the name of it?

Boy 'The Green Mile'. It's a film about …

Girl Oh no. That's a sad film. I don't like dramas. What about this? It's with Keanu Reeves.

Boy Oh yes, I know him. He was in the film 'Matrix'. Is it an adventure film?

Girl No, it isn't. It's a love story.

Boy I don't want to watch that! I hate love stories!

Girl Well, how about this then? It is really funny.

Boy OK, I like comedies.

Girl Me too. I always laugh with Jim Carrey.

Boy Yeah, he's great. Let's get this then.

Girl This one looks good too.

Boy But it's got singing and dancing in it. Boring!

Girl Well which other one do you want then?

Boy This one, 'Mission Impossible 3'.

Girl Well I don't usually like adventure films. They're all the same.

Boy But Craig says it's really exciting!

Girl Oh, OK then. Let's get these two.

Lesson 3

Man	OK, thank you Amber. That was very good.
Woman	How old are you Amber?
Amber	I'm ten.
Woman	And when did you start playing the piano?
Amber	When I was eight.
Man	Do you have piano lessons, Amber?
Amber	Yes. My mum's a music teacher.
Man	OK, thanks Amber. We're giving you a score of 9! Well done!
Amber	Thanks!
Woman	Well, Damian. That was amazing. Do you only dance hip hop?
Damian	No, I go to a dance school and we learn many other dances too.
Man	You've got talent, Damian. How old are you?
Damian	Nine.
Man	Well done, Damian. You were very calm.
Woman	The audience loved it too. Do you practise a lot?
Damian	Yes, every day. My dance teacher, Mr Simms, helps me a lot. He's very good.
Woman	Your score is 10.
Man	OK, Damian, you're on the show!
Damian	Oh! Thank you very much. That's fantastic!

Unit 11
Lesson 1

Presenter	Today in 'Animal Magic' we're talking about an animal that a lot of people find quite scary: the crocodile! Peter Horn knows a lot about crocodiles. Hello Peter. Welcome to our show.
Peter	Thanks. Hello.
Presenter	So Peter, why are crocodiles interesting?
Peter	Well, because they are very clever animals. They're also big, strong and, yes, a bit scary!
Presenter	How big are crocodiles then?
Peter	Some crocodiles are 6 metres long!
Presenter	Wow! And are crocodiles really dangerous to people?
Peter	Well, crocodiles usually eat other animals, but hungry crocodiles sometimes kill people, yes.
Presenter	What else do they eat?
Peter	They eat a lot of fish, birds, snakes, and they also eat very big animals. Zebras, and lions, for example!
Presenter	But those are bigger than crocodiles!
Peter	I know! It's amazing!
Presenter	Where do crocodiles live?
Peter	In many places all over the world, like Australia, India, America, and Africa. They live in the sea, rivers and lakes. And they live for a long time – up to 60 years.
Presenter	Well thanks for talking to us, Peter …

Lesson 2

Man	OK, Lucy, what do you want for your birthday?
Lucy	I want a pet! Let's have a look in the pet shop.
Man	OK … Oh look! This mouse is cute.
Lucy	Oh no, mice are boring.
Man	Well, I know. What about a rabbit? They're the easiest pets. They live outside.
Lucy	No, I don't like rabbits. But this puppy is beautiful!
Man	Yes, but puppies aren't the best pets.
Lucy	Why?
Man	Well, they need a lot of exercise.
Lucy	That's OK. I can take it for walks.
Man	Mmm. But there's another problem.
Lucy	What?
Man	Your mum doesn't like dogs.
Lucy	Oh. Well, what about a kitten?
Man	No, we can't have a cat.
Lucy	Why not?
Man	Cats eat fish and your brother's got a goldfish.
Lucy	Well what pet can I have?
Man	Er, I don't know. Maybe I can get you a new computer game for your birthday …
Lucy	Oh Dad!

Unit 12
Lesson 1

1

Boy	Wow! Look! Everything's white.
Girl	Fantastic! Let's go and make a snowman in the garden.
Mum	Just a minute! Put some warm clothes on. It's cold out there.
Boy	Oh come on Mum! It's nice and sunny.

2

Girl 1	We can't go to the beach today. Look at the weather!
Girl 2	Never mind. Let's go for a walk in the park.
Girl 1	But I don't want to get wet!
Girl 2	We can take our umbrellas!

3

Boy 1	Look at the weather! That man's hat is in the air! He can't catch it.
Boy 2	Oh yes! Ha ha! That's so funny. Oh no! My ticket for the concert is going to fly into the lake.
Boy 1	Run or you aren't going to go to the concert!
Boy 2	Help me!
Boy 1	I can't catch it!

4

Girl	Bye Mum!
Mum	Bye! Enjoy your swim. And don't forget to put sun cream on.
Girl	No, Mum.
Mum	And drink lots of water.
Girl	Yes, Mum.
Mum	And wear a hat on the beach.
Girl	Yes, Mum.
Mum	And don't be late.
Girl	No, Mum. Bye Mum.

Lesson 2

Are you bored with beach holidays? Then have a holiday at Nature Parks Holiday Centres this summer!

There are Nature Parks in five beautiful places in the UK. You will stay in wooden huts next to a lake and eat your meals in one of our 'Lakeside View' restaurants.

There are lots of things to do at Nature Parks. You can go walking or cycling in the forest. At some Nature Parks near the mountains you can also go mountain climbing. And why not learn something new while you're here? Choose from horse riding, dancing and tennis lessons. They're all free!

You won't have a problem with bad weather at Nature Parks either. At our beautiful indoor swimming pool, it's always nice and warm!

What are you waiting for? Call Nature Parks on 0800 450000 now!

Lesson 3

Man Do you know the story about the sun and the wind?
Girl No, I don't.
Man OK, I'll tell you because it's a good story. The wind and the sun are talking one day. The wind says he's stronger than the sun. OK, says the sun, how strong are you? I'll show you, says the wind. A man is walking down the street and he's wearing a hat. And the wind says to the sun: Do you see that man? I'm going to make his hat come off. OK, says the sun, let's see. So the wind tries to make the man's hat come off. He blows and he blows but the hat doesn't come off. The man holds it on his head.
Girl And then what happens?
Man The sun says, OK, now it's my turn. The sun shines and the man gets hot. He gets hotter and hotter and then he takes his hat off. That's the end of the story.
Girl So the sun was stronger than the wind in the end!
Man Yes.

Cartoon DVD Worksheet 1

Unit 1

Before you watch

Look at page 12 of Wonderful World 3 Pupil's Book and do the task below.

1 Point to the children and say their names.
2 Point to Uncle Oliver.
3 Where are the children?

While you watch

Who says these things? Tick (✓).

	Jake	Mandy	Kate	Robbie	Uncle Oliver
1. What's that?					
2. What a stupid trick!					
3. Hi! This is cool!					
4. We're on holiday here.					
5. Kate's crazy about science.					
6. Good idea, Jake.					

After you watch

Answer the questions below about Episode 1 of *The Cortuga Mystery*.

1 Who is in the water?

_____

2 Who are cousins?

_____

3 Who is sorry?

_____

4 Who has got a towel?

_____

5 Where is Uncle Oliver's house?

_____

6 What's Kate crazy about?

_____

7 Who has got a good idea?

_____

Cartoon DVD Worksheet 2

Unit 2

Before you watch

Look at page 20 of Wonderful World 3 Pupil's Book and answer the questions.

1 Where are the children?

_____

2 Why are they there?

_____

While you watch

Watch the DVD and complete the sentences with these words.

laptop   lizard   message   mystery   strange

1 He's got some _____ things!

2 That's Uncle Oliver's pet _____ , Henry.

3 I've got a _____ on my mobile phone.

4 This is a great _____ . Have you got any computer games?

5 Find the pieces and then see the answer to the _____ .

After you watch

Answer the questions.

1 Who has got a pet?

_____

2 Who has got a message on his mobile phone?

_____

3 Where is Uncle Oliver?

_____

4 Has Uncle Oliver's laptop got any computer games?

_____

5 What has Mandy got?

_____

6 Has she got all the pieces of the puzzle?

_____

7 Who is scared?

_____

Cartoon DVD Worksheet 3

Unit 3

Before you watch

Look at page 30 of Wonderful World 3 Pupil's Book and answer the questions.

1 Where do you think the children are?

_____

2 What is strange?

_____

While you watch

Watch the DVD and number the sentences in the correct order.

a It's a piece of the puzzle! ☐

b Hey! We're in a school. ☐

c Please have this! ☐

d It's 1885! ☐

e It's just a calculator. ☐

f That teacher isn't very nice. ☐

After you watch

A Answer the questions.

1 What year is it?

_____

2 Who isn't good at maths?

_____

3 What does Jake give the boy?

_____

B Choose the correct answer.

1 Tom is from the past / the future.

2 153 is the answer / date to a sum.

3 Tom / The teacher isn't very nice.

4 Tom thinks calculators are correct / magic machines.

5 Tom / Robbie has got a piece of the puzzle.

Cartoon DVD Worksheet 4

Unit 4

Before you watch

Look at page 38 of Wonderful World 3 Pupil's Book and answer the questions.

1 What do the children get at the end of Episode 3?

_____

2 Where are the children now?

_____

3 What is the new girl's name?

_____

While you watch

Watch the DVD and number the pictures in the correct order.

After you watch

Write T (True) or F (False).

1 The children haven't got any Chinese money. ☐

2 The kite competition is tomorrow. ☐

3 Ling's uncle has got a shop. ☐

4 Ling makes a kite. ☐

5 The kite is beautiful. ☐

6 Ling doesn't win the competition. ☐

7 The prize is a new kite. ☐

Cartoon DVD Worksheet 5

Unit 5

Before you watch

Look at page 48 of Wonderful World 3 Pupil's Book and answer the questions.

1 Where do the children go to in Episodes 2 and 3 of *The Cortuga Mystery?*

_____

2 Where do you think the children are now?

_____

While you watch

Who says these things? Tick (✓).

	Jake	Mandy	Kate	Robbie	Boy
1. There aren't any people here.					
2. Now Mandy's got red paint on her!					
3. It's that boy! Quick, catch him!					
4. Don't throw paint, please.					
5. We have paint fights.					
6. Good shot, Kate!					

After you watch

Choose the correct answer.

1 It is very cold / hot in India.

2 Robbie's clothes have got blue / red paint on them.

3 The boy throws colour / paint.

4 It's the Festival of Colour in Japan / India.

5 The festival is fun / boring.

6 The piece of the puzzle is in the paint / stall.

Cartoon DVD Worksheet 6

Unit 6

Before you watch

Look at page 56 of Wonderful World 3 Pupil's Book and answer the questions.

1 Where do the children go to in Episode 5 of The Cortuga Mystery?

_____

2 Where do you think the children are now?

_____

While you watch

Watch the DVD and complete the sentences with these words.

| amazing | chewing gum | delicious | fast food | menu | tasty |

1 We're in the future! _____!

2 Look, there's a _____ restaurant over there!

3 There aren't many things on the _____ .

4 But real food is _____!

5 Yes, but these pills aren't _____ . Yuk!

6 It's called _____ . Here you are.

After you watch

Answer the questions.

1 Where do the children go to eat?

_____

2 Who helps the children in the restaurant?

_____

3 What do people eat in the future?

_____

4 Where is a piece of the jigsaw?

_____

5 Why can't the waiter move his hands?

_____

Cartoon DVD Worksheet 7

Unit 7

Before you watch

Look at page 66 of Wonderful World 3 Pupil's Book and answer the questions.

1 Who do the children meet in Episode 6?

_____

2 How many pieces of the puzzle have the children got now?

_____

3 Where are the children now?

_____

While you watch

Watch the DVD and number the sentences in the correct order.

a But this boy is also the winner. ☐

b Get ready, set, go! ☐

c Those people are having a picnic. ☐

d Go, Jake, go! ☐

e OK. Put your eggs on your spoons. ☐

f Let's enter the egg and spoon race. ☐

After you watch

Write T (True) or F (False).

1 The children are at a sports centre. ☐

2 Mandy and Kate don't enter the race. ☐

3 Simon is number 4. ☐

4 Jake pushes Simon. ☐

5 Robbie's egg falls off his spoon. ☐

6 Jake and Simon win the race. ☐

Cartoon DVD Worksheet 8

Unit 8

Before you watch

Look at page 74 of Wonderful World 3 Pupil's Book and answer the questions.

1 Where are the children now?

_____

2 Who do they meet?

_____

While you watch

Watch the DVD and number the pictures in the correct order.

After you watch

Answer the questions.

1 What do the children see from the Tower of London?

_____

2 Who works in the Tower of London?

_____

3 How old is the Tower of London?

_____

4 Who lives in the Tower of London?

_____

5 What is the knight doing?

_____

6 Who's wearing the knight's costume?

_____

Cartoon DVD Worksheet 9

Unit 9

Before you watch

Look at page 84 of Wonderful World 3 Pupil's Book and answer the questions.

1 Where are the children now?

_____

2 How do the children travel?

_____

While you watch

Who says these things? Tick (✓).

	Jake	Mandy	Kate	Robbie	Bedouin	Asim
1. There's a lot of sand here.						
2. Yes, of course. Come with us.						
3. We're riding camels.						
4. This is my family's tent.						
5. No, just some water for me.						
6. Yes, please! It's very important to us.						

After you watch

Answer the questions.

1 Who has got some sun cream?

_____

2 Whose camp do they go to?

_____

3 What are very tall?

_____

4 What does Robbie drink?

_____

5 What does Kate want to drink?

_____

6 Where is the piece of the jigsaw?

_____

120

Cartoon DVD Worksheet 10

Unit 10

Before you watch

Look at page 92 of Wonderful World 3 Pupil's Book and answer the questions.

1 Where are the children?

   a in a film studio   **b** at a concert

2 Who do they meet?

   a a famous actor   **b** a director

While you watch

Watch the DVD and circle the correct words.

1 We're in a concert / film studio!

2 Now, go and put on your costume / lines.

3 All actors please come to the set / dressing room.

4 Kate's got talent / dinner.

5 Can I have your acting / autograph?

6 The cameraman / director gave me this beautiful bag.

After you watch

Write T (True) or F (False).

1 The children see two cameramen. ☐

2 The director thinks Kate is an actor. ☐

3 Kate makes dinner. ☐

4 Kate hasn't got talent. ☐

5 The director gave Mandy a beautiful bag. ☐

6 The children can go home because they have got the last piece of the puzzle. ☐

Cartoon DVD Worksheet 11

Unit 11

Before you watch

Look at page 102 of Wonderful World 3 Pupil's Book and answer the questions.

1 How many pieces of the puzzle have the children got?

_____

2 Where is Kate putting a torch and binoculars?

_____

While you watch

Watch the DVD and number the sentences in the correct order.

a Caves are full of horrible bats.   ☐

b Are we ready?   ☐

c We're back in Uncle Oliver's house!   ☐

d Let's stop for a few minutes.   ☐

e This cave is near Eagle Rock!   ☐

f Here, Henry, eat a worm!   ☐

After you watch

Answer the questions.

Who/What ...

1 ...is still in the same place in the hut?

_____

2 ...is good at puzzles?

_____

3 ...doesn't like bats?

_____

4 ...wants to make some sandwiches?

_____

5 ...gives the lizard food?

_____

6 ...is tired?

_____

Cartoon DVD Worksheet 12

Unit 12

Before you watch

Look at page 110 of Wonderful World 3 Pupil's Book and answer the questions.

1 Where are the children going?

_____

2 What do you think happens at the end of The Cortuga Mystery?

_____

While you watch

Watch the DVD and complete the sentences with these words.

| box   clouds   medallion   rainbow   switch on |

1 Look at the _____! It's going to rain.

2 _____ the torch, Robbie.

3 It's a gold _____! Jake, open it!

4 This is the lost _____ of Sethenca.

5 And there's a beautiful _____ in the sky.

After you watch

Answer the questions.

1 Why doesn't Mandy want it to rain?

_____

2 Where is the gold box?

_____

3 Who is also in the cave?

_____

4 How did Uncle Oliver find the children?

_____

5 What is inside the gold box?

_____

6 What are the children going to do now?

_____

Extra tasks for early finishers 1

Lesson 1

Find and circle ten words from Unit 1, Lesson 1.

A	N	S	H	A	R	K	O	L	E
C	O	U	S	I	N	T	U	P	D
L	P	B	D	Y	H	P	L	M	S
E	B	E	A	U	T	I	F	U	L
V	N	A	W	N	A	D	M	F	A
E	M	C	B	F	L	E	S	Y	S
R	D	T	E	R	L	T	T	O	B
E	A	F	A	I	R	V	U	U	X
F	F	R	C	E	B	N	P	N	K
C	L	I	H	N	G	U	I	G	J
F	R	E	I	D	D	I	D	E	A

1 _____
2 _____
3 _____
4 _____
5 _____
6 _____
7 _____
8 _____
9 _____
10 _____

Lesson 2

Complete the table with the correct subject pronouns and possessive adjectives.

Subject Pronouns	Possessive Adjectives
I	**1** _____
you	**2** _____
he	**3** _____
	her
4 _____	
it	**5** _____
	our
6 _____	
7 _____	your
they	**8** _____

Lesson 3

Circle the correct answers.

1 Michael is / Michael's mum's 30 years old.
2 This is the children's / childrens' room.
3 Is Karen your best friend. / ?
4 Parrots / Parrots' are very clever.
5 My names / name's Polly.
6 Dan's thirteen year's / years old.

 **Lesson 1**

Look at the Vocabulary tasks on page 21 and complete the puzzle. Find the extra word.

	1			E			A		
2	E		D					R	
3 G									
	4		P		O				
5	K				O				
		6		B					
	7	O							

 **Lesson 2**

Find and circle ten words from Unit 2, Lesson 2.

```
L O B E X C I T I N G
P R E S S A N T C P L
I G K C X M E S E R V
A G L O B E C D S E O
N C H M J R A V K S R
O B S I C A M R A E W
W A T C H F N P T N W
E C O U N T R Y E T P
L T S C A R Y H S L U
```

1 _____
2 _____
3 _____
4 _____
5 _____
6 _____
7 _____
8 _____
9 _____
10 _____

 **Lesson 3**

Match.

My laptop is old	**a** and a macaw parrot.
Jane has got a pet lizard	**b** and scary.
There are trees	**c** but it's very good.
The Remote Controlled Tarantula is big	**d** but my friends like board games.
I'm crazy about scary DVDs	**e** and flowers in the park.

Extra tasks for early finishers 3

 **Lesson 1**

Write the school subject.

1 You learn about the world.   g _ _ _ _ _ _ _ _ _
2 You learn about the past.   h _ _ _ _ _ _ _
3 You learn about numbers.   m _ _ _ _ _
4 You learn grammar and vocabulary.   E _ _ _ _ _ _ _
5 You play games.   s _ _ _ _ _
6 You learn how to paint and draw.   a _ _
7 You learn how to sing.   m _ _ _ _ _
8 You learn about nature.   s _ _ _ _ _ _ _

 **Lesson 2**

Write questions and short answers using the Present Simple.

1 you / like / sport and music (✓)

_____

_____

2 Mary / draw / in art class (✓)

_____

_____

3 Sam / walk / to school (✗)

_____

_____

4 the children / have lunch / in the cafeteria (✓)

_____

_____

5 wear / a uniform / you (✗)

_____

_____

6 we / study / in the library (✗)

_____

_____

Lesson 3

Complete the sentences with these words.

> always   every   never   once   usually

1 Mark goes to the library _____ a week.
2 I _____ like scary DVDs, but I don't like Creepy Creatures.
3 Mrs Green loves songs. We _____ sing in her music lessons.
4 I don't like school and I _____ do my homework.
5 We have sport _____ day.

126

Extra tasks for early finishers 4

4 Lesson 1

Circle the correct words.

1 Whose / Who's lizard is this?
2 Where / What do you do in the afternoons?
3 When / What does school start?
4 Where / When are the stamps?
5 Who / What is your name?
6 Who / Whose likes ice skating?

4 Lesson 2

Choose the correct answers.

1 Tom can _____ the piano.
   a plays   **b** does play   **c** play

2 You _____ your mobile phone at school.
   a can't use   **b** can't   **c** not use

3 _____ to the amusement park?
   a I can go   **b** Can I go   **c** Can I

4 No! You _____ go on the Kingda rollercoaster.
   a can   **b** not   **c** can't

5 She can _____ dinner at the new restaurant.
   a has   **b** to have   **c** have

6 Yes, _____ a kite.
   a you can make   **b** can you make   **c** you can

4 Lesson 3

Complete the sentences with words from Unit 4, Lesson 3.

1 I always go b _ _ _ _ _ _ on Friday evenings.
2 Here's my email address. Let's be e-_ _ _ _.
3 Are you g _ _ _ at ice-skating?
4 This adventure film is very e _ _ _ _ _ _ _ _.
5 What do you like to do in your f _ _ _ t _ _ _?

Extra tasks for early finishers 5

5 Lesson 1

Look at the Vocabulary tasks on page 49 and complete the puzzle. Find the extra word.

```
                    1        A       D
                2  F                        A
        3   T            L
        4                K
                    5        L           O
            6                Y           T
                7  P
            8        A       H
    9   A   D
```

5 Lesson 2

Choose the correct answer.

1 The treasure hunt is _____ event.
   a –   **b** an   **c** a

2 Give us _____ clue!
   a –   **b** an   **c** a

3 I can hear _____ music.
   a –   **b** an   **c** a

4 Wow! I can win _____ prize.
   a –   **b** an   **c** a

5 There are _____ workshops in different places.
   a –   **b** an   **c** a

6 Let's buy _____ food for the street stalls.
   a –   **b** an   **c** a

5 Lesson 3

Circle the odd one out.

1 fireworks   candles   jokes
2 food   meal   presents
3 April Fool's Day   Bonfire Night   barbecue
4 November   April   Australia Day
5 picnic   teacher   test

128

 **Extra tasks for early finishers 6**

 **Lesson 1**

Match.

1 How much
2 I don't have many
3 Do you drink much
4 There are a lot
5 We've got lots of

a chips.
b burgers.
c food.
d is the meal?
e orange juice?

 **Lesson 2**

Complete the crossword.

Across

1 The meal you eat in the middle of the day.
5 You cut food with this.
7 The meal you eat in the morning.
9 This food has got holes in it.

Down

2 This is a cold drink.
3 This snack is brown and delicious
4 This is a yellow fruit.
6 You make sandwiches with this.
8 This drink has got leaves.
9 You drink from this.

 **Lesson 3**

Match.

1 What's your favourite food?
2 What about frogs' legs?
3 How often do you eat spaghetti?
4 Who makes lunch in your family?
5 Is paella healthy?

a Twice a week.
b My dad.
c Fish and chips.
d Yes, it is.
e They're horrible!

Extra tasks for early finishers 7

7 Lesson 1

Find 11 words from Unit 7, Lesson 1.

C	Y	C	L	I	N	G	P	M
O	S	M	R	H	X	W	R	A
N	E	W	U	M	F	P	J	O
G	W	I	N	N	E	R	P	T
R	U	N	N	I	N	G	T	S
A	W	E	E	S	F	D	R	O
T	T	R	R	A	C	E	O	S
U	R	I	B	I	L	N	P	D
L	O	D	F	L	I	G	H	M
A	P	I	C	I	M	F	Y	X
T	H	N	A	N	B	O	I	J
I	I	G	L	G	O	N	N	I
O	D	I	V	I	N	G	P	L
N	I	V	I	N	G	S	S	F
S	C	L	I	M	B	I	N	G

1 _____
2 _____
3 _____
4 _____
5 _____
6 _____
7 _____
8 _____
9 _____
10 _____
11 _____

7 Lesson 2

Write questions and short answers using the Present Continuous.

1 the boys / play / with their skateboards (✗) _____

2 the boxer / feel / sad (✗) _____

3 Kate / train / for the competition (✓) _____

4 you / swim / in the sea (✓) _____

5 we / win / the match (✗) _____

6 I / have fun (✓) _____

7 Lesson 3

Circle the odd one out.

1	champion	winner	coach
2	train	watch	practise
3	player	competition	match
4	team	players	fans
5	ice dancing	thai boxing	sumo wrestler

130

Extra tasks for early finishers 8

8 Lesson 1

Choose the correct answers.

1 Look! The dog _____ in the river!
   a swims **b** is swimming **c** it's swimming

2 I _____ clean my bedroom at the weekend.
   a usually **b** at the moment **c** now

3 _____ the tower at the moment?
   a Are they visiting **b** Do they visit **c** They are visiting

4 _____ in a beautiful houseboat on the river.
   a We live **b** We are living **c** Do we live

5 My dad _____ in the Tower of London.
   a works **b** working **c** are working

6 _____ you hear footsteps on the stairs?
   a Are **b** Is **c** Do

8 Lesson 2

Write the name of the person who says the sentences below.

1 You must brush your teeth twice a day.   d _ _ _ _ _ _

2 You must cut your hair once a month.   h _ _ _ _ _ _ _ _ _ _

3 You mustn't start fires.   f _ _ _ _ _ _ _ _ _ _

4 You must take this medicine three times a day. d _ _ _ _ _ _

5 You mustn't smoke in my car.   t _ _ _ d _ _ _ _ _ _

6 You mustn't walk up and down the plane.   p _ _ _ _ _

7 You must pay here.   s _ _ _ a _ _ _ _ _ _ _ _

8 You must be quiet in the theatre.   a _ _ _ _ _

8 Lesson 3

Circle the correct words.

1 You can visit the castle so / because it's open for tourists.

2 People go to Loch Ness so / because they want to see Nessie.

3 I want to see the Pyramids so / because let's go to Egypt.

4 Visitors love Edinburgh so / because it is beautiful.

5 The museum is closed so / because we can't go there.

6 There's a cinema in my town so / because we can see a film tonight.

Extra tasks for early finishers 9

9 Lesson 1

Complete the sentences with these words.

> camels   desert   rucksack   seat   sun cream   swimsuit   tent

1 My _____ is next to the window, so I can see the view.

2 Jenny put her clothes into her _____ and put it on her back.

3 I can't go swimming today. I haven't got my _____!

4 We're sleeping in a _____ this weekend.

5 There is a lot of sand in the _____ .

6 It's very hot today, so we must take some _____ .

7 Bedouin use _____ to travel across the sand.

9 Lesson 2

Write sentences in the Past Simple with these words.

1 we / stay / in a hotel / last year
_____

2 the train / stop / at the platform
_____

3 Karen / travel / by car / yesterday
_____

4 you / try / to go up / in a hot air balloon
_____

5 he / carry / his rucksack / for hours
_____

6 I / wait / for the bus / for forty minutes
_____

9 Lesson 3

Complete the sentences with the Past Simple of the verbs in brackets.

1 Tom and John _____ (eat) at an expensive restaurant last night.

2 Pat _____ (sleep) in a tent on holiday.

3 I _____ (buy) a new skirt yesterday.

4 We _____ (go) to lots of museums last year.

5 The dog _____ (swim) in the sea this morning!

6 Jane _____ (see) the Eiffel Tower when she was in Paris.

Extra tasks for early finishers 10

 **Lesson 1**

Write questions and short answers using the Past Simple.

1 Robbie Williams / sing / with 'Destiny's Child' (✗)

_____

_____

2 the brothers / star / in the film (✓)

_____

_____

3 Kylie Minogue / give / you her autograph (✓)

_____

_____

4 we / get / a role in the play (✗)

_____

_____

5 the director / leave / the set (✓)

_____

_____

6 you / buy / tickets for the concert (✗)

_____

_____

 **Lesson 2**

Match.

1 When did you go to Disneyland?	**a** I like cartoons.
2 Who was the star of the film?	**b** at the supermarket
3 Why did you buy the Snow White DVD?	**c** very tired
4 Where did you see my sister?	**d** last summer
5 Whose costume is this?	**e** Leonardo de Caprio
6 How did you feel at the concert?	**f** the actor's.

 **Lesson 3**

Complete the interview with words from the interview on page 96.

Interviewer   You go to a school for singing and (1) _____, Mark. When did you start at the school.

Mark   Well, I started two years ago.

Interviewer   Did you have an (2) _____?

Mark   Yes, I did. I sang a song from _The Lion King_.

Interviewer   Really? Did you feel (3) _____?

Mark   No. I always try to (4) _____ before I sing.

Interviewer   That's good. Tell me about your school. What lessons do you have?

Mark   We have (5) _____ lessons, but we also have singing and (6) _____ lessons.

Extra tasks for early finishers 11

 **Lesson 1**

See how many words of three letters or more you can make using the letters in FAVOURITE ANIMAL. Use a dictionary to help you find words, then check your score.

_____   _____

_____   _____

_____   _____

_____   _____

_____   _____   **5 words:**   good
                                                              6 - 10 words: very good
_____   _____   **11+ words:**   excellent

 **Lesson 2**

Complete the sentences with the superlative form of the adjectives in brackets.

1 This snake is _____ (scary) animal in the zoo.

2 Monkeys are _____ (funny) animals.

3 Who has got _____ (many) pets of all?

4 Kittens are _____ (pretty) pets.

5 Mice are _____ (bad) pets.

6 Which bird is _____ (beautiful) colour?

 **Lesson 3**

Find and circle 15 animals from Unit 11.

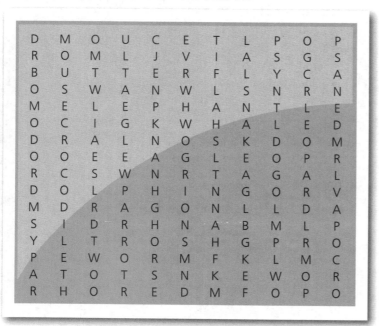

D	M	O	U	C	E	T	L	P	O	P
R	O	M	L	J	V	I	A	S	G	S
B	U	T	T	E	R	F	L	Y	C	A
O	S	W	A	N	W	L	S	N	R	N
M	E	L	E	P	H	A	N	T	L	E
O	C	I	G	K	W	H	A	L	E	D
D	R	A	L	N	O	S	K	D	O	M
O	O	E	E	A	G	L	E	O	P	R
R	C	S	W	N	R	T	A	G	A	L
D	O	L	P	H	I	N	G	O	R	V
M	D	R	A	G	O	N	L	L	D	A
S	I	D	R	H	N	A	B	M	L	P
Y	L	T	R	O	S	H	G	P	R	O
P	E	W	O	R	M	F	K	L	M	C
A	T	O	T	S	N	K	E	W	O	R
R	H	O	R	E	D	M	F	O	P	O

1 _____

2 _____

3 _____

4 _____

5 _____

6 _____

7 _____

8 _____

9 _____

10 _____

11 _____

12 _____

13 _____

14 _____

15 _____

Extra tasks for early finishers 12

12 Lesson 1

Write questions and short answers using *be going to*.

1 it / snow / this weekend (✗)

_____

_____

2 Sam and Rick / have / a party (✓)

_____

_____

3 we / win / the competition (✗)

_____

_____

4 you / buy / that medallion (✗)

_____

_____

5 I / find / the treasure (✓)

_____

_____

6 Kathy / get / wet (✓)

_____

_____

12 Lesson 2

Look at the Vocabulary tasks on pages 112 and 113 and complete the puzzle. Find the extra word.

12 Lesson 3

Complete the dialogue with words from the interview on page 114.

Interviewer You've got a very strange (1) _____ Tricia. Can you tell us about it?

Tricia Yes, I like to take (2) _____ of unusual weather.

Interviewer Unusual weather? What kind of unusual weather.

Tricia Well, last week I followed a (3) _____ – it was a very fast and strong wind and it looked like a black (4) _____ . It was amazing.

Interviewer Isn't that a bit (5) _____?

Tricia Yes, it is, but I'm always very (6) _____ so I drove away when the tornado came towards me.

Interviewer What weather will you photograph next?

Tricia I'm going to India next week because there's lots of rain there at the moment.

Extra Tasks (for early finishers) Key

Unit 1
Lesson 1

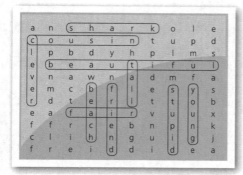

Lesson 2

1 my
2 your
3 his
4 she
5 its
6 we
7 you
8 their

Lesson 3

1 Michael's
2 children's
3 ?
4 Parrots
5 name's
6 years

Unit 2
Lesson 1

1 MESSAGE
2 TEDDY BEAR
3 GAMES
4 LAPTOP
5 SKATEBOARD
6 ROBOT
7 TOY

The missing word is *MYSTERY*.

Lesson 2

Words can appear in any order:

1 camera
2 comic
3 country
4 exciting
5 globe
6 ice skates
7 piano
8 present
9 scary
10 watch

Lesson 3

1c   **2**a   **3**e   **4**b   **5**d

Unit 3
Lesson 1

1 geography
2 history
3 maths
4 English
5 sport
6 art
7 music
8 science

Lesson 2

1 Do you like sport and music?
  Yes, I do.
2 Does Mary draw in art class?
  Yes, she does.
3 Does Sam walk to school?
  No, he / she doesn't.
4 Do the children have lunch in the cafeteria?
  Yes, they do.
5 Do you wear a uniform?
  No, I don't.
6 Do we study in the library?
  No, you / we don't.

Lesson 3

1 once
2 usually
3 always
4 never
5 every

Unit 4
Lesson 1

1 Whose
2 What
3 When
4 Where
5 What
6 Who

Lesson 2

1c   **2**a   **3**b   **4**c   **5**c   **6**a

Lesson 3

1 bowling
2 e-pals
3 good
4 exciting
5 free time

Unit 5
Lesson 1

1 CARD
2 FESTIVAL
3 STALL
4 CAKE
5 BALLOON
6 PARTY HAT
7 PAINT
8 CATCH
9 CANDLE

The missing word is *CELEBRATE*.

Lesson 2

1b   **2**c   **3**a   **4**c   **5**a   **6**a

Lesson 3

1 jokes (*The others are things you can light.*)
2 presents (*The others are things you can eat.*)
3 barbecue (*The others are special days.*)
4 Australia Day (*The others are months.*)
5 picnic (*The others are related to school.*)

Unit 6
Lesson 1

1d   **2**a   **3**e   **4**b   **5**c

Lesson 2

Across
1 LUNCH
5 KNIFE
7 BREAKFAST
9 CHEESE

Down
2 JUICE
3 CHOCOLATE
4 BANANA
6 BREAD
8 TEA
9 CUP

Lesson 3

1c   **2**e   **3**a   **4**b   **5**d

Unit 7
Lesson 1

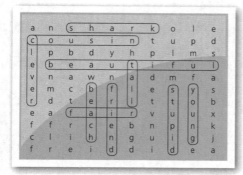

136

Lesson 2

1 Are the boys playing with their skateboards?
No, they aren't.
2 Is the boxer feeling sad?
No, he isn't.
3 Is Kate training for the competition?
Yes, she is.
4 Are you swimming in the sea?
Yes, I am / we are.
5 Are we winning the match?
No, we / you aren't.
6 Am I having fun?
Yes, I am / you are.

Lesson 3

1 coach (*The other two are people who take part in competitions or matches and are successful.*)
2 watch (*The other two are active.*)
3 player (*The other two are events.*)
4 fans (*The other two are people who do sports.*)
5 ice dancing (*The other two are sports.*)

Unit 8
Lesson 1

1b 2a 3a 4a 5a 6b

Lesson 2

1 dentist
2 hairdresser
3 firefighter
4 doctor
5 taxi driver
6 pilot
7 shop assistant
8 actor

Lesson 3

1 because
2 because
3 so
4 because
5 so
6 so

Unit 9
Lesson 1

1 seat
2 rucksack
3 swimsuit
4 tent
5 desert
6 sun cream
7 camels

Lesson 2

1 We stayed in a hotel last year.
2 The train stopped at the platform.
3 Karen travelled by car yesterday.
4 You tried to go up in a hot air balloon.
5 He carried his rucksack for hours.
6 I waited for the bus for forty minutes.

Lesson 3

1 ate
2 slept
3 bought
4 went
5 swam
6 saw

Unit 10
Lesson 1

1 Did Robbie Williams sing with Destiny's Child?
No, he didn't.
2 Did the brothers star in the film?
Yes, they did.
3 Did Kylie Minogue give you her autograph?
Yes, she did.
4 Did we get a role in the play?
No, we / you didn't.
5 Did the director leave the set?
Yes, he did.
6 Did you buy tickets for the concert?
No, I / we didn't.

Lesson 2

1d 2e 3a 4b 5f 6c

Lesson 3

1 drama
2 audition
3 nervous
4 relax
5 normal
6 acting

Unit 11
Lesson 1

Some words pupils might make from:
FAVOURITE ANIMAL

after
aunt
fair
fan
fat
five
flame
four
late
male
mate
more
rate
Rome
tail
time
tour
trail
train
van

Lesson 2

1 the scariest
2 the funniest
3 the most
4 the prettiest
5 the worst
6 the most beautiful

Lesson 3

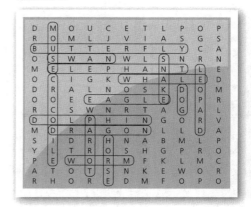

Unit 12
Lesson 1

1 Is it going to snow this weekend?
No, it isn't.
2 Are Sam and Rick going to have a party?
Yes, they are.
3 Are we going to win the competition?
No, we / you aren't.
4 Are you going to buy that medallion?
No, I'm / we're not.
5 Am I going to find the treasure?
Yes, you are.
6 Is Kathy going to get wet?
Yes, she is.

Lesson 2

1 WATERFALL
2 CANYON
3 CLIFF
4 MOUNTAIN
5 FOREST
6 OCEAN
7 ARRIVE
8 DESTROY
9 SURVIVE
10 CUT DOWN

The missing word is *RAINFOREST*.

Lesson 3

1 hobby
2 photographs
3 tornado
4 cloud
5 dangerous
6 careful

Workbook Key

Introduction

A

1d (given)   **2**c   **3**b   **4**a

B

A-a (given), B-b, C-c, D-d, E-e, F-f, G-g, H-h, I-i, J-j, K-k, L-l, M-m, N-n, O-o, P-p, Q-q, R-r, S-s, T-t, U-u, V-v, W-w, X-x, Y-y, Z-z

C

```
D O A U G U S T O T E Q N R
E K U M E P A U E V J O F O
C P T U N S D E B S A U S A
E S U Y A O E S M O N D A Y
M A M O A R X D A L U C T B
B L N L P B Z A Y K A E U C
E A F R E O Y L S R B R V O
R V L W I N T E R P Y E D P
E N O F L W O A B L V S A T
T O C T O B E R P J U L Y A
S V B D E G F J K O E J K N
E E Q S U V A X L S B F A W
P M A R C H E F L U P E S E
T B R N K S P R I N G B O D
E E J F A U V I A D P R N N
M R A G K M K D L A E U P E
B K P H A M I A U Y P A M S
E S J U N E K Y A O E R Z D
R L M A K R D M J N G Y F A
U V S P Q O T H U R S D A Y
```

D

1 five (given)
2 eight
3 seventeen
4 twenty
5 thirty-three
6 forty-eight
7 fifty
8 eighty-nine
9 a/one hundred

E

1 please (given)
2 spell
3 Open
4 answer
5 mean

F

1 an (given)
2 This
3 a
4 Those
5 this
6 an
7 That's
8 a
9 Those
10 a
11 These
12 an

G

1 first (given)
2 2nd
3 fifth
4 8th
5 tenth
6 13th
7 eighteenth
8 20th
9 twenty-second
10 31st

H

Across
2 EYE (given)
3 HAIR
4 ARM
7 FOOT
8 HAND
9 LEG

Down
1 NOSE
2 EAR
3 HEAD
4 MOUTH
6 TOE
7 FINGER

I

Singular
toy (given)
glass
country
knife
child
tomato
dog
mouse

Plural
toys (given)
glasses
countries
knives
children
tomatoes
dogs
mice

J

It's four o'clock.

It's ten to six.

It's half past twelve.

It's quarter past eight.

It's twenty-five past ten.

It's quarter to one.

It's ten to five.

It's nine o'clock.

It's quarter past seven.

K

Pupils colour the picture accordingly.

Unit 1

Lesson 1

Vocabulary

A

1d (given)   **5**b
2a   **6**c
3f   **7**h
4e   **8**g

B

1 fair (given)
2 tall
3 young
4 ugly
5 black
6 clever

C

1d (given)   **4**f
2c   **5**a
3b   **6**e

Grammar

A

1 is (given)
2 am
3 are
4 Is
5 Are
6 are

B

1 I'm (given)
2 Are
3 isn't
4 are
5 aren't
6 Is it
7 You're
8 are

C

1a (given)   **5**a
2b   **6**b
3a   **7**a
4b   **8**a

Lesson 2

Vocabulary

A

1 live (given)
2 fly
3 swim
4 have
5 keep
6 eat

B

1 stupid (given)
2 egg
3 parents
4 hungry
5 son

C

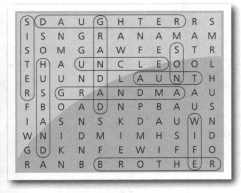

Grammar

A

I-my (given)
you-your
he-his
she-her
it-its
we-our
they-their

B

1 I (given)
2 Our
3 She
4 Your
5 He
6 Its
7 Their
8 You're

C

1 His
2 its
3 my
4 her
5 Their
6 our

Lesson 3

Vocabulary

1 email (given)
2 class
3 twins
4 matter
5 birthday

Grammar

1b (given)   **4**b
2b   **5**b
3a   **6**a

Say it like this!

1c (given)   **2**d   **3**a   **4**e   **5**b

Writing

A

hi – Hi
sally – Sally
how are you – How are you?
thank you for your email - Thank you for your email.
my best friend is liz – My best friend is Liz.
shes from america – She's from America.
shes eleven – She's eleven
her birthday – Her birthday
january – January
she is crazy about cats – She is crazy about cats.
who is your best friend – Who is your best friend?
email – Email
love – Love
melissa – Melissa

B

Pupils' own answers

Unit 2
Lesson 1

Vocabulary

A

a6 (given)   **e**2
b8   **f**7
c4   **g**3
d1   **h**5

B

1 I'm scared! (given)
2 Please don't touch.
3 Sorry!
4 I don't know.
5 Welcome!
6 Look!

C

1 message (given)
2 toys
3 museum
4 mystery
5 bike
6 pet
7 pieces
8 picture

Grammar

A

1 has got (given)
2 has got
3 have got
4 has got
5 have got
6 has got

B

1 hasn't (given)
2 haven't
3 haven't
4 got
5 It's

C

1 Has Tom got a skateboard? Yes, he has. (given)
2 Has Jane got a mobile phone? No, she hasn't.
3 Have they got pets? Yes, they have.
4 Has it got ears? No, it hasn't.
5 Has Paul got an uncle? Yes, he has.
6 Have Mum and Dad got a new car? No, they haven't.

Lesson 2

Vocabulary

A

1 watch (given)
2 globe
3 Ice skates
4 DVD
5 camera

B

Across

1 COMICS (given)
3 PRESENT
4 BIRTHDAY
5 MOON

Down

1 COUNTRY
2 SPIDER
3 PIANO

C

1 creepy (given)
2 real
3 homework
4 exciting
5 moving

Grammar

A

1 There is (given)
2 There are
3 Are there
4 Is there
5 there isn't
6 there aren't

B

Pupils' own answers

139

C

1 There is a tarantula in front of the DVDs. (given)
2 There is a pen between the globe and the DVDs.
3 There are ice skates under the piano.
4 There is a boy next to a girl.
5 There are some comics in the desk.
6 There is a laptop on the desk.
7 There is a lizard behind the laptop.
8 There is a teddy bear near the laptop.

Lesson 3

Vocabulary

1 guitar (given)
2 favourite
3 boring
4 stories
5 photo
6 fun

Speaking

Pupils' own answers

Say it like this!

1 Catch! (given)
2 Slow down!
3 Can I have a go?
4 Well done!
5 It's my turn!

Writing

A

1 and (given)
2 and
3 but
4 but
5 and
6 and

B

Pupils' own answers

Review 1

Reading

1b (given)   2a   3e   4c   5d

Vocabulary

1a (given)	7b
2b	8b
3b	9a
4a	10b
5b	11a
6a	12b

Grammar

1b (given)	7b
2a	8b
3a	9a
4b	10b
5b	11a
6a	12a

Unit 3
Lesson 1

Vocabulary

A

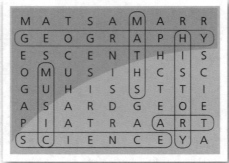

C

1 subject (given)
2 fun
3 homework
4 school
5 football
6 class

Grammar

A

1 brushes her hair (given)
2 plays football
3 walks to school
4 studies English
5 washes the car
6 teaches maths

B

1 go (given)
2 carries
3 like
4 have
5 plays
6 sit
7 has
8 does

C

1 in (given)
2 at
3 Every
4 on
5 every
6 in

Lesson 2

Vocabulary

A

1 playground (given)
2 library
3 uniform
4 cafeteria
5 classmates
6 bookcase

B

1 food (given)
2 teeth
3 fun
4 homework
5 wear
6 classroom

C

1 do (given)
2 finish
3 wear
4 clean
5 carry
6 sing

Grammar

A

1 doesn't (given)
2 Does
3 don't
4 give
5 Do
6 have

B

1 Yes, they do. (given)
2 Yes, it does.
3 No, they haven't.
4 Yes, they do.
5 No, he doesn't.
6 No, I don't./Yes, I do.

C

1 don't know (given)
2 Do you take
3 Does your father work?
4 doesn't work
5 Do you like
6 don't play

Lesson 3

Vocabulary

1b (given) 2a 3d 4c 5e

Say it like this!

Pupil's own answers

Grammar

1F (given)	4F
2T	5F
3T	6T

Writing

A

1 usually gets up (given)
2 always has
3 sometimes visits
4 usually does
5 often sends

B

Morning:

Paul usually gets up at 7 o'clock in the morning. (given) He often rides his bike to school.

Afternoon:

Paul always finishes school at 3 o'clock. He usually does his homework in the afternoon.

Evening:

In the evening, Paul often watches TV with his dad. He always goes to bed at 10 o'clock.

Unit 4

Lesson 1

Vocabulary

A

1 e (given)	**5** c
2 b	**6** f
3 h	**7** g
4 a	**8** d

B

1 winner (given)
2 watch
3 Chinese
4 need
5 competition
6 Me

C

1 You're the winner. (given)
2 Congratulations!
3 Here you are.
4 Thanks.
5 I'm happy!
6 Me too!

Grammar

A

1 What is Doug's hobby? (given)
2 Where is your school?
3 Whose kite is this?
4 When is the music competition?
5 Who is the clever boy?
6 What is her favourite thing?

B

Pupils' own answers

C

1 What's (given)
2 Who's
3 Where
4 Whose
5 When
6 Who

Lesson 2

Vocabulary

A

1 f (given)	**4** a
2 b	**5** e
3 d	**6** c

B

a 3 (given)	**d** 2
b 6	**e** 5
c 4	**f** 1

C

1 scary (given)
2 tourist
3 huge
4 famous
5 mirror
6 face

Grammar

A

1 can't (given)
2 can
3 can't
4 can't
5 can't
6 can

B

1 you can (given)
2 he can't
3 they can't
4 she can
5 I can't
6 it can't

C

1 can (given)
2 can't
3 can
4 can't
5 Can
6 can

Lesson 3

Vocabulary

1 like (given)
2 visit
3 go
4 eat
5 send
6 help
7 play
8 meet

Speaking

Pupils' own answers

Say it like this!

1 Do you like (given)
2 Are you good at
3 Are you good at
4 Do you like
5 Are you good at
6 Do you like

Writing

A

1 is good at (given)
2 goes
3 can
4 likes

B

Pupils' own answers

Review 2

Reading

1 is (given)
2 schools
3 helps
4 money
5 Children

Vocabulary

1 b (given)	**7** a
2 a	**8** a
3 b	**9** b
4 a	**10** a
5 b	**11** a
6 b	**12** b

Grammar

1 b (given)	**7** b
2 b	**8** b
3 a	**9** a
4 b	**10** a
5 a	**11** a
6 a	**12** b

Unit 5

Lesson 1

Vocabulary

A

1 balloons (given)
2 cake
3 candles
4 card
5 invitation
6 presents

B

1 stall (given)
2 catch
3 quiet
4 shot
5 Ouch!
6 festival

C

1 What's that? (given)
2 OK.
3 Look!
4 This is fun!
5 Over there!
6 Hey, you!

Grammar

A

1 Don't eat (given)
2 Catch
3 be
4 Don't go
5 clean
6 Don't throw

B

1 it (given)
2 her
3 We
4 them
5 us
6 him
7 me
8 She

C

1 b (given)	**4** f
2 e	**5** c
3 a	**6** d

Lesson 2

Vocabulary

A

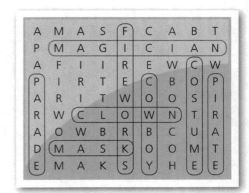

B
1 b (given)　　**4** a
2 b　　　　　**5** b
3 b　　　　　**6** b

C
1 hat (given)
2 person
3 city
4 street
5 preparations
6 king

Grammar

A
Countable
candle (given)
costume
mask
queen

Uncountable
hair
money
music
paint

B
1 b (given)　　**5** b
2 a　　　　　**6** a
3 a　　　　　**7** b
4 a　　　　　**8** b

C
1 balloons (given)
2 hair
3 masks
4 orange juice
5 bananas

Lesson 3

Vocabulary
1 give (given)
2 play
3 make
4 sing
5 light
6 laugh
7 open
8 have

Grammar
1 some (given)
2 any
3 any
4 some
5 any
6 some

Say it like this!
1 Why don't you go to bed? (given)
2 Why don't you have a party?
3 Why don't you go to the doctor?
4 Why don't you go to an Internet café?
5 Why don't you have a picnic?

Writing
A
1 She (given)
2 They
3 them
4 We
5 me

B
Pupils' own answers

Unit 6
Lesson 1

Vocabulary

A
1 c (given)　　**4** b
2 d　　　　　**5** f
3 a　　　　　**6** e

B
1 fast (given)
2 delicious
3 bill
4 hungry
5 menu
6 waiter

C
1 D (given)　　**5** D
2 F　　　　　**6** F
3 O　　　　　**7** O
4 O　　　　　**8** F

Grammar

A
1 lots of (given)
2 much
3 a lot of
4 many
5 a lot of
6 many

B
1 There aren't many oranges in this dessert. (given)
2 I haven't got many chips on my plate.
3 There isn't much ice cream on my spoon.
4 The restaurant has got many waiters.
5 There are lots of snacks on the table.
6 My cat always eats a lot of food.

C
1 How many (given)
2 How much
3 How much
4 How many
5 How much
6 How many

Lesson 2

Vocabulary

A

B
1 holes (given)
2 letters
3 answer
4 leaves
5 luck

C
1 cup (given)
2 milk
3 slice
4 Swiss
5 health
6 knife
7 plate

Grammar

A
1 b (given)　　**4** a
2 b　　　　　**5** a
3 b　　　　　**6** a

B
1 d (given)　　**4** e
2 a　　　　　**5** c
3 b　　　　　**6** f

C
1 little (given)
2 lot
3 lots
4 a few
5 lot
6 little

Lesson 3

Vocabulary
1 restaurant (given)
2 slice
3 different
4 big
5 plates
6 eat
7 rice
8 tea

Speaking
Pupils' own answers

Say it like this!
1 favourite food (given)
2 love
3 How often
4 What about
5 they're horrible

Writing

A
1 First (given)
2 Then
3 After
4 Finally

B
Pupils' own answers

Review 3
Reading
1 F (given)　**2** T　**3** T　**4** F　**5** T

142

Vocabulary

1 b (given)	**7** a
2 b	**8** b
3 b	**9** b
4 a	**10** b
5 b	**11** a
6 a	**12** a

Grammar

1 b (given)	**7** b
2 a	**8** a
3 a	**9** b
4 a	**10** a
5 b	**11** b
6 b	**12** b

Unit 7

Lesson 1

Vocabulary

A

1 e (given)	**5** a
2 b	**6** g
3 c	**7** f
4 d	**8** h

B
1 enter (given)
2 cross
3 off
4 go
5 Come
6 leave

C
1 riding (given)
2 climbing
3 cycling
4 running
5 sailing
6 diving

Grammar

A
1 am playing (given)
2 are coming
3 is running
4 is lying
5 is swimming
6 are chasing
7 are having
8 are crossing

B

1 b (given)	**5** b
2 a	**6** a
3 a	**7** a
4 b	**8** b

C
1 is running (given)
2 are swimming
3 is winning
4 am chasing
5 are having
6 is falling off

Lesson 2

Vocabulary

A
1 gymnast (given)
2 boxer
3 footballer
4 tennis player
5 cyclist
6 swimmer

B
1 use (given)
2 train
3 kick
4 get
5 want
6 feel
7 think
8 love

C
1 practises (given)
2 wins
3 calm
4 gives up
5 excited
6 champion

Grammar

A
1 I'm not pushing my sister. (given)
2 You aren't winning the game.
3 He isn't thinking about the fight.
4 She isn't wearing a helmet.
5 It isn't chasing birds.
6 We aren't watching cycling on TV.
7 You aren't feeling excited about the training.
8 They aren't giving up!

B
1 Are you playing football? (given)
2 Is your brother training?
3 Are you feeling calm?
4 Is the dog chasing him?
5 Are you practising at the moment?
6 Is Julia doing her homework?

C
1 No, they aren't. (given)
2 Yes, she is.
3 Yes, he is.
4 No, he isn't.
5 Yes, they are.
6 No, she isn't.

Lesson 3

Vocabulary
1 skater (given)
2 coach
3 work
4 country
5 film
6 competition

Say it like this!
1 like (given)
2 player
3 fan
4 team
5 match

Grammar
1 Kate is doing her homework tonight. (given)
2 Mr Brown is playing tennis on Tuesday.
3 Eric and Phil are watching a football match this evening.
4 Patty is swimming tomorrow.
5 Betty and Alex are sailing at the weekend.
6 Danny is having a riding lesson next week.

Writing

A
1 Salim is playing tennis on Friday morning. (given)
2 He's going shopping with his dad on Friday afternoon.
3 He's helping his mum cook dinner on Friday evening.
4 He's doing his homework on Saturday morning.
5 He's swimming on Saturday afternoon.

B
Pupils' own answers

Unit 8

Lesson 1

Vocabulary

A
1 live (given)
2 work
3 hear
4 hand
5 piece

B

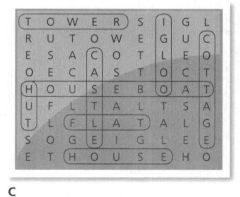

C
1 knight (given)
2 footsteps
3 view
4 monster
5 years
6 people

Grammar

A
1 lives (given)
2 am watching
3 Do / like
4 doesn't go
5 want
6 Is / eating
7 plays
8 am not doing

143

B
1 d (given)   **4** c
2 b   **5** f
3 a   **6** e

C
1 are visiting (given)
2 is
3 is wearing
4 doesn't like
5 is / holding
6 is eating

Lesson 2

Vocabulary

A
1 pilot (given)
2 actor
3 hairdresser
4 dentist
5 firefighter
6 doctor
7 taxi driver
8 shop assistant

B
1 same (given)
2 get
3 up
4 tent
5 hard
6 makes
7 on
8 cooks

C
a 4 (given)   **b** 3   **c** 1   **d** 5   **e** 2

Grammar

A
1 F (given)   **4** F
2 T   **5** T
3 F   **6** F

B
1 must (given)
2 must
3 must
4 must
5 mustn't
6 mustn't

C
1 d (given)   **4** b
2 f   **5** c
3 a   **6** e

Lesson 3

Vocabulary

1 e (given)   **4** a
2 b   **5** c
3 f   **6** d

Say it like this!

1 Where do your cousins live? (given)
2 What's it like?
3 Is it a big city?
4 What can you do there?
5 Can you go swimming?

Speaking

Pupils' own answers

Writing

A
1 because (given)
2 so
3 because
4 because

B
Pupils' own answers

Review 4

Reading

1 F (given)   **2** T   **3** T   **4** F   **5** T

Vocabulary

1 a (given)   **7** a
2 a   **8** b
3 b   **9** b
4 a   **10** b
5 b   **11** b
6 a   **12** b

Grammar

1 b   **7** b
2 b   **8** b
3 a   **9** b
4 a   **10** b
5 a   **11** a
6 b   **12** a

Unit 9

Lesson 1

Vocabulary

A
1 c (given)   **4** e
2 f   **5** d
3 a   **6** b

B
1 a (given)   **4** b
2 a   **5** b
3 b   **6** a

C
1 desert (given)
2 camel
3 sand
4 pyramid
5 hot
6 thirsty

Grammar

A
1 were (given)
2 There
3 Last month
4 Was George
5 wasn't
6 Were
7 ago
8 weren't

B
1 Was the hotel nice? No, it wasn't. (given)
2 Were the tourists happy? Yes, they were.
3 Was the leopard scary? Yes, it was.
4 Was Alice hot? No, she wasn't.
5 Was Henry excited? Yes, he was.
6 Were his climbing boots new? Yes, they were.

C
Pupils' own answers

Lesson 2

Vocabulary

A
1 ship (given)
2 chicken
3 pilot
4 inventor
5 land
6 station

B
1 basket (given)
2 start
3 air
4 smoke
5 tie
6 field
7 farmer
8 get

C
1 a (given)   **4** b
2 b   **5** a
3 b   **6** b

Grammar

A
1 lived (given)
2 carry
3 looked
4 cook
5 try
6 needed
7 used
8 play

B
1 wanted (given)
2 travelled
3 looked
4 stopped
5 liked
6 studied
7 danced
8 watched

C
1 last (given)
2 August
3 yesterday
4 in
5 ago
6 last

Lesson 3

Vocabulary

1 b (given)   **4** a
2 b   **5** a
3 b   **6** a

Grammar

1 went / had (given)
2 did / wore
3 got / bought
4 sat / ate
5 took / swam
6 saw / told

Say it like this!

1 Stephanie goes to work by taxi. (given)
2 Jason goes to school by bus.
3 The Taylors go shopping by car.
4 Alex goes to the park by bike.
5 Jenny goes to her grandparents by train.
6 The girls go to their friend's house on foot.

Writing

A

Pupils should underline: beautiful (given), amazing, big, exciting, long, huge, nice, delicious, great, friendly, fantastic.

B

Pupils' own answers

Unit 10

Lesson 1

Vocabulary

A

1 pop group (given)
2 interview
3 lines
4 acting
5 stage

B

1 studio (given)
2 shoot
3 cameraman
4 funny
5 autograph
6 talent

C

Across

2 DRESSING (given)
4 CONCERT
6 ROLE

Down

1 DIRECTOR
3 SINGER
5 READY

Grammar

A

1 didn't see (given)
2 didn't wear
3 didn't like
4 didn't have
5 didn't give
6 didn't go

B

Pupils' own answers

C

1 film did Jenny like (given)
2 did you see the play
3 did you eat
4 did Mark bring
5 did they go
6 did they leave

Lesson 2

Vocabulary

A

1 dream (given)
2 make
3 comedy
4 musical
5 adventure
6 love

B

1b (given) 4b
2a   5a
3b   6b

C

1P (given) 5P
2F   6F
3P   7P
4F   8F

Grammar

A

1 When (given)
2 How
3 What
4 Where
5 Who
6 Why
7 Which
8 How

B

1 He went to the beach. (given)
2 He went on Sunday.
3 He swam.
4 He preferred the burger.
5 Because he was cold.
6 He felt tired.

C

1c (given) 4f
2e   5a
3b   6d

Lesson 3

Vocabulary

1a (given) 5a
2a   6b
3b   7b
4b   8b

Say it like this!

1 singer (given)
2 about
3 amazing
4 songs
5 favourite
6 great

Speaking

Pupils' own answers

Writing

A

1C (given) 2A 3B 4D

B

Pupils' own answers

Review 5

Reading

1W (given) 2S 3S 4D 5W

Vocabulary

1b (given) 7a
2b   8a
3a   9b
4b   10b
5a   11b
6b   12a

Grammar

1a (given) 7b
2b   8a
3a   9a
4b   10a
5b   11a
6a   12a

Unit 11

Lesson 1

Vocabulary

A

Land
leopard (given)
lizard
worm

Air
bat
butterfly
eagle

Water
dolphin
shark
whale

B

1 torch (given)
2 tired
3 binoculars
4 short
5 birds
6 insects

C

1 caves (given)
2 dark
3 path
4 dangerous
5 strong
6 ugly

Grammar

A

1 worse (given)
2 more beautiful
3 bigger
4 better
5 more
6 nicer
7 prettier
8 taller

B

1 longer (given)
2 bigger than
3 more dangerous
4 prettier
5 faster
6 better

145

C

1 The elephant is stronger than the bird. (given)
2 The bats are uglier than the eagle.
3 The whale is bigger than the penguin.
4 The horse is faster than the turtle.
5 Katy is shorter than the dog.
6 The cat is hungrier than the mouse.

Lesson 2

Vocabulary

A

Across

2 SNAKE (given)
5 PUPPY
7 KITTEN
8 GOLDFISH

Down

1 RABBIT
3 ELEPHANT
4 PONY
6 PARROT

B

1 love (given)
2 have got
3 serve
4 bring
5 tear
6 get

C

1 fan (given)
2 sculpture
3 important
4 visitor
5 biscuits
6 desk

Grammar

A

1 the worst (given)
2 the biggest
3 the best
4 the most interesting
5 the nicest
6 the prettiest
7 the tallest
8 the most

B

1 the funniest the
2 the naughtiest
3 the best
4 the worst
5 the nicest
6 the most interesting

C

Pupils' own answers

Lesson 3

Vocabulary

1b (given) **2**a **3**b **4**b **5**a **6**b

Grammar

1F (given) **2**T **3**F **4**T **5**T **6**F

Say it like this!

Pupils' answers may vary

1 beautiful (given)
2 funny
3 ugly
4 horrible
5 clever

Writing

A

animol – animal (given)
beatiful – beautiful
usualy – usually
yeers – years
peope – people
frendly – friendly

B

Pupils' own answers

Unit 12

Lesson 1

Vocabulary

A

1 clouds (given)
2 rocks
3 medallion
4 raincoat
5 rainbow
6 boxes

B

C

1 Switch on (given)
2 see
3 look
4 know
5 rain
6 open
7 take
8 have

Grammar

A

1 to rain (given)
2 going
3 are going
4 going
5 win
6 lose

B

1 is going to be (given)
2 Are / going to take
3 aren't going to go
4 Is / going to look for
5 am not going to drive
6 are going to lose

C

1c (given)   **4**f
2a   **5**d
3b   **6**e

Lesson 2

Vocabulary

A

1 cliff (given)
2 forest
3 waterfall
4 ocean
5 canyon
6 mountain

B

1a (given)   **5**a
2b   **6**a
3b   **7**a
4b   **8**b

C

1b (given) **2**a **3**c **4**e **5**d

Grammar

A

1 won't (given)
2 will
3 will
4 will
5 won't
6 won't

B

1 Will they survive the journey? (given)
2 The team will find lots of information.
3 The dog won't destroy the garden.
4 Dr Kay will carry a rucksack.
5 Will companies cut down trees?
6 The weather won't be foggy tomorrow.

C

1 It will be sunny. (given)
2 Yes, it will.
3 It will be cloudy.
4 Yes, it will.
5 No, it won't.
6 It will be windy.

Lesson 3

Vocabulary

1 strong (given)
2 scary
3 coming towards
4 take
5 off
6 drove

Say it like this!

1 weather (given)
2 like
3 wet
4 sunny
5 winter

Speaking

Pupils' own answers

146

Writing

A

Sonday – Sunday (given)
started it - it started
wet? – wet.
run – ran
the house in - in the house
wasn't – weren't
we – We
stoped – stopped

B

Pupils' own answers

Review 6

Reading

1 are (given)
2 tails
3 Australia
4 animals
5 beautiful

Vocabulary

1 b (given)	**7** b
2 a	**8** b
3 a	**9** b
4 a	**10** b
5 b	**11** a
6 a	**12** a

Grammar

1 b (given)	**7** a
2 a	**8** a
3 b	**9** b
4 a	**10** b
5 b	**11** b
6 b	**12** b

Word searches

Units 1-2

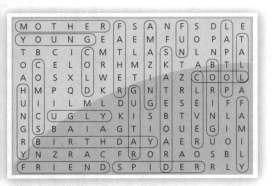

Units 3-4

Units 5-6

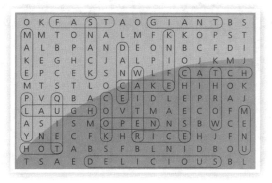

Units 7-8

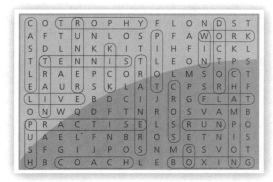

Units 9-10

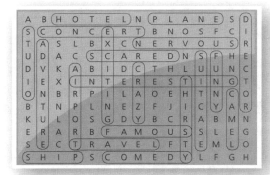

Units 11-12

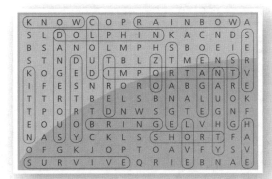

147

Project Book Key

Project 1: Antarctic animals

Activity A

1 South America
2 Africa
3 Australia

Activity B

Pupils' own answers

Activity C

Because it is very cold and snowy.

Activity D

emperor penguin
killer whale
fish
leopard seal
albatross

Activity E

1 ✓
3 ✓
4 ✓
5 ✓ (The photo tells us what colour they are, not the text itself.)
7 ✓

Activity F

Pupils' own answers.
Help the children to get started, and encourage them to think about where they can find out about these animals (books/library, TV, internet, older family member). Refer the pupils to the list in E. The children should write a sentence for each point (1–7). The children can do the research as a homework activity and combine it with Activity G, where they make a poster of their chosen animal.

Activity G

Pupils' own answers
This is designed to be a homework activity. Make sure everyone knows what to do before the end of the lesson. The children should draw a picture, or find a photo/photos of their animal in magazines and write the information they have found out underneath their picture. Set a day for the children to bring their finished posters in.

Activity H

Pupils' own answers
If you have the space, the children's posters could be displayed on the classroom walls for everyone to enjoy. Let the children walk round the class or look at the posters from where they are seated.
If space is an issue, pairs can come to the front of the class and show their posters to the rest of the class.
You can invite the children to vote for the posters they like best, or find most interesting/colourful etc. Praise those children who have clearly made an effort and good work.

Project 2: My favourite thing

Activity A

1 a pair of shoes
2 a mobile phone
3 a bike
4 a skateboard
5 a sports bag
6 a story book
7 a laptop
8 a watch
9 an MP3 player

Activity B

Pupils' own answers.
Let the children write their answers. Go round the class and help with spelling and any grammar issues. Be aware that some children may not have the more expensive items, so be sensitive in asking the class for feedback. A show of hands for each item might be the best way, rather than asking individual pupils.

Activity C

Pupils' own answers

Activity D

Pupils' own answers
1 and 2 The children could prepare their charts for homework. Make sure all the children have had a good look at the grid in the illustration, and it is clear to them what they have to do. Set a day for the class to bring in their work.

3 and 4 Make sure most children have brought in their grids. (Put any children who have forgotten theirs with a child who has done the task.) The children then move around the class and ask and answer each other:
'What's your favourite thing (name)?'
'It's my … .'
The children put a mark on the grid, as shown in the illustration. If you don't have the space for the children to move around, they can stay seated and just ask those children immediately around them.

Activity E

Pupils' own answers
Put the class into groups of four. Let them compare their charts. Are they the same?

Activity F

Pupils' own answers
The children write sentences about what they found out. The children may need to be reminded about the genitive 's after the person's name: e.g. Mariam's favourite thing is … .
Move around the class and assist with handwriting and spelling.
The children could read out their sentences as feedback to the class.

Project 3: A school day

Activity A

1 The children leave home at half past seven.
2 The children have an English lesson at two o'clock.
3 The children leave school at quarter past three.
4 The children have a maths lesson at half past eleven.
5 The children eat lunch at twelve o'clock/midday.
6 The children play football at four o'clock.

Activity B

1 The children leave home at half past seven.
2 The children have a maths lesson at half past eleven.

148

3 The children eat lunch at twelve o'clock/midday.
4 The children have an English lesson at two o'clock.
5 The children leave school at quarter past three.
6 The children play football at four o'clock.

Activity C
Pupils' own answers

Activity D
Pupils' own answers
This activity can be done as homework. Make sure everyone understands the task.
The children use their notes from Activity C as a basis for the paragraph they write. Ask some of the class to say what their favourite time of day is.
The children think about their favourite time of day and draw a picture of it to bring to school along with their writing.

Activity E
Pupils' own answers
If you have space, display the pupils' work and let the children look and admire each other's work. Otherwise, put the children into groups of four or six and let them look at each other's work and read each other's paragraphs.
Praise those who have made an effort and good work.
You may wish to correct some commonly occurring errors on the board and encourage the children to correct the errors themselves.

Project 4: Hobbies
Activity A
1 swimming
2 playing computer games
3 taking photos/photography
4 playing football
5 painting
6 skateboarding

Activity B
Pupils' own answers
Draw the children's attention to the example sentence. Put it on the board if necessary. Remind them of the 3rd person 's' at the end of the verb: likes/enjoys. Let the children write their answers. Move around the class and assist with grammar and spelling.
A few individual children could come to the front of the class and write one of their sentences on the board. Tactfully correct any errors or ask the class to check and correct any errors they can see for themselves.

Activity C
Pupils' own answers
Use the same method as described in Activity B.

Activity D
Pupils' own answers
This activity could be done as homework. Put the children into pairs – putting children who live near each other together. Each pair chooses two different hobbies – they can be different from the ones in Activity A.
At home they practise their mimes to perform to the class. Set a day for them to be ready.

Activity E
Pupils' own answers
Show the children the grid illustrated on page 11 and have them copy it in their notebooks. (They don't need to write the examples in the third column.)

When they have finished, have one or two of the stronger pairs come to the front of the class and perform their mimes. Demonstrate the task with the children, reminding them of the question and answers., e.g. 'Are you … ?' 'Yes, we are./No, we aren't. Try again!'
You could deliberately guess incorrectly to encourage more interaction and add to the fun of the activity.
Once a mime has been correctly guessed, the children write it down in the third column of their grid.
Continue with another two pairs (or more – you can make the grid bigger than is shown here) until the grid is completed.

Activity G
Pupils' own answers
Put the pupil's into pairs and let them compare their grids. Are they the same or different?

Activity H
This can either be done in class or at home. The children make a poster of two of the hobbies on their mime grids and bring them to class to display on the walls.
As always, praise effort and good work.

Project 5: Festivals
Activity A
1 fireworks
2 special food
3 balloons
4 costume
5 parade
6 music

Activity B
Pupils' own answers
Let the children write their own sentences quietly. Move around the class and assist them with their answers.
As feedback, a few of the children could either read out their answers, or write them on the board. Correct common errors tactfully, or invite the children to correct any errors themselves.

Activity C
Pupils' own answers

Activity D
Pupils' own answers
This activity can be done as homework. Before the end of class, put the children into groups of four – try to put children who live close to each other in the same group. Each group chooses a festival that they all enjoy. Each child in each group should draw a colourful picture of a different part of the festival. The children can decide who draws what part of the festival themselves – or organise each group yourself if you feel this is more appropriate. Set a day for the children to bring their work to class.

Put each group's work on the classroom walls, as indicated in the illustration. Let the children admire each other's work. You could invite them to vote on the best friezes. Praise good effort and good work.

Activity E
Pupils' own answers
Still in their groups, the children answer the questions about the festival they have drawn/painted. Each child writes a description, using their answers to the questions. Move around the class and help with handwriting, spelling and punctuation.

Activity F

The children display their descriptions with their drawings. You may want to collect their work in to correct or focus on some common errors to correct in class.

Activity G

Pupils' own answers

Project 6: Food
Activity A

1 chicken
2 bananas
3 fish
4 cake
5 bread
6 rice
7 meat
8 tomatoes
9 pasta

Activity B

Pupils' own answers
Pupils could read individual answers to the class.

Activity C

Pupils' own answers
Elicit from the children what their favourite dinner dishes are. Don't worry, as they will need to use Arabic for this. You will need to give or elicit from them some key vocabulary for specific dishes and common ingredients, e.g. beef, lamb, fish, rice, onions, garlic, peppers, tomatoes, cheese, eggs, salt, pepper, etc. Put the vocabulary items on the board with a translation if necessary. The children can listen and repeat them.
1 Ask the children to choose one favourite dish. Help them to list the ingredients they need.
2 Next, the children need to write down the steps of how to make their chosen dish. Again, put common vocabulary items on the board, e.g. wash, chop, cut, slice, cook, boil, stir, mix.
The children write down each step of their recipes – don't let them get bogged down in detail – the simpler the stages the better.

Activity D

Pupils' own answers
This may be done as a homework activity. The children make a poster of their recipes, as in the illustration, writing the recipe steps in the middle and illustrating each stage around the sides. Set a day to bring their work into school.

Activity E

Pupils' own answers
If possible, put the children's work on the classroom walls. If this is not possible, children can come out to the front of the class to show their work. Ask them to read their recipes out. Praise effort and good work.
The children could vote for whose recipe looks the nicest/tastiest.

Project 7: Sports
Activity A

- gymnastics / gymnast
- football / footballer
- cycling / cyclist
- tennis / tennis player
- running / runner

Activity B

Pupils' own answers
You may wish to demonstrate what the children have to do on the board by writing a model answer about yourself.
Give the children plenty of time to write their answers to the questions. Move around the class, assisting with spelling, punctuation and any grammar problems that may arise.

Activity C

The class will need large sheets of paper for this project. The children can work in pairs or small groups to make their games, which could be done as a homework project.
It would be a good idea to demonstrate how to make the game on the board, following steps 1–3 on page 17 (include the instructions at the foot of the page). If the project is done as a homework activity, set a day for the children to bring their work to school.

For No. 4 you will probably need to bring in dice for the children to use to play the game, or ask the children to bring in some from home. Counters can be made from coloured pieces of paper or card, small objects such as coins, water bottle caps in different colours etc.

Activity D

Let the children admire each other's board games before putting the children into pairs or groups of three or four to play the game. Make sure everyone understands the rules and everyone has a counter and each group a die.

Project 8: Interesting places
Activity A

1 The White House, Washington
2 The Pyramids, Egypt
3 The Great Wall of China
4 Edinburgh Castle, Scotland
5 The Eiffel Tower, Paris
6 The Tower of London

Activity B

Pupils' own answers
Give the class enough time to write their answers. The children can ask and answer the questions in pairs, or as a whole-class activity.

Activity C

Pupils' own answers
This activity is a preparation for the project. Brainstorm with the class some of the famous/historical places in your country. Put their answers on the board. Ask the class why the places are famous – they will need to use Arabic to answer, but don't worry. Have each pupil choose one of the places in Activities A or C.

Activity D

Pupils' own answers
Read through the questions with the children and make sure everyone understands the task. Remind them where they can find out about their chosen place: public library, encyclopaedias/books at home, internet, etc. The children complete D, E and F at home. Set a day for the children to bring in their work.

Activity E

Project work to be carried out at home.

Activity F

Project work to be carried out at home.

Activity G

If you have space, display the children's posters around the classroom and give them time to walk round and admire each other's work. Alternatively, individual children can come to the front of the class for a 'show and tell' session.

Project 9: Travelling
Activity A

1 car
2 camel
3 ship
4 plane
5 bike/bicycle
6 hot air balloon
7 train
8 bus/coach

Activity B

Pupils' own answers
Give the class enough time to write their answers. Move around the class to assist with spelling, grammar and punctuation. Individual children could read out their answers to the class, or work in pairs.

Activity C

Pupils' own answers
Give the class enough time to write their answers. Move around the class to assist with spelling, grammar and punctuation. Individual children could read out their answers to the class, or work in pairs.

Activity D

Have pupils look at the map and identify the modes of transport used in the story. Identify the places in the story. Which countries are they in?
Read the story aloud to the children and have them follow the map in their books. Read the story again, and this time the children follow the narrative. Ask the children when the story took place (last summer). Ask the children to identify the simple past verbs used in the story (travelled, stayed, was). The children could read the story aloud in pairs.

Activity E

Pupils' own answers
Tell the children that they are going to write about their own dream holiday – an imaginary holiday they enjoyed last summer. Give them some time to think about their answers to the information they need to include, before asking individual children to tell you where they went, how they got there etc.
The children will write their stories and draw their maps for homework. Remind pupils that they can look in atlases and on the internet for help. Set a day for the children to bring their work to school.

Activity F

Pupils' own answers
Put the children into pairs and have them look at and read each other's stories about their dream holidays.
If you have space, display the children's work on the classroom walls. Praise effort and good work.

Project 10: Putting on a performance
Activity A

1 an actor
2 a stage
3 a cameraman
4 an audience
5 a set
6 an audition

Activity B

Pupils' own answers
The questions (1–3) could be answered as a class, pair or group speaking activity, before the children start to write their answers. Give them time to write, and move around the class assisting with spelling, grammar and punctuation as needed.

Activity C

Pupils' own answers
1 Tell the children they are going to put on a show for the class. Put the children in groups of four, allowing children who live near each other to work together.
2 Elicit some ideas from the children as to what they might perform: e.g. tell a story or a joke, sing a song, act out a short play, recite a poem etc. Each group should do two short performances.
3 The children decide what they are going to perform for the class – give assistance where necessary. Help them decide what they need to do and who will do what.
4 Make sure the children have decided who is going to do what in the performance and who is going to go first, second etc.
5 If the children need to dress up, they could use items from home (with permission, of course!). Help the children to decide what they need and how to source the items as easily as possible.
6 The children finalise their performance scripts and ideas at home, and rehearse ready to come to class. Set a day for them to be ready by.

Activity D

Pupils' own answers
Have each group perform for the class. Make sure they have enough room at the front to do this, if at all possible. Tell the children that they are to watch carefully and make suggestions and comments on each group's performance. The children can comment after each group's performance. Encourage positive feedback and encouragement. Praise each group's efforts and enjoy!

Activity E

Pupils' own answers
After each group has performed, ask the rest of the class to be a 'director' and give their comments. If your country has talent shows on TV, the activity could be based on the same lines, with 'contestants' and 'judges' who decide who is the most talented.

Project 11: Interesting animals
Activity A

1 parrot
2 snake
3 crocodile
4 shark
5 dolphin
6 eagle
7 bat
8 lizard

Activity B

Pupils' own answers
Choose one of the animals from Activity A (perhaps one that is found in your country) and brainstorm what the children already know about the animal. Put their answers on the board. The

children then choose two of the animals and write what they already know about them and whether they like/don't like them, and why. Remind the children of 'because' to give reasons.
Give the children enough time to write. Move around the class assisting with vocabulary, spelling, grammar and punctuation.

Activity C

Pupils' own answers
Put the children into pairs, allowing children who live close to each other to work together. The children then choose another animal. You could ask each pair which animal they are going to find out about and put the names of the animal in English on the board for them to copy and to raise excitement about the project. Ask the class as a whole what they know already about each animal and put correct answers on the board. Set activity D and E as project work to do at home and set a day for the children to bring their work to class.

Activity D

Pupils' own answers

Activity E

Pupils' own answers

Activity F

Pupils' own answers
If you have space, display the children's posters around the classroom and give them time to walk round and admire each other's work. Alternatively, each pair can come to the front of the class for a 'show and tell' session.

Project 12: Wild places
Activity A

1 forest
2 ocean
3 waterfall
4 glacier
5 mountain
6 cliffs

Activity B

Pupils' own answers
The children may not be aware of environmental damage to the oceans, so you may need to help them here. Common problems include rubbish (plastic bags especially), sewage from towns and cities, chemicals from industry, land reclamation projects, tourism and over-fishing. Ask the children if they can see any effects of problems when/if they go to the seaside. Ask if the beaches are clean, for example.

Activity C

Pupils' own answers
This activity may be set for homework. Find out something about a nature reserve or conservation area in your country. Draw a map on the board and tell the children something about it: e.g. where it is, what animals and plants live there, what is being done to protect the environment.
The children may not know of any protected areas themselves, so be prepared to give them some help: e.g. the Great Barrier Reef, Australia, Yellowstone (USA), Ras Abu Galam in Egypt, Al Yasat Marine Protected Area in Abu Dhabi. Encourage them to choose one and to find out about it, using the points in Activity C.

Activity D

Pupils' own answers
The children make a poster of their chosen place, with drawings of the animals, birds, marine life plants that live there. They can write the information they have found out about each creature or plant underneath its picture. This can either be done in class or at home. Set a day for the children to bring their posters to class.

Activity E

Pupils' own answers
If you have space, display the children's posters around the classroom and give them time to walk round and admire each other's work. Alternatively, each child can come to the front of the class for a 'show and tell' session. Praise good work and effort. The children could vote for the most interesting/the most colourful posters.

Grammar Book Key

Introduction

1
1 an (given)
2 a
3 a
4 a
5 an
6 an
7 an
8 an
9 a

2
1 watches (given)
2 pencils
3 children
4 mice
5 leaves
6 boxes
7 photos
8 toys

3
1 These (given)
2 This
3 That
4 That
5 These
6 Those

4
1 She (given)
2 They
3 She
4 You
5 It
6 They
7 He
8 We

5
1 in (given)
2 on
3 at
4 on
5 at
6 on
7 on
8 in

Unit 1

Lesson 1

1
1 You're very tall. (given)
2 He's clever.
3 We aren't on holiday.
4 I'm in the garden.
5 They aren't cousins.
6 She isn't happy.
7 They're funny tricks.
8 It isn't a good idea.

2
1 's (given)
2 's
3 isn't
4 're
5 ~~'m not~~ (isn't / CG
6 are
7 're
8 are

3
1 'm (given)
2 'm
3 's
4 's
5 are
6 are
7 'm
8 is

(handwritten: I'm not h / I'm not h / etc add all)
(handwritten: Pupil's own?)

4
1 No, it isn't. (given)
2 Yes, they are.
3 No, it isn't.
4 No, they aren't.
5 Yes, it is.
6 No, it isn't.
7 Yes, he is.
8 No, it isn't. *(handwritten: ambig.)*

5
1 Is, she is (given)
2 Are, we aren't
3 Are, they are
4 Is, he isn't
5 Are, they are
6 Am, you are
7 Are, we aren't
8 Are, I'm not *(handwritten: we're)*

6
1 Are (given)
2 is
3 aren't
4 Are
5 isn't
6 am
7 aren't
8 Is

Lesson 2

1
1 your (given)
2 my
3 Our
4 her
5 our
6 His
7 their
8 Its

2
1 my (given)
2 our
3 her
4 Your
5 Their
6 Its

3
1 e (given)
2 d
3 c
4 a
5 b

4
1 Their (given)
2 Its
3 his
4 their
5 her
6 Our
7 my
8 Your

Lesson 3

1
1 girl's (given)
2 Grandma's
3 twins'
4 friends'
5 uncle's
6 children's
7 boys'
8 babies'

2
1 girls' (given)
2 boy's
3 chimps'
4 penguin's
5 men's
6 bird's

3
1 b (given)
2 b
3 a
4 a
5 a
6 a
7 b
8 a

Unit 2

Lesson 1

1
1 's got (given)
2 've got
3 've got
4 've got
5 've got
6 's got

2

1. haven't got (given)
2. haven't got
3. hasn't got
4. hasn't got
5. haven't got
6. haven't got

3

1. Have Liz and Pete got, they haven't (given)
2. Have you got, I haven't
3. Has she got, she has
4. Has Jason got, he has
5. Have we got, we haven't
6. Have I got, you have

4

1. hasn't (given)
2. Have
3. has
4. Have
5. have
6. Has
7. haven't
8. Have

5

1. Yes, he has. (given)
2. Yes, they have.
3. No, he hasn't.
4. Yes, she has.
5. Yes, she has.
6. No, he hasn't.

6

1. We have got a big dog. (given)
2. Has Aunt May got a camera?
3. My cousins haven't got a kite.
4. Our teacher has got a red pen.
5. Has Rick got an exciting DVD?
6. Have we got lots of work today?

Lesson 2

1
1. There are (given)
2. There is
3. There are
4. There are
5. There is
6. There are

2
1. There aren't (given)
2. There are
3. There is
4. There aren't
5. There is
6. There isn't

3
1. Yes, there is. (given)
2. Yes, there are.
3. No, there isn't.
4. No, there aren't.
5. No, there isn't.
6. Yes, there is.

4

1. Are there, there aren't (given)
2. Is there, there is
3. Are there, there aren't
4. Is there, there is
5. Are there, there are
6. Is there, there isn't

5

1. on (given)
2. in
3. in front of
4. behind
5. under
6. between

6

1. No, there isn't. (given)
2. Yes, there is.
3. No, there aren't.
4. Yes, there is.
5. Yes, there are.
6. No, there isn't.

Review 1

1
1. is (given)
2. aren't
3. is
4. aren't
5. aren't
6. 'm not
7. is
8. isn't

2
1. My (given)
2. His
3. Your
4. Our
5. Its
6. Their

3
1. e (given)
2. f
3. a
4. b
5. d
6. c

4
1. next to (given)
2. under (also next to)
3. on
4. behind
5. in
6. between

5
1. twins' (given)
2. children's
3. girls'
4. girl's
5. dragon's
6. boys'

6

1. Has the penguin got, it hasn't (given)
2. Have we got, we have
3. Has Uncle Tony got, he hasn't
4. Have Rick and Emily got, they have
5. Have you got, I have
6. Has Lyn got, she hasn't

7

1. 've got (given)
2. hasn't got
3. have got
4. has got
5. haven't got
6. have got

8

1. There aren't (given)
2. There are
3. Are there
4. There isn't
5. There is
6. Is there

Writing Project

1
1. have got (given)
2. are not
3. are
4. There are
5. is
6. has got
7. are not
8. Its

Unit 3

Lesson 1

1
carry / carries (given)
fix / fixes
give / gives
go / goes
like / likes
stay / stays
touch / touches
wash / washes

2
1. shows (given)
2. watches
3. stay
4. carries
5. works
6. like
7. use
8. wash

3
1. She likes art. (given)
2. On Fridays, Mark goes to the park.
3. Maria tidies her room at the weekend
4. I do my homework in my bedroom.
5. Natalie knows the correct answer.
6. We brush our teeth every morning and every evening.
7. He swims in the summer.
8. Mr Greenhalf teaches geography.

4
1 a (given)
2 b
3 a
4 b
5 b
6 a

5
1 play (given)
2 likes
3 watch
4 sits
5 brush
6 go
7 comes
8 have

Lesson 2

1
1 doesn't eat (given)
2 don't brush
3 don't have
4 don't play
5 doesn't do
6 don't sit
7 doesn't use
8 don't eat

2
1 Does, she doesn't (given)
2 Does, she does
3 Do, they do
4 Do, I don't
5 Does, he doesn't
6 Do, we do
7 Does, she does
8 Do, they don't

3
1 Do you wear a uniform at school? Yes, I do. / No, I don't. (given)
2 Does your best friend like lizards? Yes, he/she does. / No he/she doesn't.
3 Do your friends watch DVDs? Yes, they do. / No, they don't.
4 Do you have lunch at school? Yes, I do. / No, I don't.
5 Does your school have a big playground? Yes, it does. / No, it doesn't.
6 Do you like history? Yes, I do. / No, I don't.

4
1 No, he doesn't. (given)
2 Yes, they do.
3 No, they don't.
4 No, she doesn't.
5 No, they don't.
6 No, I don't.

5
1 doesn't (given)
2 do
3 doesn't
4 don't
5 doesn't
6 do
7 doesn't
8 don't

Lesson 3

1
1 We usually go to bed at 9 o'clock. (given)
2 Dad never works at the weekend.
3 How often do you read magazines?
4 We usually have a test on Tuesdays.
5 How often does your mum cook?
6 How often do they go to the park?
7 Your teacher is often in the playground.
8 How often does he go to the sports club?

2
1 never (given)
2 sometimes
3 usually
4 sometimes
5 never
6 never
7 often
8 always

3
1 a (given)
2 b
3 b
4 a
5 a
6 b

4
Pupils' own answers

Unit 4
Lesson 1

1
1 Who (given)
2 Whose
3 When
4 Which
5 What
6 How
7 Why
8 Where

2
1 g (given)
2 h
3 f
4 a
5 e
6 c
7 b
8 d

3
1 When (given)
2 What
3 Where
4 Who
5 Whose
6 Why

4
1 When is the Chinese lesson? (given)
2 What is your favourite game?
3 Whose comics are these?
4 Who has got a piece of the puzzle?
5 Where do you stay in the summer?
6 How do you make a cake?

5
1 comes from Brazil, does Liz come from (given)
2 likes puzzles, does Tom like
3 is on Friday, is the competition
4 lives in Canada, do Jamie and Helen live
5 laptop is in the classroom, is Susan's laptop

Lesson 2

1
1 can't (given)
2 can
3 can't
4 can't
5 can
6 can't

2
1 Can, cook (given)
2 can't read
3 Can, go
4 can't buy
5 can't swim
6 can have

3
1 They can play games on the computer. (given)
2 The dog can't come in.
3 Dina can play the guitar.
4 You can't eat in here.
5 The baby can't do the puzzle.
6 The girls can see the park from the ferris wheel.

4
1 b (given)
2 a
3 b
4 b
5 b
6 a
7 b
8 b

5
1 Can penguins fly? (given)
2 Can we sing?
3 Can Grandad play computer games?
4 Can robots talk?
5 Can you send an email?
6 Can Johnny use a calculator?

6
1 Yes, she can. (given)
2 Yes, he can.
3 Yes, she can.
4 No, she can't.
5 No, he can't
6 Yes, they can.

Review 2

1
1 open (given)

155

2 carries
3 do
4 don't
5 read
6 enjoy
7 work
8 tidies

(handwritten: ⑤ it doesn't)

2
1 Does it snow (given)
2 Does Dad wear, he does
3 Do they sell, they don't
4 Do you fly, I do
5 Does she go, she doesn't
6 Do we need, we do

3
1 lives in Canada, does Cathy live (given)
2 is on Saturday, is the party
3 car is in the garage, is Mr Smith's car
4 wants to buy a skateboard, does Tom want
5 is sad because he has a test, is Paul sad

4
1 On Saturdays Daniella sometimes visits her cousins. (given)
2 On Fridays Susan often goes shopping with her friends.
3 Paul usually takes his dog for a walk every night.
4 At the weekend I sometimes ride my horse.
5 Jill never goes swimming in winter.
6 Judy and Simone usually play with their doll's house after school.

5
1 can (given)
2 can't
3 can
4 can't
5 can't
6 can

6
1 how (given)
2 where
3 Whose
4 Which
5 What
6 When
7 Why
8 Who

Writing Project

1
1 think (given)
2 hear
3 visit
4 usually
5 can't
6 can

Unit 5
Lesson 1

1
1 Don't swim (given)
2 Be

3 Go
4 Don't touch
5 Don't make
6 Brush
7 Don't sit
8 Put

2
1 Don't throw (given)
2 Go
3 Don't drink
4 Finish
5 Write
6 Don't play

3
1 me (given)
2 him
3 us
4 them
5 her
6 you

4
1 it (given)
2 them
3 me
4 us
5 her
6 them

5
1 Let's go (given)
2 Let's not ride
3 Let's have
4 Let's not have
5 Let's paint
6 Let's not listen

6
1 b (given)
2 c
3 d
4 a
5 e
6 f

Lesson 2

1
countable: animal (given), clown, laptop, map, party, robot
uncountable: fun (given), hair, money, music, time, work

2
1 sandwiches (given)
2 balloons
3 spaghetti
4 hair
5 money
6 presents

3
1 b (given)
2 a
3 b
4 a
5 b
6 b

4
1 a packet of (given)
2 a carton of
3 a slice of
4 a glass of
5 a loaf of
6 a cup of

Lesson 3

1
1 some (given)
2 any
3 any
4 some
5 any
6 any
7 some
8 any
9 any
10 some

2
1 b (given)
2 b
3 b
4 a
5 b
6 b
7 b
8 b

3
1 any snow on the beach (given)
2 any maps in the classroom
3 any coffee in this restaurant
4 any presents on the table
5 some rides at the amusement park
6 any carnivals in Greece
7 some food on the plate
8 some apples in the bowl

4
1 any (given)
2 some
3 some
4 any
5 some
6 any

Unit 6
Lesson 1

1
1 many (given)
2 much
3 many
4 many
5 many
6 much
7 many
8 much

2
1 much (given)
2 many
3 much
4 many
5 many
6 much

3
1 How many (given)
2 How much
3 How many
4 How many
5 How much
6 How much
7 How many
8 How much

Lesson 2

1
1 b (given)
2 a
3 b
4 a
5 a
6 b
7 a
8 b

2
1 a lot of / lots of (given)
2 a little
3 a lot of / lots of
4 a few
5 a little
6 a lot of / lots of

3
1 a little (given)
2 a little
3 a few
4 a few
5 a few
6 a little
7 a little
8 a few

4
1 We've got a few tomatoes. (given)
2 I want a little milk in my coffee.
3 Do they eat lots of fish in Spain?
4 We need a little butter for the cake.
5 Are there a lot of people in the restaurant?
6 He drinks a little juice with his lunch.
7 Are there a lot of children in the classroom?
8 There are lots of presents under the table.

Review 3

1
1 Finish (given)
2 Don't eat
3 Don't come
4 Don't forget
5 Make
6 Buy

2
1 Let's wear (given)
2 Let's not go
3 Let's go
4 Let's give
5 Let's make
6 Let's tell

3
1 any (given)
2 some
3 any
4 some
5 some
6 any

4
1 me (given)
2 her
3 him
4 us
5 you
6 them
7 it

5
1 How many (given)
2 How much
3 How much
4 How many
5 How many
6 How much

6
1 an (given)
2 a
3 –
4 an
5 an
6 –
7 –
8 –

7
1 a cup of (given)
2 a glass of
3 a carton of
4 a slice of
5 a packet of
6 a loaf of
7 a jar of

8
1 b (given)
2 a
3 b
4 a
5 b
6 a

Writing Project

1
1 many (given)
2 some
3 lots
4 few
5 some
6 Let's
7 Remember
8 don't

Unit 7
Lesson 1

1
falling (given), playing, climbing, entering, pushing, sailing, throwing, writing (given), having, dancing, leaving, making, practising, riding, cutting (given), winning, getting, putting, sitting, stopping, swimming

2
1 're working (given)
2 's chasing
3 's buying
4 's flying
5 's fixing
6 's using
7 'm studying
8 are travelling

3
1 'm walking (given)
2 's wearing
3 's moving
4 'm writing
5 's running
6 are doing

4
1 They are running very fast. (given)
2 Todd is entering the race.
3 We are sitting in the park.
4 She is doing her homework.
5 Mandy and Dad are playing volleyball.
6 Rick is having a go at the moment.

5
1 's drinking (given)
2 's running
3 are riding
4 'm crossing
5 's giving
6 are diving

Lesson 2

1
1 The gymnast isn't training. (given)
2 She isn't swimming in the sea.
3 Sam and Bob aren't boxing.
4 I'm not wearing my new jeans.
5 You aren't practising for the competition.
6 We aren't talking to the champion now.

2
1 Yes, he is. (given)
2 No, it isn't.
3 Yes, she is.
4 No, they aren't.
5 Yes, she is.
6 No, they aren't.

3
1 Is she riding, she is (given)
2 Is he watching, he isn't
3 Are you feeling, I'm not
4 Are they playing, they are
5 Is the footballer kicking, he is
6 Are we walking, we aren't

4
1 Are, doing (given)
2 'm not studying
3 's playing
4 's cooking
5 's watching

Lesson 3

1
1. 'm washing (given)
2. 's having
3. Are, making
4. ~~are not visiting~~ aren't [given]
5. aren't taking part
6. Is, going
7. 're flying
8. 'm not studying

2
1. 'm having (given)
2. 's coming
3. are going
4. are playing
5. 's having
6. 's making
7. 're running

3
1. 's buying a present. (given)
2. 's doing homework.
3. 's going bowling.
4. 's playing volleyball.
5. 's washing his bike.
6. are going to the ~~cinema~~ theatre

4
1. 'm going (given)
2. 'm training
3. 'm watching
4. 's coming
5. 'm buying
6. 'm meeting
7. 's going
8. 're having

Unit 8

Lesson 1

1
Present simple: always (given), every day, never, on Fridays, sometimes, usually
Present continuous: now (given), at present, at the moment, this week, this year, today

2
1. On Saturdays we usually have lunch at home, but today we're having lunch in a restaurant. (given)
2. Tim often runs on the beach, but today he's running near a castle.
3. They usually play volleyball at the sports centre, but this evening they're playing in the park
4. I usually go on the ferris wheel, but this afternoon I'm going on the merry-go-round.
5. Natalie usually wears jeans, but today she's wearing a dress.
6. They often stay in a cottage in the summer, but this summer they're staying on a houseboat.

3
1. don't watch (given)

2. go
3. is climbing
4. am having
5. are painting
6. don't often go
7. Are your cousins staying
8. use

4
1. tells (given)
2. 'm talking
3. likes
4. don't stay
5. 's building
6. visit
7. ride
8. aren't going

5
1. don't go (given)
2. meet
3. play
4. ride
5. have
6. 's raining
7. 're watching
8. 're eating
9. 're having
10. isn't watching
11. 's doing

Lesson 2

1
1. mustn't (given)
2. must
3. mustn't
4. must
5. must
6. mustn't

2
1. a (given)
2. b
3. b
4. a
5. a
6. a
7. b
8. a

3
1. Must they eat a lot of vegetables? Yes, they must. (given)
2. Must they drink lots of water? Yes, they must.
3. Must they eat junk food? No, they mustn't.
4. Must they practise every day? Yes, they must.
5. Must they go to bed late? No, they mustn't.
6. Must they watch TV all day? No, they mustn't.

4
1. must do (given)
2. must buy
3. Must, take
4. must clean

5. mustn't play
6. mustn't eat

Review 4

1
1. 's using (given)
2. 's practising
3. ~~are~~ walking
4. 'm trying
5. ~~are~~ painting
6. ~~are~~ doing

2
1. The boys aren't climbing a mountain. They are climbing a tree. (given)
2. The children are not dancing on the beach. They are dancing at the parade.
3. I'm not buying a salad. I'm buying a burger.
4. Coach Stevens is not smiling at the players. He's shouting at them.
5. Paul and Amanda are not cycling on the road. They are cycling in the park.
6. Dad's not fixing his car. He's fixing Billy's bike.

3
1. mustn't (given)
2. mustn't
3. must
4. mustn't
5. mustn't
6. must

4
1. Is the girl wearing, she is (given)
2. Are you eating, I'm not
3. Are Mike and Shannon playing? they are
4. Is John drawing, he isn't
5. Are you walking, I am
6. Are we spending, we aren't

5
1. is (given)
2. isn't
3. Are you
4. are
5. aren't
6. Are they

6
1. 's buying (given)
2. 's taking
3. are singing
4. 's making
5. 'm going
6. are spending

7
1. a (given)
2. b
3. a
4. a
5. b
6. b

8
1. are you doing (given)
2. 'practising

158

3 take part
4 's studying
5 help
6 are washing

Writing Project

1
1 is (given)
2 go
3 is camping
4 aren't sleeping
5 are sitting
6 are enjoying
7 must be
8 mustn't sit

Unit 9

Lesson 1

1
1 were (given)
2 were
3 was
4 was
5 were
6 was
7 were
8 was

2
1 The skiing holiday wasn't fun. (given)
2 The girls weren't scared of the spiders.
3 The camel ride wasn't exciting.
4 I wasn't very hungry this morning.
5 Mel and Kim weren't in India a month ago.
6 We weren't in the Sahara Desert last week.

3
1 Was, Yes, it was. (given)
2 Were, No, they weren't.
3 Was, Yes, it was.
4 Were, No, it wasn't.
5 Were, No, they weren't.
6 Was, Yes, she was.
7 Were, No, I wasn't.
8 Was, Yes, he/she was.

4
1 There were (given)
2 There wasn't
3 There weren't
4 There were
5 There was
6 There were

5
1 weren't (given)
2 Was
3 were
4 Were there
5 were
6 was
7 Were
8 wasn't

6
1 were (given)
2 was

---

3 wasn't
4 were
5 was
6 weren't
7 weren't
8 was

Lesson 2

1
carried (given), chased, cried, fitted, looked, started, stayed, tied, travelled, tried, wanted, used (given)

2
1 played (given)
2 fitted
3 landed
4 lived
5 needed
6 carried
7 liked
8 washed
9 stopped
10 worked

3
1 decided (given)
2 travelled
3 arrived
4 stayed
5 visited
6 tried
7 walked
8 enjoyed

4
1 tried (given)
2 carried
3 watched
4 waited
5 climbed
6 opened
7 counted
8 cooked (or made)

Lesson 3

1
brought (given) caught, came, fell, felt, gave, held, kept, knew, put (given), rode, ran, sold, thought, threw, won (given)

2
1 found (given)
2 bought
3 ate
4 took
5 saw
6 left
7 wore
8 had

3
1 drew (given)
2 broke
3 read
4 cut

---

5 left
6 wrote

4
1 flew (given)
2 was
3 took
4 chose
5 made
6 had
7 met
8 went
9 swam
10 sat
11 drank
12 was

Unit 10

Lesson 1

1
1 didn't get (given)
2 didn't see
3 didn't go
4 didn't buy
5 didn't like
6 didn't play

2
1 She didn't want the role. (given)
2 The audience didn't enjoy the concert.
3 He didn't go for an interview.
4 We didn't find the film studio.
5 They didn't agree to shoot a film.
6 The camera man didn't look happy.

3
1 Did you meet a famous scientist? (given)
2 Did they talk to the dancer?
3 Did you travel by boat?
4 Did she take part in the competition?
5 Did we forget the tickets?
6 Did the clown do lots of tricks?

4
1 Did, meet, Yes, he did. (given)
2 Did, play, No, she didn't.
3 Did, travel, No, they didn't.
4 Did, watch, Yes, they did.
5 Did, climb, Yes, he did.
6 Did, walk, Yes, I did.

Lesson 2

1
1 What (given)
2 what/which
3 Why
4 How
5 who
6 Which/What

2
1 did they shoot (given)
2 did the children
3 did you find
4 thought
5 did she start
6 did Jane

159

7 did he eat
8 did you see

3
1 When did the dancer arrive? (given)
2 How did they travel to Italy?
3 Who did she visit in Ireland?
4 Where did the actor stay?
5 What did she miss?
6 Why did she smile?

4
1 Who did they give the award to? (given)
2 Which actor did Thomas speak to?
3 Who did he sell the company to?
4 How did I lose my laptop?
5 Where did Jake see a tiger?
6 Which medal did the champion win?
7 Why did the cameraman shout?
8 When did you have a riding lesson?

Review 5

1
1 a (given)
2 b
3 a
4 a
5 a
6 b

2
1 There was (given)
2 There were
3 There weren't
4 There was
5 There weren't
6 There wasn't

3
1 stayed (given)
2 carried
3 travelled
4 chased
5 started
6 visited
7 played
8 enjoyed

4
1 Did Oliver break a window? No, he didn't.
2 Did Sally and Ann run on the beach? No, they didn't.
3 Did Mr Baker buy a skateboard? Yes, he did.
4 Did the family drive to the airport? Yes, they did.
5 Did Paula take a picture of some penguins? No, she didn't.
6 Did Bill and Mandy have a picnic? Yes, they did.

5
1 went (given)
2 came
3 broke
4 found
5 gave
6 knew

7 saw
8 thought

6
1 They didn't walk a lot in London. (given)
2 I didn't enjoy the film.
3 She didn't take us to the theatre.
4 He didn't leave his suitcase.
5 You didn't play basketball.
6 It didn't eat my cake.

7
1 When did you go on a cruise? (given)
2 What did they visit?
3 Who did you see at the airport?
4 Where did you leave your passports?
5 Why did she choose Spanish?
6 How did he travel to France?

Writing Project

1
1 was (given)
2 became
3 died
4 discovered
5 were
6 wanted
7 filled
8 did Tutenkhamun die
9 tried

Unit 11

Lesson 1

1
bigger (given), faster, further, better, higher, more horrible, hotter, more interesting, prettier, more serious,
more amazing (given), worse, more beautiful, more boring, closer, more dangerous, more exciting, happier, harder, longer

2
1 hotter (given)
2 lazier
3 more expensive
4 wider
5 smaller
6 worse
7 more intelligent
8 shorter
9 cleaner
10 further

3
1 cheaper (given)
2 faster
3 smaller
4 heavier
5 better
6 colder

4
1 as old as (given)
2 not as tall as
3 as heavy as
4 not as clean as
5 not as expensive as

Lesson 2

1
the worst (given), the most difficult, the easiest, the best, the hardest, the hottest, the most important, most, the most popular, the strangest

2
1 the noisiest (given)
2 the fastest
3 the most boring
4 the most amazing
5 the smallest
6 the luckiest
7 the most exciting
8 The most horrible

3
1 the best (given)
2 the funniest
3 the tastiest
4 the most unusual
5 the silliest
6 the most beautiful

4
1 the longest (given)
2 the laziest
3 the strongest
4 the youngest
5 the slowest
6 the most
7 the biggest
8 the smallest

Lesson 3

1
1 friendlier (given)
2 the biggest
3 more
4 cleverer
5 easier
6 the best
7 brighter
8 warmer

2
1 b (given)
2 a
3 b
4 b
5 a
6 a
7 b
8 b

3
1 best (given)
2 nearest
3 quickest
4 prettiest
5 scarier
6 the biggest
7 most delicious
8 more interesting

Unit 12

Lesson 1

1
1 's going to rain (given)
2 are going to stay
3 are going to get
4 are going to find
5 are going to have
6 's going to visit
7 are going to fall
8 are going to go

2
1 'm not going to tidy (given)
2 isn't going to go
3 aren't going to go
4 aren't going to win
5 isn't going to buy
6 'm not going to wear

3
1 Is Max going to take, he isn't (given)
2 Are you going to do, I am
3 Are they going to sleep, they aren't
4 Is the astronaut going to travel, he/she is
5 Are you going to send, I'm not
6 Is Vicky going to visit, she is

4
1 aren't going to play (given)
2 are going to take
3 It's going to snow
4 are going to wake up
5 's going to drive
6 are going to go
7 aren't going to try
8 's going to be

5
1 'm going to ride (given)
2 are going to make
3 'm going to go
4 're going to watch
5 're going to have
6 'm going to visit

Lesson 2

1
1 c (given)
2 a
3 d
4 e
5 f
6 b

2
1 Mum and Dad won't put up our tent. (given)
2 Uncle Todd won't take us to the amusement park.
3 They won't sleep in the igloo.
4 It won't be foggy tomorrow morning.
5 Isabel won't win the race.
6 We won't look for information about the planets.

3
1 Will Amy talk about rainforests? she will (given)
2 Will Josh and Kate bring photos of waterfalls? No, they won't
3 Will Susie and I talk about our holiday? No, you won't
4 Will Robbie give me a book about wild animals? Yes, he will
5 Will Mum walk in the forest with me? Yes, she will
6 Will you show us pictures of the canyon? No, I won't

4
1 'll carry (given)
2 won't have
3 'll get
4 'll fly
5 won't swim
6 'll buy

Review 6

1
1 lower (given)
2 better
3 more difficult
4 more exciting
5 heavier
6 further / (farther?)

2
1 the most popular (given)
2 the best
3 the cloudiest
4 the most expensive
5 the scariest
6 the tallest

3
1 not as young as (given)
2 not as hot as
3 as tall as
4 not as popular as
5 as heavy as
6 not as cheap as

4
1 'll give (given)
2 won't play
3 won't tell
4 Will you open
5 Will they sell
6 Will we get
7 will drive
8 will be

5
1 Is Luke going to win, No, he isn't. (given)
2 Are you going to study, Yes, we are.
3 Are they going to catch, No, they aren't.
4 Is it going to be, Yes, it is.
5 Is Nadia going to have, Yes, she is.
6 Are they going to plant, Yes, they are.

6
1 are going to go (given)
2 isn't going to drive
3 are going to travel
4 are going to stop
5 are not going to sleep
6 are going to stay
7 are going to take part
8 am not going to cycle
9 are going to have

Writing Project

1
1 the highest (given)
2 more difficult
3 harder
4 more exciting
5 the youngest
6 oldest

Unit Tests Key

Test 1

Vocabulary

A

1d 2e 3b 4a 5c

B
1 son
2 brother
3 aunt
4 grandma
5 wife

C
1 shark
2 bird
3 parents
4 grey
5 friend

Grammar

A
1 am
2 are not/aren't
3 is/'s
4 Are
5 is not/isn't

B
1 his
2 my
3 our
4 your
5 Their

C
1 Gary's
2 children's
3 babies'
4 Rita's
5 twins'

Comprehension

B
1 England
2 is
3 horse
4 Jack's
5 twenty

Test 2

Vocabulary

A
1 teddy bear
2 skateboard
3 laptop
4 puzzle
5 pet

B
1 globe
2 scary
3 camera
4 ice
5 present

C
1 game
2 message
3 piano
4 watch
5 comic

Grammar

A
1 has got/'s got
2 haven't
3 has not/hasn't got
4 have got/'ve got
5 Has … got

B
1 Are
2 There's
3 aren't
4 there is
5 There are

C
1 under
2 in front of
3 on
4 between
5 behind

Comprehension

B 1F 2T 3T 4F 5T

Test 3

Vocabulary

A 1a 2b 3b 4a 5a
B 1c 2d 3e 4a 5b

C
1 maths
2 geography
3 history
4 science
5 music

Grammar

A
1 walk
2 has
3 doesn't
4 speak
5 does

B
1 do not/don't go
2 Does … like
3 brushes
4 does not/doesn't walk
5 Do … speak

C
1 Does Tina always clean her room?
2 We sometimes use a calculator.
3 She usually rides her bike to school.
4 I am often at school at 8 o'clock.
5 They never have lessons at the weekend.

Comprehension

B
1D 2A 3R 4S 5D

Test 4

Vocabulary

A

1d 2a 3c 4e 5b

B

1a 2a 3b 4a 5b

C
1 go
2 piano
3 watch
4 fly
5 ride

Grammar

A
1 Who
2 What
3 Where
4 Whose
5 When

B
1 can't (cannot)
2 can't (cannot)
3 can
4 can
5 can't (cannot)

C
1 Yes, you can.
2 No, he can't (cannot).
3 No, she can't (cannot).
4 Yes, I can.
5 Yes, they can.

Comprehension

B
1F 2T 3T 4F 5F

162

Test 5

Vocabulary

A
1 costume
2 parade
3 invitation
4 mask
5 fireworks

B
1 preparations
2 party hats
3 balloons
4 treasure
5 adults

C
1 street
2 catch
3 king
4 parade
5 cake

Grammar

A
1b 2b 3a 4b 5a
6a 7b 8b 9b 10a

B
1 him
2 her
3 me
4 them
5 us

Comprehension

B
1 the 4th of July
2 in the morning
3 great costumes
4 in the(ir) garden
5 in the evening

Test 6

Vocabulary

A
1c 2e 3b 4a 5d

B
1 pills
2 butter
3 snack
4 rice
5 menu

C
1 cheese
2 hungry
3 breakfast
4 fast food
5 delicious

Grammar

A
1a 2b 3a 4a 5b

B
1 a little
2 a little
3 a few
4 a few
5 a little

C
1 Tina drinks lots of water.
2 Mark makes a lot of sandwiches.
3 Have we got a lot of water?
4 Ann hasn't got a lot of chips.
5 Do we need a few plates?

Comprehension

B
1M 2B 3L 4B 5M

Test 7

Vocabulary

A
1 Cycling
2 trainers
3 Climbing
4 give up
5 Sailing

B
1 gymnast
2 boxer
3 footballer
4 swimmer
5 cyclist

C
1 feel
2 use
3 train
4 enter
5 leave

Grammar

A
1 Are
2 are
3 playing
4 They are
5 Is

B
1 am/'m watching
2 are/'re playing
3 is/'s running
4 are chasing
5 is/'s kicking

C
1 now
2 Saturday
3 moment
4 3 o'clock
5 tonight

Comprehension

B
1 this week

2 at the weekends
3 excited
4 years
5 money

Test 8

Vocabulary

A
1 houseboat
2 dentist
3 ghosts
4 stairs
5 flats

B
1 cottage
2 view
3 get up
4 make
5 get

C
1 horse
2 river
3 actor
4 footsteps
5 igloo

Grammar

A
1 is visiting
2 Do you go
3 am getting
4 walks
5 goes
6 is helping
7 work
8 are cleaning
9 Are you having
10 Do you cook

B
1 must
2 mustn't
3 must
4 mustn't
5 must

Comprehension

B 1S 2J 3C 4S 5J

Test 9

Vocabulary

A
1 village
2 smoke
3 bus
4 tent
5 port

B 1d 2e 3a 4c 5b

C
1 flight
2 passenger
3 station

163

4 airport
5 seat

Grammar

A
1 Were
2 were not/weren't
3 was
4 was
5 was not/wasn't

B
1 went
2 wore
3 got
4 had
5 did

C
1 wanted
2 stopped
3 danced
4 watched
5 carried

Comprehension

B
1F **2**F **3**F **4**T **5**T

Test 10
Vocabulary

A
1a **2**b **3**a **4**a **5**a

B
1 autograph
2 stage
3 adventure
4 singer
5 garage

C
1 character
2 director
3 comedy
4 cameraman
5 cartoon

Grammar

A
1 I didn't like the film on TV last night.
2 They didn't sell the photo for a lot of money.
3 Steve didn't speak to the famous actor.
4 The singers didn't sing for two hours.
5 Leslie didn't buy tickets for the theatre.

B
1 Did Stella go
2 No, she didn't.
3 Did you call
4 Yes, I did
5 Did she give

C
1 did he go
2 did Dad see
3 film did she like
4 did it start
5 did she buy you a ticket

Comprehension

B
1 in 1889
2 a black hat
3 because his mother was sick
4 to America
5 He made films.

Test 11
Vocabulary

A
1 parrots
2 unusual
3 map
4 worms
5 important

B
1 leopard
2 goldfish
3 eagle
4 swan
5 dolphin

C **1**c **2**e **3**d **4**b **5**a

Grammar

A
1 Butterflies are more beautiful than worms.
2 Cats are cleverer than birds.
3 Lions are stronger than monkeys.
4 Bats are more interesting than insects.
5 Ponies are nicer than crocodiles.

B
1 the best
2 the biggest
3 the ugliest
4 the worst
5 the scariest

C
1a **2**b **3**a **4**b **5**a

Comprehension

B
1a **2**c **3**d **4**b **5**e

Test 12
Vocabulary

A
1b **2**d **3**e **4**a **5**c

B
1 mountains
2 sunny

3 cloud
4 waterfall
5 rainy

C
1 cut down
2 foggy
3 rainbow
4 snowy
5 carry

Grammar

A
1 Is Jack going to go on holiday?
2 They aren't going to invite many friends.
3 Is the weather going to be bad tomorrow?
4 Caroline is going to buy a rucksack.
5 Is Kevin going to climb a cliff?

B
1 will/'ll fly
2 will/'ll have
3 will not/won't be
4 will/'ll survive
5 will not/won't take

C
1 Yes, they are.
2 No, it won't.
3 Yes, they will.
4 No, we aren't.
5 Yes, I am.

Comprehension

B
1 New Forest
2 at 8.15 am
3 because the weather will be cold
4 because they are going to collect leaves and other interesting things
5 £10

End-of-Year Test
Vocabulary

A
1 swans
2 unusual
3 swimmer
4 cloudy
5 landed

B
1 cycling
2 firefighter
3 train
4 audience
5 cliff

C
1 actor
2 role
3 theatre
4 stage
5 dream

164

D

1 survive
2 playground
3 robot
4 menu
5 tent

Grammar

A

1 is jumping
2 Is … watching
3 is not/isn't working
4 are sitting
5 Are … cooking

B

1 Did you go
2 went
3 wanted
4 did you stay
5 took

C

1b **2**a **3**b **4**b **5**b
6a **7**a **8**b **9**b **10**b

Comprehension

B

1 beautiful
2 garden
3 summer
4 shops
5 river

Writing

Model Letter
Hi Jason,
How are you? I want to tell you about my holiday.
I went to Scotland and I visited Edinburgh Castle. It was amazing! The castle is very big and old. I went there with my mum, my dad and my sister. We went in June and we stayed in Edinburgh for a week. The weather was rainy and cloudy, but it didn't matter. It was a good holiday!
How was your holiday?
Write back soon!
Jordan

Family and Friends

Name: _____ Date: _____

Vocabulary

A Match.

1 hungry ☐
2 cold ☐
3 old ☐
4 tall ☐
5 beautiful ☐

◯ / 5

B Complete the sentences with these words.

| aunt brother grandma son wife |

1 My grandad's _____ is my dad.
2 I'm ten, but my _____ Jason is only two.
3 My dad's sister is my _____ .
4 Polly is 7, her mum is 37 and her _____ is 67!
5 My mum is my dad's _____ .

◯ / 5

C Write the missing letters.

1 This is a big fish.   s _ _ _ _
2 A penguin is one.   b _ _ _
3 Your mum and dad are these.   p _ _ _ _ _ _
4 Old people's hair is this colour. g _ _ _
5 This person is good to you.   f _ _ _ _ _

◯ / 5

Grammar

A Complete the sentences with the correct form of be.

1 'Are you Jill's grandad?' 'Yes, I _____ .'
2 Sarah and I _____ sisters. We're cousins.
3 Paul _____ my best friend. He's great.
4 _____ they new pupils?
5 Peter _____ 5 years old. He's 6.

 / 5

B Circle the correct words.

1 Dad is tall and his / her hair is dark.
2 Hi, I'm Tracy and that's my / its mum over there.
3 We're Janet and Pauline and these are your / our brothers.
4 What's you're / your name?
5 Look at these babies. Their / Its hands are really small.

/ 5

C Write the apostrophe (') in the correct place.

1 This is Garys bike.
2 The childrens aunt is a teacher.
3 The babies eyes are blue.
4 Ritas mum is a scientist.
5 The twins names are Bob and Will.

/ 5

Reading

A Read the description of a best friend.

My name is Nevine and I'm eleven years old. I'm Egyptian and my home is in Alexandria. Anna is my best friend. She isn't from Egypt. She's from England, but her home is in Alexandria. She's twelve years old, she's tall and her hair is short and dark. She's very clever, but she isn't crazy about school. She's crazy about animals and she's got a great horse. Its name is Rufus. We visit Rufus every day. Anna's family is nice too. Anna's brother, Jack, is sixteen and he likes tricks. His tricks are really funny! Her sister is twenty and her name is Lisa. She's cool. Anna's mum and dad are scientists. They are very nice people. I'm happy that Anna is my friend!

Comprehension

B Circle the correct words.

1 Anna is from Egypt / England.
2 Anna is / isn't crazy about animals.
3 Rufus is Anna's brother / horse.
4 Jack's / Lisa's tricks are funny.
5 Lisa is sixteen / twenty.

/ 10

 Total ⬭ / 40

My Favourite Things

Name: _____   Date: _____

Vocabulary

A Write the missing letters.

1 This is a small, soft toy.   t _ _ _ _ b _ _ _
2 This has got wheels.   s _ _ _ _ _ _ _ _ _
3 This is a small computer.   l _ _ _ _ _ _
4 This game has got many pieces.   p _ _ _ _ _ _
5 This is an animal in your home.   p _ _

 / 5

B Circle the correct words.

1 I've got a country / globe in my bedroom.
2 This book isn't good for children. It's very exciting / scary.
3 Look at the photos on Dad's camera / bike.
4 Jackie's new ice / moving skates are great.
5 Thank you for the birthday picture / present.

 / 5

C Complete the sentences with these words.

comic   game   message   piano   watch

1 My new computer _____ is great.
2 There is a _____ on your mobile phone.
3 Kate's crazy about music. She's got a _____ and a guitar.
4 Look at my _____ . It's three o'clock.
5 This Spiderman _____ has got 16 pages.

/ 5

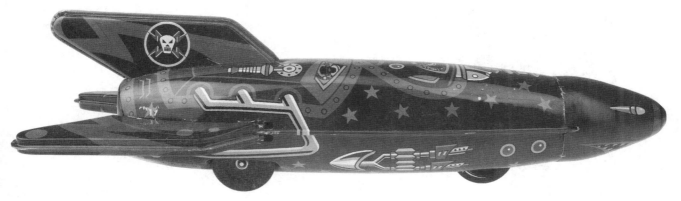

Grammar

A Complete the sentences with the correct form of have/has got.

1 John is very happy. He _____ a new pet.
2 'Have you got a laptop?' 'No, I _____ .'
3 Julie _____ a big bike. It's small.
4 We _____ two cars, one for Mum and one for Dad.
5 _____ your grandad _____ a pet?

 / 5

B Circle the correct words.

1 Is / Are there any toys in the classroom?
2 There's / There are a map in my bedroom.
3 There isn't / aren't any books in your bag.
4 'Is there a pencil under my desk?' 'Yes, there's / there is.'
5 There's / There are three balls in the garden.

/ 5

C Look at the pictures and complete the sentences with these prepositions of place.

> behind between in front of on under

1 The ball is _____ the table.

2 The ball is _____ the chair.

3 The ball is _____ the table.

4 The ball is _____ the chairs.

5 The ball is _____ the chair.

/ 5

Reading

A Read about these cool toys.

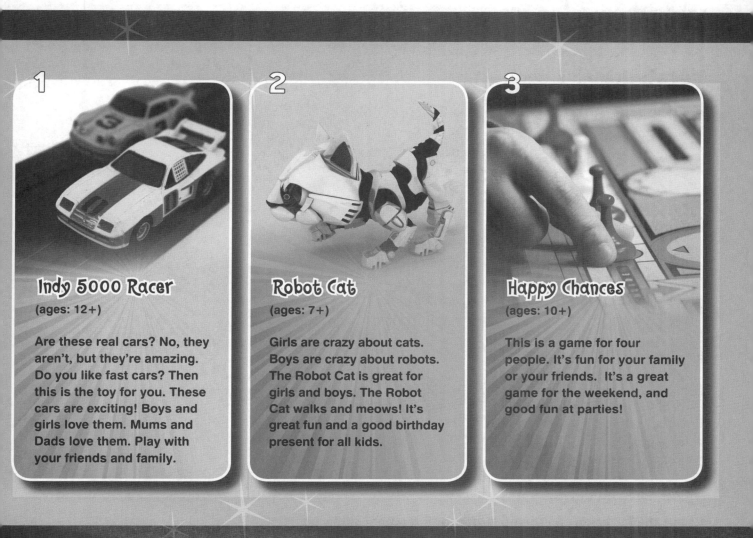

1 Indy 5000 Racer
(ages: 12+)

Are these real cars? No, they aren't, but they're amazing. Do you like fast cars? Then this is the toy for you. These cars are exciting! Boys and girls love them. Mums and Dads love them. Play with your friends and family.

2 Robot Cat
(ages: 7+)

Girls are crazy about cats. Boys are crazy about robots. The Robot Cat is great for girls and boys. The Robot Cat walks and meows! It's great fun and a good birthday present for all kids.

3 Happy Chances
(ages: 10+)

This is a game for four people. It's fun for your family or your friends. It's a great game for the weekend, and good fun at parties!

Comprehension

B Write **T** (true) or **F** (false).

1 *Indy 5000 Racer* is a board game. ☐
2 *Indy 5000 Racer* is exciting and fast. ☐
3 The Robot Cat is for boys. ☐
4 *Happy Chances* is for two people. ☐
5 *Happy Chances* is a game for parties. ☐

◯ / 10

Total ◯ / 40

3 School Life

Name: _____ Date: _____

Vocabulary

A Choose the correct answers.

1 12 + 9 is a _____ .
   a sum   b date

2 The _____ near my house is great fun.
   a bookcase   b playground

3 Sarah's art _____ isn't nice.
   a classmate   b teacher

4 Students have lunch in the _____ .
   a cafeteria   b library

5 Mike's got a new _____ for maths class.
   a calculator   b answer   / 5

B Match.

1 read   a a bicycle
2 sing   b a uniform
3 do   c a comic
4 ride   d a song
5 wear   e homework   / 5

C Put the letters in the correct order to find school subjects.

1 s t a h m   _____
2 h a p o g g r e y _____
3 s i t h r y o   _____
4 n i c c e s e   _____
5 s i m c u   _____   / 5

Grammar

A Circle the correct words.

1 Ted and Carol walk / walks to school every day.
2 He have / has lunch at 12 o'clock.
3 Cindy don't / doesn't talk on the phone.
4 I speak / speaks English and French.
5 'Does Robert like maths?' 'Yes, he do / does.'   / 5

B Complete the sentences with the Present Simple of the verbs in brackets.

1 We _____ (not go) to school on Friday.
2 _____ John _____ (like) history?
3 Lisa _____ (brush) her teeth before school.
4 Ron _____ (not walk) to school.
5 _____ they _____ (speak) English?   / 5

C Put the words in the correct order to make sentences and questions.

1 ? / room / Tina / clean / always / her / does
   _____

2 a / we / calculator / use / sometimes
   _____

3 her / usually / she / bike / school / rides / to
   _____

4 at / I / often / am / o'clock / 8 / school / at
   _____

5 weekend / they / never / at / the / have / lessons
   _____   / 5

Reading

A Read about different children and their schools.

Ann
(10 years old)

I always get up at 7 o'clock in the morning. I always have breakfast and I walk to school. We start lessons at 8 o'clock and we finish school at 3 o'clock. I usually do my homework after school, but I sometimes watch a DVD.

Doug
(13 years old)

I love school! I meet my friend Joe and we walk to school together. We always play football in the playground before our lessons. Joe never does his homework, but I always do my homework.

Rachel
(7 years old)

I finish school at 2 o'clock. Then Mum and I walk home and we have lunch together. I like books, and I often listen to music. I sometimes sing songs!

Sam
(16 years old)

School is great! My favourite subject is maths. I always study maths, but I never study history. I often walk to school, but I sometimes ride my bike.

Comprehension

B Write **A** (Ann), **D** (Doug), **R** (Rachel) or **S** (Sam).

Who ...

1 always does their homework? ☐

2 finishes school at 3 o'clock? ☐

3 reads books? ☐

4 loves maths? ☐

5 goes to school with a friend? ☐

/ 10

Total / 40

Hobbies

Name: _____ Date: _____

Vocabulary

A Match.

a

b

c

d

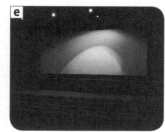
e

1 tourist   ☐
2 mirror   ☐
3 entrance   ☐
4 cinema   ☐
5 restaurant   ☐

◯ / 5

B Choose the correct answers.

1 _____ You're the winner!
   a Congratulations!   b Thanks!

2 Do you _____ stamps?
   a collect   b do

3 We go to the sports _____ every Saturday.
   a park   b centre

4 We often see plays at the _____ .
   a theatre   b café

5 My uncle _____ the guitar.
   a makes   b plays

◯ / 5

C Complete the sentences with these words.

| fly   go   piano   ride   watch |

1 Janet and I _____ ice-skating on Sundays.
2 My sister plays the _____ with my mum.
3 Do you _____ DVDs at the weekend?
4 We can't _____ a kite today. It's very cold.
5 Rachel doesn't like that _____ at the amusement park.

◯ / 5

Grammar

A Complete the sentences with these words.

> What   When   Where   Who   Whose

1 '_____ is that woman?' 'That's our new teacher.'
2 '_____ is your friend's name?' 'Sophie.'
3 '_____ are you from, Pedro?' 'Spain.'
4 '_____ bag is this?' 'It's Fred's.'
5 '_____ is the party?' 'It's tomorrow.'

/ 5

B Complete the sentences with **can** or **can't**.

1 Cats _____ play football.
2 Babies _____ write their names.
3 John _____ read books. He usually reads in the library.
4 My sister _____ ride a bike. She rides her bike every weekend.
5 A dog _____ use a computer.

/ 5

C Write short answers.

1 Dad, can I go swimming?   _____ (✓)
2 Can Jack go on this ride?   _____ (✗)
3 Can Sally have lunch now?   _____ (✗)
4 Can you drive us to school, Mum?   _____ (✓)
5 Can they watch TV this evening?   _____ (✓)

/ 5

Reading

A Read about Rebecca and her family.

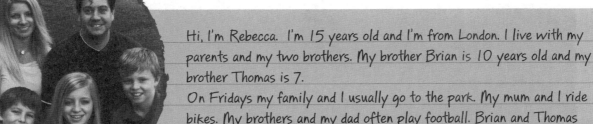

Hi, I'm Rebecca. I'm 15 years old and I'm from London. I live with my parents and my two brothers. My brother Brian is 10 years old and my brother Thomas is 7.

On Fridays my family and I usually go to the park. My mum and I ride bikes. My brothers and my dad often play football. Brian and Thomas are crazy about football. Mum and I like swimming. We go to the sports centre on Friday evenings. The sports centre is great for swimming. Brian and Thomas can't swim. They usually stay at home and play computer games.

On Saturdays we visit my grandma and we play tennis in the park near her house. My brothers are very good at tennis and they usually win!

Comprehension

B Write T (true) or F (false).

1 Rebecca's brothers are the same age. ☐
2 Rebecca's dad can play football. ☐
3 Rebecca goes to the sport centre. ☐
4 Rebecca's brothers can swim. ☐
5 Rebecca usually wins at tennis. ☐

/ 10

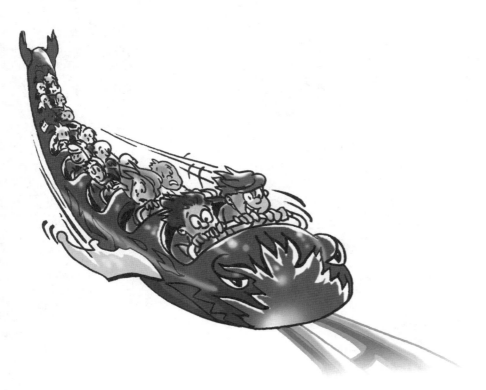

Total / 40

Vocabulary

A Write the missing letters.

1 You can wear this at a carnival.   c _ _ _ _ _ _ _
2 A celebration where people walk in the street.   p _ _ _ _ _ _
3 You ask a friend to a party with this.   i _ _ _ _ _ _ _ _ _ _
4 You can wear this on your face.   m _ _ _
5 These make red, green and blue lights in the sky.   f _ _ _ _ _ _ _ _ _

/ 5

B Complete the paragraph with these words.

> adults   balloons   party hats   preparations   treasure

A party for a young child is a great idea, but there are many (1) _____ before the event. Here are some ideas. First, make lots of (2) _____ for all the children. They can wear them on their heads. Also, make many (3) _____ so the children can throw and catch them. Hide (4) _____ in the garden for children to find – chocolates or small toys are a good idea. Finally, invite some (5) _____ to the party. They can help you!

/ 5

C Circle the correct words.

1 This house is in a nice beach / street.
2 The young girl can throw / catch the ball.
3 This person is a funny king / queen.
4 There are many people at this stall / parade.
5 The cake / candle is for the party tonight.

/ 5

Grammar

A Choose the correct answers.

1 Let's _____ to the carnival this weekend.
  a to go   b go

2 _____ eat all the cake!
  a Not   b Don't

3 Don't _____ the ball to Stevie because he can't catch.
  a throw   b throws

4 It's a nice day. _____ swimming.
  a Let go   b Let's go

5 Let's _____ a party!
  a have   b has

6 Has Derek got _____ for the festival?
  a a costume   b costume

7 There's _____ invitation for you on your desk.
  a a   b an

8 I want _____ music at my party.
  a a great   b great

9 We haven't got _____ party hats.
  a some   b any

10 I need _____ money for Mike's present.
  a some   b any

 / 10

B Complete the sentences with these words.

> her   him   me   them   us

1 Paul isn't at the festival. Let's phone _____ .
2 Where's Grandma? I want to give _____ this invitation.
3 When's the party? Send _____ a message, please.
4 Look at all these presents. Let's open _____!
5 We want a cake, Mum. Can you make a cake for _____?

/ 5

Reading

A Read about a special day in the USA.

**The 4th of July
(Jason, 8, USA)**

The 4th of July is my favourite day of the year. In America we call this day Independence Day. People have fun and lots of families have parties. I send invitations to all my cousins and they come to our house. They like coming to my city, Atlanta, because there is a big carnival here. In the morning we watch the parade. Lots of people wear great costumes. There are red, white and blue balloons in the streets and the city looks great. Some people have picnics in the park, but we go home and we have lunch in our garden. Dad makes burgers and we have ice cream. We sing songs and we have fun! In the evening there are fireworks in the city. They're amazing! People in my street watch the fireworks and we have a huge street party. I always love it!

Comprehension

B Answer the questions.

1 Which is Jason's favourite day?   _____

2 When do Jason and his family watch the parade?   _____

3 What do people wear to the carnival?   _____

4 Where do Jason and his family have lunch?   _____

5 When do they watch fireworks?   _____   / 10

Total / 40

Food!

Name: _____ Date: _____

Vocabulary

A Match.

a

b

c

d

e

1 bill ☐
2 water ☐
3 chicken ☐
4 waiter ☐
5 bread ☐

◯ / 5

B Circle the odd one out.

1 pills   chips   meat
2 lunch   dinner   butter
3 plate   snack   bowl
4 rice   milk   juice
5 fork   knife   menu

◯ / 5

C Complete the sentences with these words.

breakfast   cheese   delicious   fast food   hungry

1 Do you want _____ on your spaghetti?
2 Is lunch ready? I'm really _____ .
3 We often have eggs for _____ .
4 Burgers are my favourite _____ .
5 I love chocolate. It's _____ .

◯ / 5

Grammar

A Choose the correct answers.

1 There aren't _____ meals on this menu.
   a many   b much

2 I'm sorry, but we haven't got _____ orange juice.
   a many   b much

3 This fast food restaurant sells _____ burgers.
   a many   b much

4 _____ sandwiches do you want?
   a How many   b How much

5 '_____ are these apples?' 'Two pounds.'
   a How many   b How much   / 5

B Complete the sentences with a few or a little.

1 Does the baby want _____ milk?

2 Can we have _____ tea, please?

3 There are _____ bananas here for you.

4 Do you have _____ cakes for me and my friends, Mum?

5 Grandma loves _____ coffee with her breakfast.   / 5

C Put the words in the correct order to make sentences and questions.

1 water / drinks / of / Tina / lots

   _____

2 a / Mark / lot / sandwiches / makes / of

   _____

3 ? / lot / water / got / a / of / have / we

   _____

4 got / Ann / lot / chips / of / hasn't / a

   _____

5 ? / plates / need / a / do / we / few

   _____   / 5

Reading

A Read these descriptions of favourite foods.

Maria, 8, Mexico

In Mexico we've got lots of great food. My dad has got a restaurant and he makes delicious meals. He also makes a drink with bananas. It's sweet and I love it! I also like cakes and chocolate. My sister likes them too. We eat these desserts every week!

Benito, 12, Italy

We eat a lot of Italian food in my family. It's great, but my favourite food is eggs and chips. My uncle is from England and he loves eggs and chips too. We eat this meal together at my house! My sister doesn't like eggs, so she usually eats fish or meat.

Laura, 10, Australia

In my family we eat a lot of fish. My dad buys the fish and Mum cooks it! I like fish, but it isn't my favourite food. My favourite meal is chicken and rice. My grandma often makes this meal for me at her house. It's delicious!

Comprehension

B Write M (Maria), B (Benito) or L (Laura).

Who ...

1 likes a sweet drink?

2 is crazy about eggs and chips?

3 eats at his / her grandma's home?

4 has a meal at home with his / her uncle?

5 eats dessert with his / her sister?

/ 10

 Total / 40

7 Sport

Name: _____ Date: _____

Vocabulary

A Circle the correct words.

1 Cycling / Running is Mike's favourite sport. He rides his bike every day.
2 These trainers / players are great for my feet.
3 Diving / Climbing is an exciting sport, but you need good boots.
4 You're great at football. Don't drop / give up!
5 Sailing / Riding is great fun. We go in my dad's boat at the weekends.

/ 5

B Put the letters in the correct order to find sports people.

1 nymstag _____
2 rexbo _____
3 botolelraf _____
4 mimswer _____
5 ytcsilc _____

/ 5

C Complete the dialogues with these words.

enter   feel   leave   train   use

Jeff: Thomas is in a boxing match this weekend.
Bobby: Really? Does he (1) _____ scared?
Jeff: No! He's excited!

Jill: Stan, can I (2) _____ your bike for an hour?
Stan: Of course, Jill. Here you are.

Mike: Can I (3) _____ at the sports centre?
Ryan: Yes, of course you can.

Mary: Can you (4) _____ the running competition?
Kate: No. I've got lots of homework this week.

Frank: Lisa, please play basketball with me today!
Lisa: Frank, (5) _____ me alone! I'm studying.

/ 5

Grammar

A Circle the correct words.

1 Are / Am you talking to your mum?
2 John and I is / are watching football.
3 Grandad is play / playing tennis with Dad.
4 Are they / They are chasing the cat.
5 Is / Are Katie wearing her helmet?

/ 5

B Complete the paragraph with the Present Continuous of the verbs in brackets.

I (1) _____ (watch) Sam and his friends in the park today.
They (2) _____ (play) football. Sam has got the ball and he
(3) _____ (run) very fast. His friends (4) _____
(chase) him! He (5) _____ (kick) the ball. Yes, it's a goal! Well
done, Sam. What a great day for him!

/ 5

C Complete the sentences with these words.

3 o'clock   moment   now   Saturday   tonight

1 Please be quiet. Dad is sleeping _____ .
2 I'm having a party on _____ . Can you come?
3 Pauline is studying at the _____ .
4 I can't come to your game. I have a lesson at _____ .
5 Grandma's visiting at 6 o'clock _____ .

/ 5

Reading

A Read the interview about a horse riding competition.

Reporter: Hello, Katie. Can you tell us about the horse riding competition?

Katie: Yes, of course. I'm entering a competition in my town this week. I'm practising at the moment because I'm getting ready for it.

Reporter: Great! How often do you practise, Katie?

Katie: I sometimes practise after school, but I always practise at the weekends.

Reporter: It's hard work, then! How do you feel about the competition?

Katie: Well, I'm excited and I'm thinking about it a lot. My horse is a fantastic animal. He's five years old and he's a champion. I know we can win!

Reporter: And what is the prize for the winner?

Katie: The winner gets £500! But my dad is getting me a beautiful new helmet, so I'm happy with that.

Reporter: That's great! Good luck, Katie!

Katie: Thank you!

Comprehension

B Circle the correct words.

1 Katie is entering the competition this week / at the moment.

2 She always practises after school / at the weekends.

3 She is excited / scared about the competition.

4 Katie's horse is five months / years old.

5 The prize for the competition is money / a helmet.

 / 10

Total  / 40

Vocabulary

A Write the missing letters.

1 You can live on a river in this.   h _ _ _ _ _ _ _ _ _
2 This person looks at your teeth.   d _ _ _ _ _ _ _
3 You read about these in scary stories.   g _ _ _ _ _ _
4 You can walk up or down these.   s _ _ _ _ _
5 You can live in these and there are many in one building. f _ _ _ _ _    / 5

B Complete the dialogue with these words.

> cottage   get   get up   make   view

Bobby: Welcome to my (1) _____ .
Stella: Thanks. It's got a lovely (2) _____ of the sea.
Bobby: Yes, it's great! Every day I (3) _____ early, I drink coffee and I look at the sea from the kitchen.
Stella: You're very lucky. But it isn't warm here.
Bobby: Oh, sorry. Are you cold? I can (4) _____ a fire.
Stella: Yes, please. I don't want to (5) _____ sick.
Bobby: Of course!   / 5

C Circle the odd one out.

1 house   horse   hut
2 doctor   pilot   river
3 actor   castle   tower
4 taxi driver   shop assistant   footsteps
5 fire fighter   igloo   hairdresser   / 5

Grammar

A Circle the correct words.

1 Diana visits / is visiting London at the moment.
2 Do you go / Are you going to the shops often?
3 I get / am getting sick, so I must see a doctor.
4 Sam usually walks / is walking to work.
5 Michelle often goes / is going to Spain for her holidays.
6 'Where's the teacher?' 'She helps / is helping a student.'
7 Doctors rarely work / are working at night.
8 Bob and Jane clean / are cleaning their cottage this weekend.
9 'We're at the amusement park.' 'Do you have / Are you having fun?'
10 Do you cook / Are you cooking breakfast every day?

/ 10

B Complete the dialogue with must or mustn't.

Paul: My friends and I are visiting the museum today. Is the museum free?
Lisa: No, you (1) _____ pay at the entrance. It's £5 for a ticket.
Paul: Can we bring food inside?
Lisa: No, I'm sorry. You (2) _____ eat in the museum.
Paul: Are you open at night?
Lisa: No. All visitors (3) _____ leave at 5 o'clock. The museum closes.
Paul: Can we touch the things in the museum?
Lisa: No, you (4) _____ . You can break them.
Paul: Can we take bags into the museum?
Lisa: Yes, you can, but you (5) _____ leave them at the entrance.
Paul: OK. Thank you!

/ 5

Reading

A Read about different jobs.

John, 45

I'm a taxi driver. I like my job, but sometimes I am tired after work. I work for 12 hours every day. I work at night and at the weekends too, but it's a good job because I make lots of money.

Sandra, 23

I'm a hairdresser. I love my job because I see lots of people. I work with three other hairdressers, and one of them is my sister, Jill. We have great fun!

Carlos, 33

I'm an actor. I like my job, but I don't work very much. I sometimes work on TV programmes and in theatres, but I want to be in a film. My mum doesn't like my job. She wanted me to be a doctor!

Comprehension

B Write J (John), S (Sandra) or C (Carlos).

Who ...

1 likes other people at his / her job?

2 works in a car?

3 wants a job in film?

4 works with a person from his / her family?

5 works at night?

 / 10

Total ⬭ / 40

Holidays and Travel

Name: _____ Date: _____

Vocabulary

A Complete the sentences with these words.

| bus   port   smoke   tent   village |

1 My aunt lives in a _____ with many fields around it.
2 The _____ from that fire is really hot!
3 Let's go by _____ and leave the car at home.
4 Jason's got a new _____, so he's camping this weekend.
5 The ship leaves the _____ in the morning.

⬤ / 5

B Match.

1 pyramid   ☐
2 suitcase   ☐
3 train   ☐
4 camel   ☐
5 bus stop   ☐

⬤ / 5

C Write the missing letters.

1 You take this from London to New York.   f _ _ _ _ _ _
2 A person on a bus is this.   p _ _ _ _ _ _ _ _ _
3 Trains leave from here.   s _ _ _ _ _ _ _
4 There are many planes in this place.   a _ _ _ _ _ _ _
5 A person sits in this on a plane.   s _ _ _

⬤ / 5

Grammar

A **Complete the sentences with the correct form of be in the Past Simple.**

1 _____ you on holiday last week?

2 'Were the camels scary?' 'No, they _____ .'

3 I _____ in France for a month and it was great!

4 There _____ a hot air balloon in the sky yesterday.

5 'Was he at the station?' 'No, he _____ .'   / 5

B **Complete the sentences with the Past Simple of the verbs in brackets.**

1 We _____ (go) to Italy by ship.

2 Harold _____ (wear) shorts and a T-shirt to the beach.

3 I _____ (get) sick on the plane.

4 They _____ (have) a great time on holiday in Crete.

5 Sophie _____ (do) all her shopping yesterday.   / 5

C **Complete the sentences with these verbs in the Past Simple.**

| carry | dance | stop | want | watch |

1 He _____ a new shirt, but he didn't have any money.

2 They _____ at the restaurant for a meal.

3 I _____ at the party last night.

4 Fiona _____ a good film yesterday.

5 Mark _____ his books in his rucksack.   / 5

Reading

A Read a story about Nancy's holiday.

Last summer my family and I spent a week in a village in France. The village was beautiful. We stayed in a small hotel with nice rooms and big beds. We walked around the village in the day and stopped at cafés for coffee. On the second day we visited a castle near the village. The castle was fantastic! We went inside the castle and we saw many old things. Later, we camped in tents for a night. It was very cold! We had sleeping bags, but Mum was still cold. I was OK because I wore all my clothes. The next day we went back to the village. Mum and my sister did lots of shopping. Boring! Dad and I sat at a café and we had chocolate ice cream. I wanted to stay for another week, but Dad said no!

Comprehension

B Write T (true) or F (false).

1 The family stayed in a hotel with small beds.

2 They went to the castle on the first day.

3 Nancy's mum was warm in her sleeping bag.

4 Nancy's sister went shopping.

5 Nancy and her dad had a nice snack.

/ 10

Total ( ) / 40

10 Fame!

Vocabulary

A Choose the correct answers.

1 My _____ invited me to the cinema yesterday.
   a neighbour   b pop group
2 The actor talked about the new film in a TV _____ .
   a concert   b interview
3 The play is a very sad _____ .
   a drama   b dream
4 I didn't like the songs in that _____ .
   a musical   b audience
5 My cousin's got a small _____ in a film!
   a role   b set

/ 5

B Complete the sentences with these words.

adventure autograph garage singer stage

1 The actress gave fans her _____ in front of her hotel.
2 We didn't see the group because we weren't near the _____ .
3 Do you like _____ films?
4 Jennifer Lopez is a famous _____ .
5 That film star has got three cars in his _____ !

/ 5

C Put the letters in the correct order to find film words.

1 ratacrech   _____
2 tedirroc   _____
3 yemcod   _____
4 macremana   _____
5 notorac   _____

/ 5

Grammar

A Rewrite the sentences with the verbs in bold in the negative form of the Past Simple.

1 I **liked** the film on TV last night.

_____

2 They **sold** the photo for a lot of money.

_____

3 Steve **spoke** to the famous actor.

_____

4 The singers **sang** for two hours.

_____

5 Leslie **bought** tickets for the theatre.

_____

/ 5

B Complete the dialogue with the correct form of the Past Simple.

Ann: (1) _____ (Stella / go) to the concert yesterday?

George: (2) _____. She was sick, so she didn't go.

Ann: Oh, no! (3) _____ (you / call) her this morning?

George: (4) _____, but I spoke to her mum because Stella was in bed.

Ann: Hmm. (5) _____ (she / give) her ticket to a friend?

George: No, but she gave it to her brother Oliver, and he came to the concert with me!

/ 5

C Complete the questions.

1 'Where _____?'   'He went to the cinema.'
2 'Who _____?'   'Dad saw Uncle Jack.'
3 'Which _____?'   'She liked the adventure film.'
4 'When _____?'   'It started at 7 o'clock.'
5 'Why _____?'   'She bought me a ticket because she's nice.'

/ 5

Reading

A   Read about Charlie Chaplin.

Charlie Chaplin was a famous actor and film director. He was born in London in 1889. His famous character was a very funny man. He wore big trousers, big shoes and a black hat. He did crazy things on stage. Audiences loved his character!

Charlie Chaplin started his work in London theatres. His mother was a singer. One night she was sick, so Charlie went on the stage and sang. He was only five!

He went to America at age 21. He found a job at the Keystone Film Company. He was in his first comedy in 1914. He never spoke, of course, because characters didn't speak in the old films.

Charlie Chaplin made films for 65 years. His films are famous all over the world. He died in 1977. He was 88 years old.

Comprehension

B   Answer the questions.

1   When was Charlie Chaplin born?

_____

2   What did his famous character wear on his head?

_____

3   Why did Charlie sing on stage at age five?

_____

4   Where did he go at age 21?

_____

5   What did he do for 65 years?

_____   / 10

Total / 40

Animals

Name: _____ Date: _____

Vocabulary

A Circle the correct words.

Joe: What are you reading?

Tina: It's an article about (1) parrots / puppies. They're amazing birds!

Joe: What does the article say?

Tina: Well, they are (2) unusual / tired birds. They can talk!

Joe: Really? Where do they live?

Tina: Look here. There is a (3) path / map in the book.

Joe: Ah, yes. They live in warm places. And what do they eat?

Tina: Many things! They eat small things like fruit and (4) worms / whales.

Joe: Are they good pets?

Tina: Yes, but they must stay inside the house. That is very (5) important / dangerous!   / 5

B Write the missing letters.

1 This animal is a big cat and it can run fast.   l _ _ _ _ _ _

2 This lives in water.   g _ _ _ _ _ _ _

3 This is a large bird and it flies high in the sky.   e _ _ _ _ _

4 You can see this beautiful white bird in parks.   s _ _ _

5 This clever animal lives in the sea.   d _ _ _ _ _ _   / 5

C Match.

1 cave   ☐

2 rabbit ☐

3 lift   ☐

4 bat   ☐

5 torch   ☐

/ 5

Grammar

A Write sentences about these animals. Use the comparative form.

1 butterflies / beautiful / worms

   _____

2 cats / clever / birds

   _____

3 lions / strong / monkeys

   _____

4 bats / interesting / insects

   _____

5 ponies / nice / crocodiles

   _____   ◯ / 5

B Complete the sentences with the superlative forms of the adjectives in brackets.

1 My cat is _____ (good) pet in our house!
2 Whales are _____ (big) animals in the sea.
3 I don't like lizards. They're _____ (ugly) animals on the planet!
4 My neighbour's cat is _____ (bad) cat in our neighbourhood!
5 Crocodiles are _____ (scary) animals in the world.   ◯ / 5

C Choose the correct answers.

1 Which animal is the _____ one?
   a tallest   b taller
2 Elephants are _____ than leopards.
   a largest   b larger
3 Do you think zoos are _____ interesting than amusement parks?
   a more   b the most
4 Insects are _____ things in the world!
   a more horrible   b the most horrible
5 I like monkeys. They are _____ animals in a zoo.   ◯ / 5
   a the funniest   b funnier than

Reading

A Read about a person with many pets.

Kathryn Johns loves animals. She likes big animals and small animals, pretty animals and even ugly animals! Kathryn lives in a village and she has got a very big garden. (1) _____

At the moment, Kathryn has got four dogs, five cats and three rabbits. (2) _____ That's a lot of pets! How did she get all these pets? (3) _____ The dog needed a home, so she took him to her home. (4) _____ So she took the kitten too! Later, a neighbour visited her. He had a sick rabbit, so she took it. The rabbit is fine now, and very happy!

Now, Kathryn looks after lots of sick animals. (5) _____ They are the happiest animals in the world!

Comprehension

B Complete the article with the sentences below.

a   So, she can have many pets!

b   But the dog also had a little friend – a kitten!

c   She's also got a mouse and a lizard.

d   She found her first pet, a dog, in a field near her house.

e   She gives them a fantastic home.

 / 10

 / 40

Weather and Nature

Name: _____ Date: _____

Vocabulary

A Match.

1 cliff ☐
2 ocean ☐
3 forest ☐
4 raincoat ☐
5 rocks ☐

/ 5

B Complete the email with these words.

cloud   mountains   rainy   sunny   waterfall

E-mail

New   Reply   Forward   Print   Delete   Send & Receive

▶ Attachments:

Hi John,

How are you? Do you want to drive to the (1) _____ this week? It's beautiful up there with nice views of the area, and it's going to be warm and (2) _____. There won't be a (3) _____ in the sky, so it will be a great day. We can walk to a small (4) _____ . It's a great place for a picnic. It's going to be (5) _____ and wet next week, so we must go before then!

Write soon,

Rob

/ 5

C Circle the correct words.

1 Who cut down / switched on the trees in the park?
2 I can't see a thing! It's very foggy / windy outside.
3 Look at that canyon / rainbow in the sky!
4 We like snowy / cloudy weather because we can go skiing.
5 Stan, can you destroy / carry the suitcase? It's very big.

/ 5

Grammar

A Put the words in the correct order to make sentences and questions.

1 ? / to / Jack / on / going / holiday / is / go

_____

2 going / they / invite / to / many / friends / aren't

_____

3 ? / to / weather / be / bad / the / going / is / tomorrow

_____

4 rucksack / buy / a / going / Caroline / is / to

_____

5 ? / is / cliff / to / Kevin / going / a / climb

_____   / 5

B Complete the sentences with will or won't and the verbs in brackets.

1 Michelle has a plane ticket for Paris. She _____ (fly) on Tuesday.
2 It's beautiful in the rainforest. You _____ (have) a great time.
3 It never rains here. Soon, there _____ (be) any water.
4 They don't have much food, but they _____ (survive).
5 Mike's house is near here. The journey _____ (take) a long time.   / 5

C Write short answers.

1 Are scientists going to be there?   _____ [✓]
2 Will the weather be good tomorrow?   _____ [✗]
3 Will they make a tree house?   _____ [✓]
4 Are we going to look for tornados?   _____ [✗]
5 Are you going on a trip, Thomas?   _____ [✓]   / 5

Reading

A Read this letter from a teacher to his pupils parents.

Dear parents,

On the 16th of October the pupils in Class 5A are going to visit the New Forest. They're going to study the different kinds of plants in the forest. It'll be an exciting event!

Here is the information for the event. We're going to leave at 8.15 am, so please arrive at the school 20 minutes before then. All pupils must bring their lunch.

The weather will be cold, so pupils must wear warm clothes and boots. We're going to collect leaves and other interesting things, so students must bring small boxes or bags. Pupils can't take their mobile phones. I'll have my mobile phone, so parents can call me at 0778833222.

The price of the trip is £10. Please send the money before the 12th of October.

Thank you!

Mr Richards

Comprehension

B Answer the questions.

1 Where are the pupils going to go for their trip?

_____

2 When are the pupils going to leave for the trip?

_____

3 Why must they wear warm clothes?

_____

4 Why do the pupils need boxes?

_____

5 How much does the trip cost?

_____

 / 10

  / 40

End-of-Year Test

Name: _____ Date: _____

Vocabulary

A **Circle the correct words.**

1 We gave bread to the swans / sharks on the lake.
2 This is an unusual / important toy. It talks!
3 My uncle is a good swimsuit / swimmer.
4 It's very cloudy / snowy today. It's going to rain.
5 The plane carried / landed at 9 o'clock in the morning.

/ 5

B **Complete the word groups.**

audience cliff cycling firefighter train

1 climbing, riding, _____
2 pilot, hairdresser, _____
3 platform, station, _____
4 concert, singer, _____
5 mountain, canyon, _____

/ 5

C **Complete the paragraph with these words.**

actor dream role stage theatre

One day Michael wants to be a great (1) _____ . He loves films, plays and television
shows. He wants to play an exciting (2) _____ in a drama or musical. Michael
goes to a drama club once a week and he works in a (3) _____ on Friday and
Saturday nights. He sometimes practises on the (4) _____ after work with his
friends. Acting is Michael's (5) _____ !

 / 5

D Circle the odd one out.

1 train   survive   practise
2 cottage   igloo   playground
3 eagle   robot   leopard
4 menu   chips   rice
5 suitcase   basket   tent

/ 5

Grammar

A Complete the sentences with the Present Continuous of the verbs in brackets.

1 Look! That dolphin _____ (jump) out of the water!
2 _____ James _____ (watch) football on TV?
3 The lift _____ (not work), so you must take the stairs.
4 The passengers _____ (sit) in their seats.
5 _____ you _____ (cook) breakfast now?

/ 5

B Complete the dialogue with the Past Simple of the verbs in brackets.

Mario: Hi Nelly. (1) _____ (you / go) to an island for your holiday?

Nelly: No. I (2) _____ (go) to the mountains with some friends.

We (3) _____ (want) to see forests and snow.

Mario: Where (4) _____ (you / stay)?

Nelly: We (5) _____ (take) our tents.

Mario: Oh, great! I love camping.

/ 5

C Choose the correct answers.

1 My flat is _____ than Pat's flat, but I like it.
   a smallest   b smaller

2 Anita _____ at work today because she is on holiday.
   a wasn't   b weren't

3 She usually _____ sick on ships.
   a is getting   b gets

4 My brother thinks parrots are the _____ animals in the world.
   a cleverer   b cleverest

5 The children must _____ their rooms today.
   a to clean   b clean

6 Look at that cat! _____ head is very big!
   a Its   b It's

7 We _____ to Grandma's house on Sundays.
   a usually go   b go usually

8 My brother _____ read a book. He's only two.
   a can   b can't

9 Rachel has got _____ books in her bag.
   a a little   b a few

10 Grandad _____ to cook burgers this evening.
   a will   b is going

/ 10

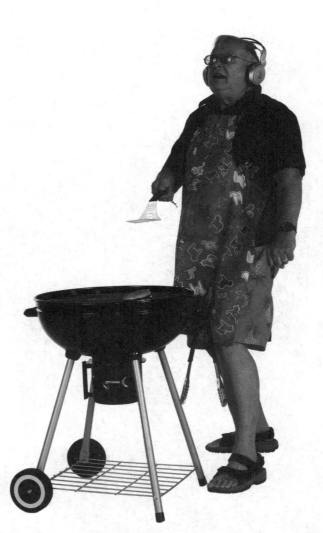

Reading

A Read the article about kinds of holidays.

For a quiet holiday, you can stay in a cottage. Cottages are usually old and very beautiful. You can stay in a cottage in a village or near a forest. You can have meals in the garden of the cottage and you can go for a walk in the area. You'll have a lovely time!

Camping is good because it isn't expensive. Summer is the best time of the year for camping because it's warm. You can camp in many places. You can make a fire and cook meals. It's great fun! You must bring a tent and a sleeping bag. You must also bring a lot of food because there aren't usually many shops near camping areas.

Houseboats are very exciting. You can stay in a houseboat on a river and you can travel to other places near the river! You can also go swimming on warm days. It's fantastic!

Comprehension

B Complete the sentences with words from the article.

1 Cottages are usually old and very _____ .

2 You can have meals in the _____ of a cottage.

3 The best time for camping is in the _____ .

4 There aren't usually many _____ near a camping area.

5 You can stay in a houseboat on a _____ .

/ 10

Writing

Write a letter to a friend about your last holiday. Use the plan to help you.

Begin like this:
Hi _____,

Paragraph 1
Ask how he/she is.
Say you want to tell him/her about
  your holiday.

Paragraph 2
Say where you went.
Say who you went with.
Say when you went on holiday.
Talk about the things you did.
Say what the weather was like.
Say your holiday was/wasn't great.

Paragraph 3
Ask him/her about his/her holiday.

Finish like this:
Write back soon!
_____ (your name)

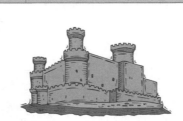

 / 10

 / 60

Notes

Notes